# Spanish
# Easy & Fun

# Visit **SpanishEasyAndFun.com**
## to access the online content

Spanish
Easy and Fun
First Edition: July 2023

© 2023 Spanish in 100 Days

This program was conceptualized by TRIALTEA USA, LC:
© 2023 TRIALTEA USA, LC

© 2023, of this edition, Penguin Random House Grupo Editorial USA, LLC.
8950 SW 74th Court, Suite 2010
Miami FL 33156

Photographs and illustrators: See page 318 for copyright list.

ISBN: 978-1-644737-32-3

Printed in Mexico.

Penguin
Random House
Grupo Editorial

# Spanish
# Easy & Fun

Welcome to Spanish: Easy & Fun!
For a full Spanish immersion, visit
SpanishEasyAndFun.com
to access online classes, videos,
activities, and interactive exercises.

# Introduction

If you are looking for a Spanish course that is fun,
easy, and entertaining, look no further.
***Spanish: Easy and Fun*** is an immersive experience in the world of
Spanish via language, culture, film, music, news, and community.

Speak the language, watch the films, listen to and sing the music, read the news, write to your community. Live in Spanish on your time and in your way.

***Spanish: Easy and Fun*** is a Spanish course developed by experts in the field of Foreign Language Education with experience in teaching Spanish to adults. The content, structure, and sequence of instruction are all based on Second Language Acquisition (SLA) research findings. Based on real-life situations, songs, movies, TV series and descriptions of captivating tourist destinations, you'll learn to keep fluent conversations in Spanish. And you'll comfortably understand Spanish in everyday situations, mastering the language from the basic to the advanced level.

**ENGAGING DESIGN**

The intuitive course design makes learning easier and faster, with visually rich materials to master essential vocabulary, uses of the language and grammar in record time.

## ONLINE COURSE

To get the most out of *Spanish: Easy and Fun*, make the book come alive take advantage of the online resources. It features hundreds of videos, audios, interactive exercises, live classes, and online activities to put into practice everything you learned in the book. You will also receive the constant support of our teachers, always available to answer any questions our students may have.

## COURSE STRUCTURE

We designed *Spanish: Easy and Fun* with ACTFL's (the American Council on the Teaching of Foreign Languages) 5 Cs in mind: Communication, Cultures, Connections, Comparisons, and Communities. The course is made up of 30 units, with each unit organized into three or four segments called Study Classrooms (Aulas de Estudio), totaling 100 Aulas de Estudio. By studying one Aula per day, you will complete the course in just 100 days.

## DISCOVER THE WORLD IN SPANISH

Each unit transports you to a Spanish-speaking destination. Throughout the course you will tour the principal destinations across Spain and Latin America, no passport required!

## EMPHASIS ON COMMUNICATION

Learn Spanish with realistic dialogues, crafted to highlight the use of the language and vocabulary, both peninsular and Latin American. You will also learn the grammar, in a simplified and easy way. And you will practice the four communication skills: you will read, write, listen and speak Spanish in no time, from the very first unit.

## SING AND DANCE IN SPANISH

Each of the 100 Aulas will feature a song in Spanish to practice communication skills, gain vocabulary and master the use of the language. And, most importantly, you will have a great time listening to, singing and dancing to these songs!

## WATCH GREAT MOVIES AND TV SERIES

Included are Aulas that feature a selection of the most successful films and TV series in Spanish, immersing you in the lifestyle and customs across Spanish-speaking countries. Learning Spanish has never been so much fun!

### So, it's time to join the party and learn Spanish.
### Let's start *Spanish: Easy and Fun!*

# Índice de contenidos

 **Unidad 1**
Barcelona

**Pág. 22**

**En esta unidad estudiaremos:**

pág. 22 ● **Diálogo**

pág. 24 ● **Hablemos español: a)** Greetings. **b)** Saying good-bye.
**c)** Exclamation and question marks. **d)** Asking someone's name.

pág. 26 ● **Gramática fácil: a)** Subject pronouns. **b)** Informal and
formal treatment: "Tú" and "Usted". **c)** The verb "ser". Present
indicative.

pág. 29 ● **Ejercicios**

 **Unidad 2**
Buenos Aires

**Pág. 30**

**En esta unidad estudiaremos:**

pág. 30 ● **Diálogo**

pág. 32 ● **Hablemos español: a)** Pronouncing and spelling words:
the alphabet. **b)** Asking how people are. **c)** Thanking and
responding expressions.

pág. 34 ● **Gramática fácil: a)** The verb "estar" (to be). Present
indicative. **b)** Structuring sentences. **c)** Yes-no answers.

pág. 37 ● **Ejercicios**

 **Unidad 3**
Madrid

**Pág. 38**

**En esta unidad estudiaremos:**

pág. 38 ● **Diálogo**

pág. 40 ● **Hablemos español: a)** Asking for and giving personal
information. **b)** Vocabulario: Objetos cotidianos (Everyday
objects). **c)** Asking and telling where things are.
**d)** Adverbs of place: "aquí", "acá", "allí", "allá", "ahí".

pág. 42 ● **Gramática fácil: a)** The definite article. **b)** Uses of
definite articles. **c)** Contractions. **d)** The verb "llamarse"
(to be called/named).

pág. 45 ● **Ejercicios**

SpanishEasyAndFun.com

# Unidad 4
## Ciudad de México

Pág. 46

**En esta unidad estudiaremos:**

pág. 46 ● **Diálogo**

pág. 48 ● **Hablemos español: a)** Introducing oneself and others.
**b)** Spanish titles. **c)** Vocabulario: La familia (The family).

pág. 50 ● **Gramática fácil: a)** Possessive adjectives.
**b)** Nouns: gender and number.

pág. 53 ● **Ejercicios**

# Unidad 5
## Granada

Pág. 54

**En esta unidad estudiaremos:**

pág. 54 ● **Diálogo**

pág. 56 ● **Hablemos español: a)** Asking and telling where people
or things are from. **b)** Vocabulario: Países y nacionalidades
(Countries and nationalities). **c)** Apologizing.
**d)** Askingsomeone to repeat and to speak more slowly.
**e)** Asking formeanings.

pág. 59 ● **Gramática fácil: a)** The indefinite article. **b)** Stressing
words and written accent marks. **c)** Dipthongs.

pág. 61 ● **Ejercicios**

# Unidad 6
## Cartagena

Pág. 62

**En esta unidad estudiaremos:**

pág. 62 ● **Diálogo**

pág. 64 ● **Hablemos español: a)** Spelling. **b)** Indicating one's
age. **c)** Telephone numbers. **d)** Vocabulario: Habitaciones,
muebles y objetos de casa (Rooms, pieces of furniture and
household objects).

pág. 66 ● **Gramática fácil: a)** The verb "tener" (to have). Present
indicative. **b)** Position of descriptive adjectives (I).
**c)** Cardinal numbers [0-99].

pág. 69 ● **Ejercicios**

 **Unidad 7**
Salamanca

**En esta unidad estudiaremos:**

**pág. 70** ◉ **Diálogo**

**pág. 72** ◉ **Hablemos español: a)** Question words. **b)** Vocabulario: Los colores (The colors).

**pág. 74** ◉ **Gramática fácil: a)** The verb "ser" vs. the verb "estar". **b)** Agreement of adjectives and nouns.

**pág. 77** ◉ **Ejercicios**

 **Unidad 8**
Machu Picchu

**En esta unidad estudiaremos:**

**pág. 78** ◉ **Diálogo**

**pág. 80** ◉ **Hablemos español: a)** Asking and answering about jobs and occupations. **b)** Vocabulario: Trabajos (Jobs).

**pág. 81** ◉ **Gramática fácil: a)** Spanish verbs. **b)** Presentindicative of regular verbs: "-ar" verbs. **c)** Present indicative of regular verbs: "-er" verbs. **d)** Present indicative of regular verbs: "-ir" verbs.

**pág. 85** ◉ **Ejercicios**

 **Unidad 9**
Santiago de Compostela

**En esta unidad estudiaremos:**

**pág. 86** ◉ **Diálogo**

**pág. 88** ◉ **Hablemos español: a)** Structuring sentences. **b)** The verb "llevar puesto" (to be wearing). **c)** Vocabulario: La ropa (Clothes).

**pág. 90** ◉ **Gramática fácil: a)** Uses of the present indicative. **b)** Questions beginning with a preposition. **c)** Asking about reasons. **d)** Position of descriptive adjectives (II): «bueno/buen»; «malo/mal»; «grande/gran».

**pág. 93** ◉ **Ejercicios**

 SpanishEasyAndFun.com

# Unidad 10
## Santiago de Chile

**Pág. 94**

**En esta unidad estudiaremos:**

**pág. 94** ● **Diálogo**

**pág. 96** ● **Hablemos español: a)** The present tense: time markers.
**b)** Vocabulario: Los días de la semana (The days of the week);
Los meses del año (The months).

**pág. 98** ● **Gramática fácil: a)** Irregular verbs. **b)** Present indicative
of irregular verbs (I). **c)** The conjunctions "o", "u", "o... o...",
"ni... ni...".

**pág. 101** ● **Ejercicios**

# Unidad 11
## San Sebastián

**Pág. 102**

**En esta unidad estudiaremos:**

**pág. 102** ● **Diálogo**

**pág. 104** ● **Hablemos español: a)** Demonstrative adjectives and
pronouns.

**pág. 106** ● **Gramática fácil: a)** Present indicative of irregular
verbs (II). **b)** Changes in spelling to maintain the pronunciation
of some verbs.

**pág. 111** ● **Ejercicios**

# Unidad 12
## La Habana

**Pág. 112**

**En esta unidad estudiaremos:**

**pág. 112** ● **Diálogo**

**pág. 114** ● **Hablemos español: a)** Expressing likes and dislikes:
the verb "gustar". **b)** The time (La hora).

**pág. 117** ● **Gramática fácil: a)** Indirect object pronouns.
**b)** The verbs "saber" and "conocer".

**pág. 119** ● **Ejercicios**

## Unidad 13
### Valencia

**En esta unidad estudiaremos:**

**pág. 120** ● **Diálogo**

**pág. 122** ● **Hablemos español: a)** The verb "hacer" (to do / to make).
**b)** Expressions with the verb "hacer". **c)** Vocabulario:
El tiempo (The weather); Las estaciones (The seasons).

**pág. 125** ● **Gramática fácil: a)** The impersonal form "hay".
**b)** Indefinite pronouns.

**pág. 127** ● **Ejercicios**


## Unidad 14
### Costa Rica

**Pág. 128**

**En esta unidad estudiaremos:**

**pág. 128** ● **Diálogo**

**pág. 130** ● **Hablemos español: a)** The verb "poder". Present indicative.
**b)** Making requests, asking for and borrowing things. **c)** Asking
for a favor. **d)** Expressions to confirm and excuse.

**pág. 133** ● **Gramática fácil: a)** The verb "venir".
**b)** The adverbs "también" and "tampoco".

**pág. 135** ● **Ejercicios**


## Unidad 15
### Islas Canarias

**Pág. 136**

**En esta unidad estudiaremos:**

**pág. 136** ● **Diálogo**

**pág. 138** ● **Hablemos español: a)** Expressing how often an action
occurs: adverbs of frequency. **b)** The verb "soler".
**c)** Vocabulario: Hábitos y rutinas (Habits and routines).

**pág. 140** ● **Gramática fácil: a)** Reflexive verbs. **b)** The conjunctions
"pero" and "sino".

**pág. 143** ● **Ejercicios**

 SpanishEasyAndFun.com

 # Unidad 16
## La Patagonia

 **Pág. 144**

**En esta unidad estudiaremos:**

**pág. 144** ● Diálogo

**pág. 146** ● **Hablemos español: a)** Prepositions and adverbs of place. **b)** Vocabulario: La ciudad (The city); Objetos de la calle (Objects on the street).

**pág. 148** ● **Gramática fácil: a)** The present participle (gerund). **b)** The present progressive: estar + present participle. **c)** The adverbs "todavía", "aún" and "ya".

**pág. 151** ● **Ejercicios**


# Unidad 17
## La Rioja

**Pág. 152**

**En esta unidad estudiaremos:**

**pág. 152** ● Diálogo

**pág. 154** ● **Hablemos español: a)** Expressing opinions. **b)** Expressing quantity: adverbs of quantity. **c)** Vocabulario: La lista de la compra [I] (The shopping list [I]).

**pág. 156** ● **Gramática fácil: a)** Direct object pronouns. **b)** The personal "a". **c)** Cardinal numbers (100-999).

**pág. 159** ● **Ejercicios**


# Unidad 18
## Potosí

**Pág. 160**

**En esta unidad estudiaremos:**

**pág. 160** ● Diálogo

**pág. 162** ● **Hablemos español: a)** Asking about quantity. **b)** Vocabulario: La lista de la compra [II] (The shopping list [II]).

**pág. 164** ● **Gramática fácil: a)** The adverbs "muy" and "mucho". **b)** Other expressions of quantity. **c)** The use of "lo". **d)** Cardinal numbers (1000-millions).

**pág. 167** ● **Ejercicios**

# Unidad 19
### Sevilla

**Pág. 168**

**En esta unidad estudiaremos:**

**pág. 168** ● **Diálogo**

**pág. 170** ● **Hablemos español: a)** The preposition "de". **b)** The date.
**c)** Vocabulario: La cara (The face). **d)** Tag questions: "¿no?",
"¿verdad?".

**pág. 173** ● **Gramática fácil: a)** The past tense. **b)** The preterite.
**c)** The preterite of regular verbs. **d)** The past tense: time
markers.

**pág. 175** ● **Ejercicios**

# Unidad 20
### Quito

**Pág. 176**

**En esta unidad estudiaremos:**

**pág. 176** ● **Diálogo**

**pág. 178** ● **Hablemos español: a)** "Desde", "hasta" and "durante".
**b)** Adverbs of time: "antes", "después" / "más tarde" / "luego".
**c)** Vocabulario: La computadora/el ordenador (The computer).

**pág. 180** ● **Gramática fácil: a)** The preterite of irregular verbs.
**b)** The verb "dar" (to give). **c)** The verb "tener" (to have).

**pág. 183** ● **Ejercicios**

# Unidad 21
### Extremadura

**Pág. 184**

**En esta unidad estudiaremos:**

**pág. 184** ● **Diálogo**

**pág. 186** ● **Hablemos español: a)** Making suggestions.
**b)** Adverbs of manner. **c)** Adverbs ending in "-mente".
**d)** Vocabulario: Tiendas y comercios (Shops and stores).

**pág. 188** ● **Gramática fácil: a)** The imperfect. **b)** Joining
sentences: "mientras" and "cuando".

**pág. 191** ● **Ejercicios**

SpanishEasyAndFun.com

 **Unidad 22**
Santo Domingo

**Pág. 192**

**En esta unidad estudiaremos:**

**pág. 192** ◉ **Diálogo**

**pág. 194** ◉ **Hablemos español: a)** The imperfect versus the preterite. **b)** Vocabulario: El cuerpo humano (The human body). **c)** The verb "doler". **d)** Giving advice.

**pág. 197** ◉ **Gramática fácil: a)** Relative pronouns. **b)** The relative pronoun "que". **c)** The relative pronoun "lo que". **d)** The relative pronoun "quien".

**pág. 199** ◉ **Ejercicios**

 **Unidad 23**
Costa del Sol

**Pág. 200**

**En esta unidad estudiaremos:**

**pág. 200** ◉ **Diálogo**

**pág. 202** ◉ **Hablemos español: a)** Expressing possession. **b)** Possessive pronouns. **c)** Vocabulario: La escuela (The school).

**pág. 204** ◉ **Gramática fácil: a)** Durative actions in the past. **b)** The past participle.

**pág. 207** ◉ **Ejercicios**

 **Unidad 24**
Tikal

**Pág. 208**

**En esta unidad estudiaremos:**

**pág. 208** ◉ **Diálogo**

**pág. 210** ◉ **Hablemos español: a)** Verbs followed by prepositions. **b)** Vocabulario: Actividades de ocio (Leisure activities).

**pág. 211** ◉ **Gramática fácil: a)** The present perfect. **b)** Uses of the present perfect. **c)** The adverbs "ya", "todavía" and "aún" + the present perfect.

**pág. 215** ◉ **Ejercicios**

 **Unidad 25**
Segovia

**En esta unidad estudiaremos:**

**pág. 216** ◉ **Diálogo**

**pág. 218** ◉ **Hablemos español: a)** The imperative. **b)** Asking for and giving directions.

**pág. 221** ◉ **Gramática fácil: a)** The comparative of equality.

**pág. 223** ◉ **Ejercicios**

**Unidad 26** **Pág. 224**
Isla de Pascua

**En esta unidad estudiaremos:**

**pág. 224** ◉ **Diálogo**

**pág. 226** ◉ **Hablemos español: a)** Adjectives followed by prepositions. **b)** Uses of "algún", "ningún" and "cualquier". **c)** Vocabulario: Medios de transporte (Means of transport).

**pág. 228** ◉ **Gramática fácil: a)** The comparative of superiority and inferiority. **b)** Irregular comparatives. **c)** The verbs "quedar" and "quedarse".

**pág. 231** ◉ **Ejercicios**

**Unidad 27** **Pág. 232**
Toledo

**En esta unidad estudiaremos:**

**pág. 232** ◉ **Diálogo**

**pág. 234** ◉ **Hablemos español: a)** Exclamaciones con "¡qué!". **b)** Expressing obligation and prohibition. **c)** Vocabulario: En el restaurante (At the restaurant).

**pág. 237** ◉ **Gramática fácil: a)** Pronouns preceded by prepositions. **b)** The relative superlative.

**pág. 239** ◉ **Ejercicios**

# Unidad 28

**Chichén Itzá**

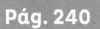

**En esta unidad estudiaremos:**

**pág. 240** ◉ **Diálogo**

**pág. 242** ◉ **Hablemos español: a)** Expressing certainty and probability. **b)** Expressing future plans and intentions. **c)** "Ir a + infinitive». **d)** "Querer + infinitive". **e)** Vocabulario: El medio ambiente (The environment).

**pág. 244** ◉ **Gramática fácil: a)** The future tense. **b)** The future tense: time markers. **c)** Combining pronouns.

**pág. 247** ◉ **Ejercicios**

# Unidad 29

**Ibiza**

Pág. 248

**En esta unidad estudiaremos:**

**pág. 248** ◉ **Diálogo**

**pág. 250** ◉ **Hablemos español: a)** The prepositions "para" and "por". **b)** Uses of the preposition "para". **c)** Uses of the preposition "por". **d)** Vocabulario: En el hotel (At the hotel).

**pág. 253** ◉ **Gramática fácil: a)** Infinitives used as nouns. **b)** Ordinal numbers.

**pág. 255** ◉ **Ejercicios**

# Unidad 30

**Lago Titicaca**

Pág. 256

**En esta unidad estudiaremos:**

**pág. 256** ◉ **Diálogo**

**pág. 258** ◉ **Hablemos español: a)** Expressions on the telephone. **b)** Vocabulario: La salud y las enfermedades (Health and illnesses).

**pág. 260** ◉ **Gramática fácil: a)** The conditional mood. **b)** The absolute superlative.

**pág. 263** ◉ **Ejercicios**

**pág. 264** ◉ **Spanish Verbs**
**pág. 304** ◉ **Conversion Charts**

# Units

# Unidad 1
## Barcelona

### En esta unidad estudiaremos:

- **Diálogo**
- **Hablemos español:**
  a) Greetings. b) Saying good-bye. c) Exclamation and question marks.
  d) Asking someone's name.
- **Gramática fácil:**
  a) Subject pronouns. b) Informal and formal treatment:"Tú" and "Usted". c) The verb "ser". Present indicative.
- **Ejercicios**

---

*Francisco es estudiante en la universidad y va a compartir el apartamento con Natalia y otras personas. Va a la vivienda por primera vez.*

Natalia: **¡Hola! ¡Buenas tardes!**
Francisco: **¡Buenas tardes!**
N:  **Me llamo** Natalia. ¿Y tú? **¿Cómo te llamas?**
F:  **Yo me llamo** Francisco. **¿Qué tal,** Natalia**?**
N:  Bien, gracias. ¡Encantada!
F:  ¡Mucho gusto!
N:  **Yo soy** de Colombia. **Tú eres** español, ¿verdad?
F:  Sí, **soy** español.
N:  [Señalando a otras personas]. Mira, **ellos son** mis amigos. Él es Tomás y **ella es** Silvia. **Ellos son** colombianos. Bueno, **nosotros somos** colombianos. ¡Ah! Y allí está Rufo. **Es** mi perro.
F:  **Ustedes** también **son** estudiantes de arte, supongo.
N:  **Yo soy** estudiante de arte, pero **ellos son** estudiantes de arquitectura. ¡Pasa! Te enseñaré el apartamento.
F:  Gracias.
N:  De nada. **Es** un apartamento grande. Hay cuatro dormitorios y dos cuartos de baño.
F:  ¡Estupendo! Además, las vistas **son** fantásticas.
N:  Así **es**. **Somos** muy afortunados. Mira, este **es** tu dormitorio.
F:  ¡Wow! **Es** muy bonito.
N:  Espero que te sientas cómodo aquí.
F:  Seguro que sí. Muchas gracias, Natalia.
N:  No hay de qué. Bueno, yo tengo que salir ahora, pero nos volveremos a ver después.
F:  De acuerdo. **¡Hasta luego,** Natalia**!**
N:  **¡Hasta luego!**

SpanishEasyAndFun.com

Parque Güell, Barcelona, España.

*Francisco is a college student and is going to share an apartment with Natalia and a few others. He is going there for the first time.*

*Natalia: Hello! Good afternoon!*
*Francisco: Good afternoon!*
N: My name is Natalia. And you? What's your name?
F: My name is Francisco. How is it going, Natalia?
N: Fine, thank you. Nice to meet you!
F: Nice to meet you, too!
N: I am from Colombia. You are Spanish, aren't you?
F: Yes, I'm Spanish.
N: [Pointing at some people]. Look, they are my friends. He is Tomás and she is Silvia. The are Colombian. Well, we all are Colombian. Ah! And there is Rufo. He's my dog.
F: You are also art students, I guess.
N: I am an art student but they are architecture students. Come on in! I'll show you around the apartment.
F: Thanks.
N: You're welcome. It's a big apartment. There are four bedrooms and two bathrooms.
F: Great! Besides, the views are fantastic.
N: Yes, they are. We're very lucky. Look, this is your bedroom.
F: Wow! It's very nice.
N: I hope you feel comfortable here.
F: I'm sure I will. Thanks a lot, Natalia.
N: Don't mention it!. Well, I have to leave now but we'll meet again later.

F: Alright. See you later, Natalia!
N: See you later!

# Hablemos español

## a Greetings

Greeting expressions vary with location, but some of the most common in Spanish are the following:

| | | |
|---|---|---|
| **¡Hola!** | > | *Hello! / Hi!* |
| **¡Buenas!** | > | *Hello! / Hi!* |
| **¿Qué tal?** | > | *How do you do? / How is it going? / What's up?* |
| | | |
| **¿Cómo estás?** | > | *How are you? (informal)* |
| **¿Cómo está usted?** | > | *How are you? (formal)* |

Depending on the time of day when we use the greeting expression, we can also say:

| | | |
|---|---|---|
| **¡Buenos días!** | > | *Good morning!* |
| **¡Buenas tardes!** | > | *Good afternoon! / Good evening! (early evening)* |
| **¡Buenas noches!** | > | *Good evening!* |

## b Saying good-bye

In order to say good-bye we can use the following expressions:

| | | |
|---|---|---|
| **¡Adiós!** | > | *Good-bye!* |
| **¡Hasta pronto!** | > | *See you soon!* |
| **¡Hasta luego!** | > | *See you later!* |
| **¡Hasta mañana!** | > | *See you tomorrow!* |
| **¡Buenas noches!** | > | *Good night!* |
| **¡Cuídate!** | > | *Take care!* |

## c Exclamation and question marks

In Spanish, exclamation and question marks are used both at the beginning and end of the sentence or expression. They are inverted when used at the beginning (¡...!, ¿...?).

¡Hola! ¿Cómo estás?

SpanishEasyAndFun.com

## d  Asking someone's name

The most common ways to ask someone's name are:

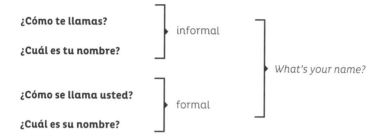

**¿Cómo te llamas?**

**¿Cuál es tu nombre?**

informal

**¿Cómo se llama usted?**

**¿Cuál es su nombre?**

formal

What's your name?

And the answer may be:

**Me llamo** Pedro.  >  *My name is Pedro.*
**Soy** Luisa.  >  *I am Luisa.*

# Gramática fácil

## a Subject pronouns

### Singular

| yo | > | I |
|---|---|---|
| tú | > | you (informal) |
| usted | > | you (formal) |
| él | > | he |
| ella | > | she |
| - | > | it |

| | | |
|---|---|---|
| **Yo** soy español. | > | I am Spanish. |
| **Tú** eres alto. | > | You are tall. |
| **Usted** es profesor. | > | You are a teacher. |
| **Él** es Fernando. | > | He is Fernando. |
| **Ella** es mi madre. | > | She is my mother. |

In Spanish there is no equivalent for the English neuter pronoun **"it"**. In most cases no pronoun is used when referring to animals, things or places, but sometimes we can use "él" or "ella".

Es una mesa.
*It is a table.*

### Plural

| nosotros, nosotras | > | we |
|---|---|---|
| vosotros, vosotras * | > | you (informal) |
| ustedes * | > | you (formal and informal) |
| ellos, ellas | > | they |

¿Dónde está Madrid? Está en España.
*Where is Madrid? It is in Spain.*

⭐ "**Vosotros/vosotras**" is used for informal treatment in Spain only. Its formal equivalent is "**ustedes**", which is used for both formal and informal treatment in Latin American countries.

| | | |
|---|---|---|
| **Nosotros** somos brasileños. | > | We are Brazilian. |
| **Vosotros** sois altos. | > | You are tall. |
| **Ustedes** son hermanos. | > | You are brothers. |
| **Ellas** son estudiantes. | > | They are students. |

In Spanish, all persons in plural have both masculine and feminine forms, except for "ustedes":

**nosotros, vosotros, ellos** (masc.)    **nosotras, vosotras, ellas** (fem.)

SpanishEasyAndFun.com

**Nosotros, vosotros** and **ellos** are used when the people or things that we refer to are <u>all masculine or if the group is mixed</u>.

**Nosotros** somos Francisco y Ricardo.   >   *We are Francisco and Ricardo.*
**Vosotros** sois dominicanos.   >   *You are Dominican.*
**Ellos** son Lidia y Rafael.   >   *They are Lidia and Rafael.*

**Nosotras, vosotras** and **ellas** are used when the people or things that we refer to are <u>all feminine</u>.

**Nosotras** somos hermanas.   >   *We are sisters.*
**Vosotras** sois mejicanas.   >   *You are Mexican.*
**Ellas** son Natalia y Mercedes.   >   *They are Natalia and Mercedes.*

## b   Informal and formal treatment "Tú" and "Usted"

"**Tú**" is the pronoun used informally when addressing:

- a friend,
- a member of one's family,
- a workmate,
- someone of the same age or status,
- a child.

**Tú** eres mi amigo.   >   *You are my friend.*

In some countries, like Argentina and Uruguay, "**vos**" is used instead of "**tú**".

Although "**usted**"/ "**ustedes**" refer to the second person (singular and plural), the verb they precede is conjugated as for "él/ella" in singular or "ellos/ellas" in plural.

"**Usted**" and "**ustedes**" (abbreviated **Ud**. and **Uds**. respectively) are used in a formal context to show respect, as well as to put a little distance between you and the person or people you are addressing. "**Usted**" and "**ustedes**" are used when addressing:

- someone with whom the speaker is not personally familiar,
- someone much older,
- someone in a position of authority or higher rank,
- someone for the first time (in most cases).

**Usted** es el director.   >   *You are the director.*

After using the formal treatment "**usted**", we may be asked to use the informal "**tú**". That is what in Spanish is called "tutearse" (to address each other as "**tú**").

## c The verb "ser" (*to be*). Present indicative

The verb "**ser**" is equivalent to "*to be*". In the present indicative it is conjugated as follows:

| | | | | | |
|---|---|---|---|---|---|
| yo | **soy** | *I am* | nosotros/as | **somos** | *we are* |
| tú | **eres** | *you are* | vosotros/as | **sois** | *you are* |
| usted | **es** | *you are* | ustedes | **son** | *you are* |
| él | **es** | *he is* | | | |
| ella | **es** | *she is* | ellos/as | **son** | *they are* |

The verb "**ser**" is used, among other things, to give the following information:

🔹 permanent state:

| Argentina **es** un país. | > | *Argentina is a country.* |
|---|---|---|
| **Es** un libro. | > | *It is a book.* |

🔹 name or identity:

| Yo **soy** Pedro. | > | *I am Pedro.* |
|---|---|---|
| Ellas **son** mis hermanas. | > | *They are my sisters.* |
| Mi apellido **es** García. | > | *My surname es García.* |

🔹 origin or nationality:

| Tú **eres** de Colombia. | > | *You are from Colombia.* |
|---|---|---|
| Él es estadounidense. | > | *He is American.* |

🔹 job:

| Nosotros **somos** arquitectos. | > | *We are architects.* |
|---|---|---|
| Ella **es** estudiante. | > | *She is a student.* |

🔹 (personal) features:

| Ustedes son altos. | > | *You are tall.* |
|---|---|---|
| Nueva York **es** una ciudad grande. | > | *New York is a big city.* |

SpanishEasyAndFun.com

# Ejercicios de la **Unidad 1**

**a** Choose the correct subject pronoun.

**1** _____ soy español. (Él / Ellos / Yo)
**2** _____ eres arquitecto. (Tú / Usted / Yo)
**3** _____ es Jorge. (Él / Ella / Nosotros)
**4** _____ son Julia y Marta. (Nosotras / Ustedes / Él)
**5** _____ somos mejicanos. (Ellos / Nosotros / Nosotras)

**b** Fill in the gaps with the correct form of the verb "ser".

**1** Ustedes _____ italianos.
**2** Yo _____ estudiante.
**3** Ellas _____ secretarias.
**4** Nosotros _____ Eduardo y Ángel.
**5** Tú _____ alto.

**c** Which of the following expressions can be used as a greeting and to say good-bye?

**1** ¡Buenos días!
**2** ¡Buenas noches!
**3** ¡Hasta luego!
**4** ¡Buenas!

**d** Choose the right question to go with the answer: "María".

**1** ¿Cómo estás?
**2** ¿Cómo eres?
**3** ¿Cómo te llamas?
**4** ¿Cómo?

· · · · · · · · · · · · · · · · · · · · · · · · · · · · · · · · · · · · · · · · · · · · · · · · · · · · · ·

**d:** 3
**c:** 3
**b:** 1.- son; 2.- soy; 3.- son; 4.- somos; 5.- eres.
**a:** 1.- Yo; 2.- Tú; 3.- Él; 4.- Ustedes; 5.- Nosotros.
**Key**

Spanish: Easy and Fun

# Unidad 2
## Buenos Aires

### En esta unidad estudiaremos:

- ◉ **Diálogo**
- ◉ **Hablemos español:**
  **a)** Pronouncing and spelling words: the alphabet. **b)** Asking how people are. **c)** Thanking and responding expressions.
- ◉ **Gramática fácil:**
  **a)** The verb "estar" (to be). Present indicative. **b)** Structuring sentences. **c)** Yes-no answers.
- ◉ **Ejercicios**

---

*Lucas ha pasado la primera noche en el apartamento que comparte con otros estudiantes y se levanta por la mañana.*

Teresa: ¡Buenos días!
Lucas: ¡Buenos días, Teresa!
T:    **¿Cómo estás?** ¿Dormiste bien?
L:    **Sí, muy bien**, **gracias**. ¿Y tú?
T:    Yo también. Por eso **estoy** contenta hoy.
L:    ¡Estupendo! Oye, no escucho ningún ruido. **¿Está** el perro en el apartamento?
T:    No, **no está** aquí. **Está** en la calle. **Está** con Roberto.
L:    ¡Ah!
T:    Pero **no estamos** solos. Marina también **está** en el apartamento ahora. **Está** en mi dormitorio. Quiere que le preste una blusa y está mirando en mi armario.
L:    Mi ropa **no está** en mi armario. **Está** en mi maleta todavía.
T:    Bueno, ya la pondrás en su sitio. No te preocupes. ¿Quieres desayunar ahora?
L:    Mmm... Es una buena idea.
T:    Todo **está** en la cocina: leche, mantequilla, mermelada, jugo...
L:    Solo tomaré un poco de jugo y unas galletas.
T:    El jugo **está** en el refrigerador y las galletas **están** en la mesa.
L:    **¡Muchas gracias**, Teresa!
T:    **¡De nada!**

🖑 SpanishEasyAndFun.com

Avenida 9 de Julio, Buenos Aires, Argentina.

Lucas has spent the first night in the apartment he shares with other students and has just got up in the morning.

Teresa: Good morning!
Lucas: Good morning, Teresa!
T:  How are you? Did you sleep well?
L:  Yes, very well, thank you. And you?
T:  Me, too. That's why I'm happy today.
L:  Great! Hey, I don't hear a thing. Is the dog in the apartment?

T:  No, it isn't here. It's outside. It's with Roberto.
L:  Ah!
T:  But we are not alone. Marina is also in the apartment now. She is in my bedroom. She wants me to lend her a blouse and is looking in my closet.

L:  My clothes are not in my closet. They are still in my suitcase.
T:  Well, you'll put them away. Don't worry. Do you want to have breakfast now?
L:  Mmm... It's a good idea.
T:  Everything is in the kitchen: milk, butter, jam, juice...
L:  I'll only have a little juice and some cookies.
T:  The juice is in the fridge and the cookies are on the table.
L:  Thank you very much, Teresa!
T:  You're welcome!

# Hablemos español

| A | B | C | D | E | F | G | H | I | J |
|---|---|---|---|---|---|---|---|---|---|
| a | be | ce | de | e | efe | ge | h | i | jota |

| K | L | M | N | Ñ | O | P | Q | R | S |
|---|---|---|---|---|---|---|---|---|---|
| ka | ele | eme | ene | eñe | o | pe | cu | ere | ese |

| T | U | V | W | X | Y | Z | | | |
|---|---|---|---|---|---|---|---|---|---|
| te | u | uve | uve doble | equis | ye | zeta | | | |

### Pronunciation

How to pronounce some of the most confusing Spanish letters are detailed here for your review.

- "b" and "v" are pronounced the same (like a "b").
- before "e" and "i", "c" is pronounced as an "s" (in Latin American countries and some areas in southern Spain) or as "th" in "three" (in the rest of Spain). It is always pronounced as a "k" before "a", "o" and "u".
- "g" sounds like a heavily aspirated "h" before "e" and "i" (like "h" in "hot") but, to make it sound the same as in "get" or "give", a silent "u" is needed between the "g" and the "e" or "i" [guerra (war), guitarra (guitar)]. When marked by a diaeresis (¨), this "u" is pronounced [antigüedad (antiquity), cigüeña (stork)].
- "h" is always silent.
- "j" sounds like a heavily aspirated "h" (like "h" in "hot") in all cases.
- "ñ" is a typical Spanish letter that sounds like "in" in "onion" or "ny" in "canyon".
- "q" always precedes "ue" or "ui", sounding "ke" or "ki".
- "r" is pronounced similarly to the American pronunciation of "tt" in "better". But after "l", "n", "s" or at the start of a word, it sounds stronger (the same as "rr" – see "double letters" below).
- "z" is pronounced as an "s" (in Latin American countries and some areas in southern Spain) or like "th" in "three" (in the rest of Spain).

### Double letters

- "ch" sounds like "ch" in "church".
- "ll" sounds like "y" in "you".
- "rr" is a strong trill of the tip of the tongue against the front part of the palate.

SpanishEasyAndFun.com

## b  Asking how people are

- The interrogative pronoun "**¿Cómo?**" *(How?)* is used to ask how people are:

| | | |
|---|---|---|
| **¿Cómo estás? / ¿Cómo está usted?** | > | *How are you?* |
| **¿Cómo está ella?** | > | *How is she?* |

- To answer, you can use these expressions:

| | | |
|---|---|---|
| **Estoy muy bien.** | > | *I am very well.* |
| **Ella está bien.** | > | *She is well/fine/ok.* |
| **No estoy muy bien.** | > | *I am not very well.* |

- And also:

| | | |
|---|---|---|
| **Más o menos.** | > | *So, so.* |
| **Regular.** | > | *Not so good.* |
| **Mal.** | > | *Lousy / Awful.* |

## c  Thanking and responding expressions

- When giving thanks (for something), we can use any of these expressions:

| | | |
|---|---|---|
| **Gracias.** | > | *Thank you.* |
| **Muchas gracias.** | > | *Thank you very much. / Thanks a lot.* |
| **Muchísimas gracias.** | > | *Thank you very much indeed.* |
| **Muchas gracias por tu invitación.** | > | *Thank you very much for your invitation.* |

- To respond, say:

| | | |
|---|---|---|
| **De nada.** | > | *You're welcome.* |
| **No hay de qué.** | > | *Don't mention it. / Not at all.* |

# Gramática fácil

## a The verb "estar" (*to be*). Present indicative

The verb "**estar**" (the same as "ser") is another equivalent to the verb "*to be*". In the present indicative it is conjugated as follows:

| yo | **estoy** | *I am* | nosotros/nosotras | **estamos** | *we are* |
|----|-----------|--------|-------------------|-------------|----------|
| tú | **estás** | *you are* | vosotros/as | **estáis** | *you are* |
| usted | **está** | *you are* | ustedes | **están** | *you are* |
| él | **está** | *he is* | | | |
| ella | **está** | *she is* | ellos/ellas | **están** | *they are* |

The verb "**estar**" is used, among other things, to give the following information:

location:

| Ellos **están** en Bogotá. | > | *They are in Bogota.* |
|---|---|---|
| **Está** en la mesa (el libro). | > | *It is on the table (the book).* |

[But "ser" is used to tell where an event is taking place].

| El concierto **es** en el auditorio. | > | *The concert is at the auditorium.* |
|---|---|---|

temporary states or situations:

| Yo **estoy** contento. | > | *I am happy.* |
|---|---|---|
| Ustedes **están** delgados ahora. | > | *You are thin now.* |

how someone or something is:

| ¿Cómo **está** usted? | > | *How are you?* |
|---|---|---|
| La sopa **está** fría. | > | *The soup is cold.* |

before the adverbs "bien" (*well, fine*) and "mal" (*badly*):

| ¿**Estás** bien? | > | *Are you okay?* |
|---|---|---|
| Nosotros no **estamos** mal. | > | *We don't feel too bad.* |

Although "**usted**"/ "**ustedes**" refer to the second person (singular and plural), the verb they precede is conjugated as for "él/ella" in singular or "ellos/ellas" in plural.

SpanishEasyAndFun.com

## b    Structuring sentences

When structuring sentences we have to consider that:

🔹 In many cases the subject does not appear in the sentence:

| | | |
|---|---|---|
| Cómo estás **(tú)**? | > | *How are you?* |
| **(Yo)** Estoy bien. | > | *I am fine.* |

The subject pronouns are not always used in Spanish because the verb itself has a different ending for each person (both in singular and plural), thus revealing the subject. But these pronouns are commonly used for emphasis, clarity and contrast.

| | | |
|---|---|---|
| **(Nosotros)** Somos José y Miguel. | > | *We are José and Miguel.* |
| ¿Cómo está él? | > | *How are you?* |
| **Nosotras** estamos aquí. | > | *We are here.* |

🔹 When structuring negative sentences, simply add "**no**" before the verb:

| | | |
|---|---|---|
| **No** estoy muy bien. | > | *I am not very well.* |
| Ustedes **no** están en la escuela. | > | *You are not at school.* |

🔹 When asking questions, the position of the subject and verb may change:

| | | | |
|---|---|---|---|
| | Ella **está** bien. | > | *She is fine* |
| | ¿**Está** ella bien? | > | *Is she fine?* |
| But also: | ¿**Ella está** bien? * | > | *Is she fine?* |

✪ You can ask a question simply by altering the intonation of your words. Unlike in other languages, you don't need to change the order of the words.

# Yes-no answers

In many cases questions can simply be answered affirmatively ("**Sí**") or negatively ("**No**").

| | | |
|---|---|---|
| —¿Está Miguel en Perú? | > | —*Is Miguel in Peru?* |
| —**Sí**. | > | —*Yes.* |
| | | |
| —¿Están los libros en la mesa? | > | —*Are the books on the table?* |
| —**No**, están en los estantes. | > | —*No, they are on the shelves.* |
| | | |
| —¿Eres tú Rafael? | > | —*Are you Rafael?* |
| —**Sí**, lo soy. | > | —*Yes, I am.* |

In a negative answer to a Spanish question sometimes two "nos" are needed:

| | | |
|---|---|---|
| —¿Es un libro? | > | —*Is it a book?* |
| —**No**, **no** es un libro. | > | —*No, it isn't.* |

If a question begins with a questioning word ("¿Qué?", "¿Cómo?", etc.), then a simple "sí" or "no" answer alone is not possible.

The affirmative adverb "**sí**" *(yes)* is written with an accent mark not to be confused with the condicional "**si**" *(if)*.

SpanishEasyAndFun.com

# Ejercicios de la **Unidad 2**

**a** Which of the following expressions are not used after saying "¡Gracias!"?

1 No hay de qué.
2 Bien.
3 De nada.
4 Más o menos.

**b** Fill in the gaps with the following expressions: **Muchas gracias, Regular, ¿Cómo estás?, No hay de qué**.

1 ¿_____? Estoy bien, gracias.
2 ¿Cómo está Juan? _____
3 Gracias por la invitación. _____
4 _____. De nada.

**c** Fill in the gaps with the correct form of the verb "estar".

1 ¿Cómo _____ ustedes? Muy bien, gracias.
2 ¿_____ en Canadá? No, yo _____ en Brasil.
3 Lucía _____ mal.
4 Nosotras _____ en Colombia.

**d** Match the questions and the answers.

1 ¿Está bien María?
2 ¿Es un libro?
3 ¿Estás en casa?
4 ¿Cómo está ella?
5 ¿Cómo te llamas?

a Sí, ella está bien, gracias.
b Manuel.
c No, no es un libro.
d Ella está bien, gracias.
e No, estoy en la escuela.

# Unidad 3
## Madrid

### En esta unidad estudiaremos:

◉ **Diálogo**

◉ **Hablemos español:**
   **a)** Asking for and giving personal information. **b)** Vocabulario: Objetos cotidianos (Everyday objects. **c)** Asking and telling where things are. **d)** Adverbs of place: "aquí", "acá", "allí", "allá", "ahí".

◉ **Gramática fácil:**
   **a)** The definite article. **b)** Uses of definite articles. **c)** Contractions. **d)** The verb "llamarse" (to be called/named).

◉ **Ejercicios**

---

*Pedro ha ido a la biblioteca a pedir prestado un libro. El auxiliar de la biblioteca le está pidiendo algunos datos personales.*

Pedro: ¡Buenas! Quisiera pedir prestado un libro de esta biblioteca.
Auxiliar: ¿Tiene **el** carnet de préstamo?
P:   No, todavía no.
A:   Bueno, entonces debo tomar sus datos. **¿Cuál es su nombre?**
P:   **Me llamo** Pedro.
A:   **¿Y cuáles son sus apellidos?**
P:   Cortázar Oldenburg.
A:   ¿Olden...? ¿Cómo se escribe?
P:   O-L-D-E-N-B-U-R-G
A:   Es un apellido extraño.
P:   Sí, bueno... Mi madre es alemana.
A:   Bien, sigamos. **¿Cuál es su dirección?**
P:   **Mi dirección** es: Avenida Independencia, número 32.
A:   Bueno, ya están todos **los** datos. ¡Acompáñeme, por favor! [Entran en la biblioteca]. Señor Cortázar, **las revistas y los periódicos** están **aquí; los libros** están **allí y los diccionarios** están **por allá**, en otra habitación. ¡Ah! **Y** no olvide apagar su **celular**. Yo he de volver **al** despacho.
P:   ¡Muchas gracias por su ayuda!
A:   No hay de qué. Estaré en mi despacho por si necesita algo.
P:   Muy bien. ¡Hasta luego!
A:   ¡Adiós!

SpanishEasyAndFun.com

Fuente de Cibeles, Madrid, España.

Pedro has gone to the library to borrow a book. The library assistant is asking him for some personal information.

Pedro: Hello! I would like to borrow a book from this library.
Assisstant: Do you have a library card?
P:  No, not yet.
A:  Then I must take down of some personal information. What's your name?
P:  My name is Pedro.
A:  And what is your last name?
P:  Cortázar Oldenburg.
A:  Olden...? How do you spell it?
P:  O-L-D-E-N-B-U-R-G
A:  It's a strange last name.
P:  Yes, well... My mother is German.
A:  Okay, let's continue. What's your address?
P:  My address is: 32, Avenida Independencia.
A:  Well. That is all. Come with me, please! [They enter the library]. Mr. Cortázar, the magazines and the newspapers are here; the books are there and the dictionaries are over there, in another room. Ah! And don't forget to switch off your cell phone. I must go back to my office.
P:  Thank you very much for your help!
A:  Don't mention it! I'll be in my office in case you need something.
P:  Alright. See you later!
A:  Good-bye!

# Hablemos español

## a  Asking for and giving personal information

When asking for someone's name or address, you can say:

| | | |
|---|---|---|
| ¿Cuál es **tu nombre?** | > | *What's your name?* |
| ¿Cuál es tu **dirección?** | > | *What's your address?* |

And also:

| | | |
|---|---|---|
| **¿Cómo te llamas?** | > | *What's your name?* |
| **¿Cuáles son tus apellidos?** | > | *What are your last names?* |

When speaking to someone formally, it is better to say:

| | | |
|---|---|---|
| **¿Cuál es <u>su</u> nombre / dirección?** | > | *What's your name / address?* |

To answer, say:

| | | |
|---|---|---|
| **Mi nombre es** Lucas. | > | *My name is Lucas.* |
| **Me llamo** Ramón. | > | *My name is Ramón.* |
| **Mi dirección es** calle Ríos, 24. | > | *My address is calle Ríos, 24.* |

In Spanish-speaking countries people have two last names or surnames. Their first last name is their father's first last name and their second last name is their mother's first last name.

Roberto **Sánchez** García (*father*)     Margarita **Fernández** Ruiz (*mother*)

Luis **Sánchez Fernández** (*son*)

## b  Vocabulario: Objetos cotidianos  (Everyday objects)

| | | |
|---|---|---|
| **libro**: *book* | **carta**: *letter* | **gafas, lentes**: *glasses* |
| **diccionario**: *dictionary* | **periódico**: *newspaper* | **revista**: *magazine* |
| **llave**: *key* | **llavero**: *key ring* | **teléfono**: *telephone* |
| **móvil, celular**: *cell phone* | **agenda**: *notebook* | **maletín**: *briefcase* |
| **collar**: *necklace* | **ordenador**: *computer* | **portátil**: *laptop* |
| **reloj**: *watch, clock* | **bolso**: *purse, handbag* | **cámara**: *camera* |

SpanishEasyAndFun.com

**pulsera**: *bracelet*      **anillo**: *ring*     **aretes, pendientes**: *earrings*
**cadena**: *chain*     **auto\***: *car*     **billetera, cartera**: *wallet*

🔧 The word **auto** (automóvil) is common to all Spanish-speaking countries, although in each country there may be a different more commonly used name (carro, coche, etc.).

## c   Asking and telling where things are

🔹 In order to ask where things are, use these questions:

**¿Dónde está** + singular noun?

**¿Dónde está** el diccionario?    >    *Where is the dictionary?*

**¿Dónde están** + plural noun?

**¿Dónde están** las llaves?    >    *Where are the keys?*

🔹 A common preposition used to say where things are is "**en**" *(in, on, at)*.

La cámara está **en** la bolsa.    >    *The camera is in the bag.*
Los periódicos están **en** la mesa.    >    *The newspapers are on the table.*

## d   Adverbs of place: "aquí", "acá", "allí", "allá", "ahí"

Adverbs of place are used to say where things or people are. The following ones show proximity to or distance from the speaker.

🔹 **Aquí** and **acá** *(here)* are used to indicate a place near the speaker:

La pulsera está **aquí /acá.**    >    *The bracelet is here.*

🔹 **Allí, allá** and **ahí** *(there)* are used to indicate a place away from the speaker:

María y Lidia están **allí/allá/ahí.**    >    *María and Lidia are there.*

🔹 These adverbs can also be used in other expressions:

🔹 **por aquí/acá**:                *over here*
El llavero está **por aquí.**    >    *The key ring is over here.*

🔹 **por allí/allá/ahí**:           *over there*
Ellos están **por allá.**    >    *They are over there.*

# Gramática fácil

## a The definite article

The definite article is used to mention something specific, already quoted, or understood. In Spanish it has two forms in singular and another two in plural.

|  | SINGULAR | PLURAL |
|---|---|---|
| masculine | el | los |
| feminine | la | las |

All Spanish nouns have a gender: they are either masculine or feminine. The article must agree with the noun it comes before in gender and in number.

**el** periódico *(the newspaper)*      **los** periódicos *(the newspapers)*
**la** revista *(the magazine)*      **las** revistas *(the magazines)*

When a feminine noun begins with a stressed "a" or "ha", the article changes into masculine in singular.

**el** agua *(the water)*      **las** aguas *(the waters)*
**el** hacha *(the ax)*      **las** hachas *(the axes)*

Do not mistake the article **el** *(the)* for the subject pronoun **él** *(he)*. The accent mark on the personal pronoun is used to show this difference.

**El** niño está en la escuela.      *The boy is at school.*
**Él** está en la escuela.      *He is at school.*

## b · Uses of definite articles

Apart from the uses already quoted, the definite articles can be found in many contexts. In other units we will deal with some of them but basically they are used:

● before names of languages except after the preposition "en" (and sometimes "de") and the verbs "hablar" *(to speak)*, "enseñar" *(to teach)* or "aprender" *(to learn)* :

| | | |
|---|---|---|
| **El** español no es difícil. | > | *Spanish is not difficult.* |
| No entiendo **el** chino. | > | *I don't understand Chinese.* |
| Tú estudias los artículos en español. | > | *You're studying the Spanish articles.* |
| Ella habla inglés. | > | *She speaks English.* |

● before most titles, except when speaking directly to the person:

| | | |
|---|---|---|
| **El** señor García está en la oficina. | > | *Mr. García is in the office.* |
| **El** profesor Vives es famoso. | > | *Professor Vives is famous.* |

● with the parts of the body and clothing:

| | | |
|---|---|---|
| Me lavo **las** manos. | > | *I wash my hands.* |
| Ponte **el** abrigo. | > | *Put on your coat.* |

● before the names of the days of the week and dates, except after the verb "ser" in some cases:

| | | |
|---|---|---|
| Mi cumpleaños es **el** 5 de mayo. | > | *My birthday is on May 5th.* |
| Juego un partido **el** martes. | > | *I'm playing a match on Tuesday.* |
| Hoy es jueves. | > | *It's Thursday today.* |
| Hoy es 3 de abril. | > | *Today is April 3rd.* |

● The plural of the days of the week is revealed by the article:

| | | |
|---|---|---|
| Juego al tenis **los** martes. | > | *I play tennis on Tuesdays.* |

● when referring to the time:

| | | |
|---|---|---|
| El programa es a **las** 9. | > | *The program is at 9:00.* |
| Son **las** 2 en punto. | > | *It's 2 o'clock.* |

● before nouns of a general or abstract nature.

| | | |
|---|---|---|
| **La** vida es maravillosa. | > | *Life is wonderful.* |
| Me gusta **el** baloncesto. | > | *I like basketball.* |

## c  Contractions

When the article "**el**" is preceded by the prepositions "**a**" *(to)* or "**de**" *(of, from)*, they contract to become:

a + el
*(to + the)*  ·····➤  **al**   Voy **al** cine.   ➤   *I am going to the movie theatre.*

de + el  ·····➤  **del**   Vengo **del** cine.   ➤   *I am coming from the movie theater.*


## d  The verb "llamarse" (*to be called/named*)

**PRESENT INDICATIVE**

| yo | **me llamo** | nosotros/nosotras | **nos llamamos** |
|---|---|---|---|
| tú | **te llamas** | vosotros/as | **os llamáis** |
| usted | **se llama** | ustedes | **se llaman** |
| él | **se llama** | | |
| ella | **se llama** | ellos/ellas | **se llaman** |

The verb "**llamarse**" is commonly used to express someone's name.

¿Cómo **te llamas**? **Me llamo** Claudia.  ➤  *What's your name? My name is Claudia.*
¿Cómo **se llama** él? Él **se llama** Alberto.  ➤  *What's his name? His name's Alberto.*
¿Cómo **se llaman** ustedes?  ➤  *What are your names?*
**Nos llamamos** Pablo y Lola.  ➤  *Our names are Pablo and Lola.*


## e  The conjunctions "y" and "e"

The conjunction "**y**" *(and)* is used to list things or join some elements:

Ellos son Francisco **y** Carlos.  ➤  *They are Francisco and Carlos.*
El libro **y** las fotos están en el estante.  ➤  *The book and the photos are on the shelf.*

When the conjunction "**y**" is followed by a word that begins with "i" or "hi", it changes into "**e**".

Ricardo **e** Ignacio están aquí.  ➤  *Ricardo and Ignacio are here.*
Es un problema de padres **e** hijos.  ➤  *It's a problem of parents and children.*

# Ejercicios de la **Unidad 3**

## a

Match the questions with the correct answers:

**1** ¿Dónde están los niños?
**2** ¿Cuáles son tus apellidos?
**3** ¿Cómo se llaman ustedes?
**4** ¿Cuál es tu dirección?
**5** ¿Cómo se llaman ellos?

**a** Se llaman José y Paz.
**b** En la casa.
**c** Nos llamamos Marcos y Luis.
**d** Monegro Estévez.
**e** Calle Sol, número 3.

## b

Fill in the gaps with the correct form of the verbs "ser" and "llamarse".

**1** ¿Cómo _____ usted? _____ Manuel Jiménez.
**2** ¿_____ ellas canadienses? No, _____ estadounidenses.
**3** ¡Hola! ¿Cómo _____? _____ Sara.
**4** Nosotras _____ de Colombia.

## c

How do you ask where the watch is?

**1** ¿De dónde es el reloj?
**2** ¿Cómo es el reloj?
**3** ¿Dónde está el reloj?
**4** ¿Cuál es el reloj?

## d

Fill in the gaps with the suitable article (el, la, los, las) or conjunction (y, e).

**1** _____ niñas están en _____ auto.
**2** Carlos _____ Iván son amigos.
**3** Peter es inglés _____ Paolo es brasileño.
**4** Me llamo Roberto _____ soy mejicano.
**5** ¿Dónde está _____ teléfono? Está en _____ mesa.

**Key**

**a:** 1.– b; 2.– d; 3.– c; 4.– e; 5.– a.
**b:** 1.– se llama, Me llamo; 2.– Son, son; 3.– te llamas, Me llamo; 4.– somos
**c:** 3
**d:** 1.– Las, el; 2.– e; 3.– y; 4.– y; 5.– el, la.

# Unidad 4
## Ciudad de México

### En esta unidad estudiaremos:

⦿ **Diálogo**

⦿ **Hablemos español:**
    **a)** Introducing oneself and others. **b)** Spanish titles.
    **c)** Vocabulario: La familia (The family).

⦿ **Gramática fácil:**
    **a)** Possessive adjectives. **b)** Nouns: gender and number.

⦿ **Ejercicios**

---

*Es sábado. Silvia sabe que su amigo Fernando no conoce a nadie más en la ciudad y por ello le invita a pasar una velada con su familia.*

Silvia: Fernando, hoy es sábado. Yo quiero ir a visitar a **mi hermana**. Ha tenido **su** primer **hijo** y hoy irá toda la **familia** a cenar a **su** casa. ¿Te apetece venir conmigo?

Fernando: De acuerdo. Así podré conocer a **tu hermano,** a **tu hermana** y a **tus padres**.

Silvia: Bueno... y a más **parientes**.
    [Llegan a la casa de la hermana de Silvia].

Raúl: ¡Silvia! ¡Qué alegría de verte! Pasen, por favor.

S:  ¡Hola, Raúl! **Te presento a mi** compañero de apartamento. Se llama Fernando y es español. Fernando, **este es** Raúl, mi **cuñado**.

F:  ¡**Encantado de conocerle!**

R:  **Igualmente**.

S:  ¿Y dónde está **mi sobrino**?

R:  Está con **tu hermana** en el dormitorio. **Tus padres, tu hermano, su novia, tus tíos** y **tus primos** están en el salón.

S:  ¿Están también **mis abuelos** aquí?

R:  **Tu abuelo**, no, pero **tu abuela** vino con **doña** Paquita. Están en la cocina.

F:  ¿Quién es **doña** Paquita?

S:  Es una vecina.

R:  Silvia, ve al salón con Fernando y preséntale a la **familia**.

S:  ¡Ven, Fernando! Voy a presentarte a **mi madre**, a **mi padre**, a **mi abuela**, a la **suegra** de **mi hermana**...

F:  ¡Dios mío! ¡No podré recordar tantos nombres!

S:  No te preocupes. Por cierto, ¿tienes hambre? Mi **tía** es la mejor cocinera del mundo...

La Catedral, El Zócalo, Ciudad de México.

*It is Saturday. Silvia knows that her friend Fernando doesn't know anyone else in the city and invites him to spend the evening with her family.*

*Silvia: Fernando, today is Saturday. I want to visit my sister. She has had her first son and all the family is going to have dinner in her house. Would you like to come with me?*

*Fernando: Alright. Then I'll be able to meet your brother, your sister and your parents.*

*Silvia: Well... and more relatives.*
  *[They arrive at Silvia's sister's house].*

*Raúl: Silvia! How nice to see you! Come in, please.*

*S:   Hello, Raúl! Let me introduce you to my roommate. His name is Fernando and he is Spanish. Fernando, this is Raúl, my brother-in-law.*

*F:   Pleased to meet you!*

*R:   Pleased to meet you, too!*

*S:   And where is my nephew?*

*R:   He is with your sister in the bedroom. Your parents, your brother, his girlfriend, your uncle and aunt and your cousins are in the living-room.*

*S:   Are my grandparents also here?*

*R:   Your grandfather isn't, but your grandmother came with doña Paquita. They are in the kitchen.*

*F:   Who is doña Paquita?*

*S:   She is a neighbor.*

*R:   Silvia, go to the living-room with Fernando and introduce him to the family.*

*S:   Come on, Fernando! I'll introduce you to my mother, my father, my grandmother, my sister's mother-in-law...*

*F:   Oh, my God! I won't remember so many names!*

*S:   Don't worry. By the way, are you hungry? My aunt is the best cook in the world...*

# Hablemos español

## a Introducing oneself and others

🔲 In order to introduce ourselves to other people we can say:

| | | |
|---|---|---|
| **Soy** Luis Ramos. | > | *I'm Luis Ramos.* |
| **Me llamo** Carla. | > | *My name is Carla.* |
| **Mi nombre es** Alberto. | > | *My name is Alberto.* |

🔲 And when we introduce other people:

| | | |
|---|---|---|
| **Este / Él es** Miguel. | > | *This is Miguel.* |
| **Esta / Ella es** la Sra. López. | > | *This is Mrs. López.* |
| **Te/le presento a** Silvia Pérez. | > | *Let me introduce you to Silvia Pérez.* |
| **¿Conoces a** Guadalupe? | > | *Do you know Guadalupe?* |

🔲 Some common expressions said by those who have just been introduced are:

| | | |
|---|---|---|
| **Encantado/a (de conocerte/le)**. | > | *Nice to meet you.* |
| **¡Mucho gusto!** | > | *Nice to meet you.* |
| **Un placer (conocerte/le)**. | > | *Pleased to meet you.* |
| **Igualmente**. | > | *Nice to meet you, too.* |
| Paco: Luis, **este es** Pedro. | > | *Paco: Luis, this is Pedro.* |
| Luis: Hola, Pedro. **Encantado de conocerte**. | > | *Luis: Hello, Pedro. Nice to meet you.* |
| Pedro: **Igualmente**. ¿Cómo estás? | > | *Pedro: Nice to meet you, too.How are you?* |

## b Spanish titles

Spanish titles are used somewhat differently than their English counterparts.

🔲 Spanish titles are not capitalized (though their abbreviations are).
🔲 When they are used before a name they are preceded by the definite article except when speaking to the person.
🔲 There are masculine and feminine versions of most titles.

### Abbreviation

| | | | | | |
|---|---|---|---|---|---|
| **señor** | **Sr.** | *Mr.* | **doctor** | **Dr.** | *Dr.* |
| **señora** | **Sra.** | *Mrs., Ms.* | **doctora** | **Dra.** | *Dr. (female)* |
| **señorita** | **Srta.** | *Miss, Ms.* | **profesor** | **Prof.** | *Professor* |
| **don** | **D.** | | **profesora** | **Profa.** | *Professor* |
| **doña** | **Dª / Dña.** | | | | *(female)* |

SpanishEasyAndFun.com

- The tiles "Sr.", "Sra.", "Srta.", "Dr.", "Dra.", "Prof." and "Profa." usually precede a surname, though they can also be used with a name and surname.

La **Srta.** Ruiz no está aquí.     >     *Miss Ruiz isn't here.*

- "Don" is the most common courtesy title or form of address for a man and "doña" for a woman. They are followed by the person's first name, or first name and surname, and have no real equivalent in English.

¿Conoces a **don** Pedro?     >     *Do you know don Pedro?*
**Dr.** Sánchez, ¿cómo está usted?     >     *Dr. Sánchez, how are you?*

## C   Vocabulario: La familia (The family)

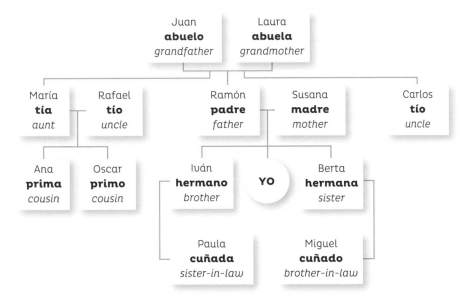

**padres**: *parents*
**hijo**: *son*
**abuelos**: *grandparents*
**nieto**: *grandson*
**sobrino**: *nephew*
**suegro**: *father-in-law*
**novio**: *boyfriend*
**parientes**: *relatives*

**hijos/as**: *children*
**hija**: *daughter*
**nietos**: *grandchildren*
**nieta**: *granddaughter*
**sobrina**: *niece*
**suegra**: *mother-in-law*
**novia**: *girlfriend*

The father and mother are colloquially called **"papá"** *(dad, daddy)* and **"mamá"** *(mom, mommy)*.

# Gramática fácil

## a Possessive adjectives

Possessive adjectives are used to show ownership.
They are:

| | | | |
|---|---|---|---|
| **mi** | *my* | **nuestro-nuestra** | *our* |
| **tu** | *your* | **vuestro-vuestra**\*\* | *your* |
| **su (de usted)** | *your* | **su (de ustedes)**\*\* | *your* |
| **su (de él)** | *his* | | |
| **su (de ella)** | *her* | **su (de ellos/as)** | *their* |
| **su (de ello)**\* | *its* | | |

🔄 **Su** is the possessive adjective for animals, things or places.
🔄🔄 In Spain this possessive is **vuestro-vuestra**, but **su** is the one used in Latin American countries.

🔵 Possessive adjectives are always followed by a noun.

**Mi** <u>apartamento</u> es grande.
*My apartment is big.*

**Su** <u>diccionario</u> (de ella) es caro.
*Her dictionary is expensive.*

**Nuestro** <u>idioma</u> es el español.
*Our language is Spanish.*

¿**Su** <u>habitación</u> (de ustedes) está cerrada?
*Is your room closed?*

Daniel no es **su** <u>hijo</u> (de ellos).
*Daniel isn't their son.*

🔵 The possessives "**nuestro**", "**vuestro**" (masculine)
and "**nuestra**", "**vuestra**" (feminine), agree with
the gender of the noun they precede.

**Nuestro** <u>auto</u> es grande.
*Our car is big.*

Estamos en **vuestra** <u>casa</u>.
*We are in your house.*

Do not mistake the
possessive **tu** *(your)* for the
personal pronoun **tú** *(you)*.
The accent mark is used on
the personal pronoun to
stress this difference.

**Tu** nombre es Federico.
*Your name is Federico.*

**Tú** eres Federico.
*You are Federico.*

🖐 SpanishEasyAndFun.com

● If a plural noun follows the possessive, a plural possessive is needed: **mis**, **tus**, **sus**, **nuestros / nuestras, vuestros / vuestras** or **sus**.

| | | |
|---|---|---|
| **Mis** <u>padres</u> son Pablo y María. | > | *My parents are Pablo and María.* |
| **Tus** <u>abuelos</u> son argentinos. | > | *Your grandparents are Argentinian.* |
| **Sus** <u>hijos</u> (de él) son altos. | > | *His children are tall.* |
| **Sus** <u>calles</u> (de Nueva York) son largas. | > | *Its streets are long.* |
| **Nuestras** <u>madres</u> están en **sus** casas. | > | *Our mothers are in their houses.* |
| **Vuestros** <u>libros</u> son interesantes. | > | *Your books are interesting.* |
| No son **sus** <u>primos</u> (de ustedes). | > | *They aren't your cousins.* |
| ¿Dónde están **sus** <u>autos</u> (de ellos)? | > | *Where are their cars?* |

## b Nouns: gender and number

All Spanish nouns have a gender and are either masculine or feminine.

el **hermano** (masc.) *the brother*          la **hermana** (fem.) *the sister*

● Regarding the **gender of nouns** (note the article has been added in order to stress the difference):

▪ Words ending in "-o" are usually masculine: el **gato** *(cat)*, el **amigo** *(friend)*. But there are some exceptions: la **mano** *(hand)*, la **foto** *(photo)*, etc.

▪ Words ending in "-a" are usually feminine: la **gata** *(cat)*, la **amiga** *(friend)*. But there are also some exceptions: el **día** *(day)*, el **atleta** *(male athlete)*, etc.

▪ Words ending in "-e" or in a consonant can be either masculine or feminine: el **hombre** (man), la **mujer** (woman), el **padre** (father), la **madre** (mother), el **calor** (heat), la **flor** (flower).

▪ Words ending in "-ema" are masculine: el **tema** *(topic)*, el **problema** *(problem)*.

▪ Words ending in "-dad" are feminine: la **amistad** *(friendship)*, la **verdad** *(truth)*.

▪ Words ending in "-ción" and "-sión" are also feminine: la **solución** *(solution)*, la **información** *(information)*, la **televisión** *(television)*.

▪ Words referring to jobs or occupations that end in "or" in masculine add "a" in feminine: el **pintor** (male painter) – la **pintora** (female painter)

▪ Words that describe people and end in "-ista" can be either masculine or feminine: el **periodista** *(male journalist)* – la **periodista** *(female journalist)*, el **especialista** *(male specialist)* – la **especialista** *(female specialist)*.

● Regarding the **number of nouns**, to make the plural forms:
If the singular noun ends in a vowel, simply add an "-s":

casa – casa**s** (*house – houses*)      hombre – hombre**s** (*man – men*)

Except when the word ends with a stressed "-í" or "-ú", that both "**-s**" and "**-es**" can be added (depending on the cases):

esquí – esquí**s** [*ski – a pair of skis*]    menú – menú**s** [*menu(s)*]
jabalí - jabalí**es** [*wild boar(s)*]        hindú – hindú**es** [*Hindu(s)*]

● If a noun ends in a consonant, make it plural by adding "**-es**":

profesor – profesor**es**  (*teacher – teachers*)
árbol – árbol**es** (*tree – trees*)

● If a noun ends in a "-z", it becomes a "c" before adding "**-es**":

lápiz – lápi**ces** (*pencil – pencils*)      pez – pe**ces** (*fish – fish*)

● If the plural refers to a mixed group, it has the masculine form:

2 gat**os** + 5 gat**as** = 7 gat**os**

● There are some nouns that are normally used in plural form, although they refer to a single object: las lente**s** / gafa**s** (*a pair of glasses*), las tijera**s** (*a pair of scissors*), los pantalon**es** (*a pair of trousers*), etc.

SpanishEasyAndFun.com

**a** Fill in the gaps with the following expressions to complete the dialogue:

| te presento a | Encantada | Igualmente | este es |
|---|---|---|---|

**1** Juan, _____ Luisa.

**2** Luisa, _____ Juan.

**a** _____

**b** _____

**b** Match the numbers and the letters.

**1** My mother's mother is

**2** My aunt's son is

**3** My aunt's husband is

**4** My sister's husband is

**5** My sister's son is

**a** mi primo

**b** mi tío

**c** mi cuñado

**d** mi sobrino

**e** mi abuela

**c** Fill in the gaps with the suitable possessive adjective.

**1** Él es argentino. _____ nombre es Pedro.

**2** Miguel y Antonio son _____ primos (de Lidia).

**3** Nosotros somos hermanos. _____. casa es grande.

**4** Nosotros somos hermanos. _____ autos son grandes.

**d** What is the plural form for the following nouns?

**1** sobrina _____

**2** calle _____

**3** profesor _____

**4** marido _____

**5** mujer _____

**6** señor _____

**e** Use the definite article (el, la, los, las) to indicate the gender and number of the following nouns.

**1** _____ libros

**2** _____ días

**3** _____ estudiante

**4** _____ artistas

**5** _____ agua

# Unidad 5
## Granada

**En esta unidad estudiaremos:**

● **Diálogo**

● **Hablemos español:**
   **a)** Asking and telling where people or things are from.
   **b)** Vocabulario: Países y nacionalidades (Countries and nationalities).
   **c)** Apologizing. **d)** Asking someone to repeat and to speak more slowly.
   **e)** Asking for meanings.

● **Gramática fácil:**
   **a)** The indefinite article. **b)** Stressing words and written accent marks.
   **c)** Dipthongs.

● **Ejercicios**

*Francisco y Linda se conocen en la universidad. Hoy es el primer día del curso.*

Francisco: ¡Hola! Me llamo Francisco.
Linda: ¡Hola! Yo soy Linda.
F:   **¿De dónde eres?**
L:   Soy **de Canadá**.
F:   **¿Qué?**
L:   Soy **canadiense**, ¿y tú?
F:   Yo soy **español**. Soy **de** Barcelona.
L:   ¡Ah! Me gusta **España**. Es **un país** bonito y tiene **una** historia interesante.
F:   Sí, es cierto. Bueno, en nuestra clase hay gente **de** muchos **países**: de **Colombia, Argentina, Brasil, Estados Unidos**...
L:   Sí, y también hay **ingleses, italianos, franceses, un chino** y **unas** muchachas **alemanas**. Tenemos diferentes **nacionalidades.**
F:   Ah!, ya los conoces. Y, **¿de dónde** son nuestros profesores**?** ¿Lo sabes?
L:   **¿Cómo? ¿Puedes repetir?**
F:   No sé **de dónde son** nuestros profesores. ¿Lo sabes tú?
L:   Sé que **unos** profesores son **estadounidenses**. Bueno, Francisco, tengo que irme ahora ¿**Cómo se dice** "It's late!" en **español**?

SpanishEasyAndFun.com

Patio de los Leones en la Alhambra, Granada, España.

*Francisco and Linda meet each other at the university. Today is the first day of the semester.*

Francisco: Hello! My name is Francisco.
Linda: Hello! I am Linda.
F:  Where are you from?
L:  I am from Canada.
F:  What?
L:  I am Canadian, and you?
F:  I am Spanish. I'm from Barcelona.
L:  Ah! I like Spain. It is a nice country and has an interesting history.
F:  Yes, it's true. Well, in our class there are people from many countries: from Colombia, Argentina, Brazil, the United States...
L:  Yes, and there are also English, Italians, French, a Chinese guy and some German girls. We have different nationalities.
F:  Ah, you already know them. And, where are our teachers from? Do you know?
L:  What? Can you repeat that?
F:  I don't know where our teachers are from. Do you know?
L:  I know some teachers are American. Well, Francisco, I have to go now. How do you say "It's late" in Spanish?

# Hablemos español

**Asking and telling where people or things are from**

To ask about the place of origin of people or things you can use the following expression:

> **¿De dónde +** present of "to be" + (subject)**?**
> *Where + present of "to be" + subject + from?*

Remember that the preposition "**de**" is used before the interrogative "**¿dónde?**", whereas in other languages this preposition is used at the end of the question.

| | | |
|---|---|---|
| ¿**De dónde** eres (tú)? | > | *Where are you from?* |
| ¿**De dónde** es usted? | > | *Where are you from?* |
| ¿**De dónde** es tu madre? | > | *Where is your mother from?* |
| ¿**De dónde** son ellos? | > | *Where are they from?* |

And to answer:

| | | |
|---|---|---|
| Soy **de** México. | > | *I'm from Mexico.* |
| Mi madre es **de** España. | > | *My mother is from Spain.* |
| Ellos son **de** Nueva York. | > | *They're from New York.* |

In order to ask and answer where people or things are from, it is important to know some vocabulary about countries and nationalities.

**b** **vocabulario: Países y nacionalidades (Countries and nationalities)**

| **Países** *(Countries)* | **Nacionalidades** *(Nationalities)* |
|---|---|
| México *(Mexico)* | mexicano-mexicana *(Mexican)* |
| Colombia *(Colombia)* | colombiano-colombiana *(Colombian)* |
| Cuba *(Cuba)* | cubano-cubana *(Cuban)* |
| Argentina *(Argentina)* | argentino-argentina *(Argentinian)* |
| Brasil *(Brazil)* | brasileño-brasileña *(Brazilian)* |
| Estados Unidos *(The United States)* | estadounidense *(American)* |
| Canadá *(Canada)* | canadiense *(Canadian)* |

 SpanishEasyAndFun.com

| Países (Countries) | Nacionalidades (Nationalities) |
|---|---|
| España (Spain) | español-española (Spanish) |
| Francia (France) | francés-francesa (French) |
| Inglaterra (England) | inglés-inglesa (English) |
| Alemania (Germany) | alemán-alemana (German) |
| Holanda (The Netherlands) | holandés-holandesa (Dutch) |
| Bélgica (Belgium) | belga (Belgian) |
| Italia (Italy) | italiano-italiana (Italian) |
| China (China) | chino-china (Chinese) |
| Japón (Japan) | japonés-japonesa |

When speaking about someone's origin you can use:

**ser** + <u>nationality</u>
**ser de** + <u>city or country</u>

Nationalities (and languages) are always written in lower case letters. In Spanish there are masculine and feminine forms to express nationalities, except for those ending with "-e" (estadounidense, canadiense, etc.), and some others (belga, iraní, etc.).

Thus, you can say:

| | | |
|---|---|---|
| ¿De dónde eres? | > | *Where are you from?* |
| **Soy de** <u>Brasil</u>. **Soy** <u>brasileño</u>. | > | *I'm from Brazil. I'm Brazilian.* |
| | | |
| ¿De dónde es tu profesor? | > | *Where is your teacher from?* |
| **Es de** <u>Alemania</u>. **Es** <u>alemán</u>. | > | *He's from Germany. He's German.* |
| | | |
| Su madre (de él) **es** <u>francesa</u>. | > | *His mother is French.* |
| Yo **soy de** <u>Miami</u>. **Soy** <u>estadounidense</u>. | > | *I'm from Miami. I'm American.* |

## c Apologizing

When apologizing we can use the following expressions:

**Perdón**
**Perdona** (informal) - **Perdone** (formal)
**Disculpa** (informal) - **Disculpe** (formal)  ⟩  *Excuse me*

These expressions are also used when we mean *"Sorry"*, but in this case, we can also say **"Lo siento"** or **"Lo lamento"**.

| | | |
|---|---|---|
| —Hola ¿Está José? | > | —*Hello Is José there?* |
| —No. Se ha confundido. | > | —*No. You have the wrong number.* |
| —¡Oh! **Lo siento***. | > | —*Oh! I'm sorry.* |

✪ You could also say "**lo lamento**", "**perdón**", "**perdone**" or "**disculpe**".

## d Asking someone to repeat and to speak more slowly

When we don't understand someone and want them to repeat what they have just said or to speak more slowly, we can use any of the following expressions.

🖐 Colloquially we can say:

| | | |
|---|---|---|
| **¿Qué? / ¿Cómo?** | > | *What? (What did you say?)* |
| **¿Puedes repetir?** | > | *Can you repeat (that)?* |
| **¿Puedes hablar más despacio?** | > | *Can you speak more slowly?* |

🖐 But in a formal situation we use:

| | | |
|---|---|---|
| **¿Perdón?** | > | *I beg your pardon?* |
| **¿Podría hablar más despacio?** | > | *Could you speak more slowly?* |
| **Perdone, pero no entiendo**. | > | *Sorry, I don't understand.* |

## e Asking for meanings

In order to ask for the meaning of a word or expression or how something is said in another language, we use:

| | | |
|---|---|---|
| **¿Qué significa... (en...)?** | > | *What does... mean (in...)?* |
| **¿Cómo se dice... en...?** | > | *How do you say... in... ?* |
| **¿Qué significa** "calabaza" (**en** español)**?** | > | *What does "pumpkin" mean (in Spanish)?* |
| **¿Cómo se dice** "table" **en** español**?** | > | *How do you say "table" in Spanish?* |

🖐 SpanishEasyAndFun.com

# Gramática fácil

## a The indefinite article

The indefinite article is used to identify what something is, therefore it is used when talking about something or someone for the first time.

| | | |
|---|---|---|
| Soy **un** hombre. | > | *I am a man.* |
| Es **una** mesa. | > | *It is a table.* |

In Spanish, the indefinite article has four forms, depending on whether the noun it precedes is masculine, feminine, singular or plural.

| | MASCULINE | FEMININE | |
|---|---|---|---|
| **singular** | un | una | *a* |
| **plural** | unos | unas | *some* |

| | | |
|---|---|---|
| **un** gato | > | *a male cat* |
| **unos** gatos | > | *some male cats (or a mixed group)* |
| **una** gata | > | *a female cat* |
| **unas** gatas | > | *some female cats* |

"**Un**" and "**una**" are also equivalent to the number "*one*".

| | | |
|---|---|---|
| **un** libro | > | *one book, a book* |
| **una** manzana | > | *one apple, an apple* |

Remember, as long as the group has at least one male member, the masculine plural article is used. Thus, "unos gatos" could refer to a group of male cats, or it could refer to a group of male and female cats.

## b  Stressing words and written accent marks

In order to have the correct pronunciation, we need to know the stress patterns in Spanish.

■ If a word ends in a vowel, "n" or "s", stress falls upon the second-to-last syllable.

**ca**sa (*house*)          e**xa**men (*exam*)          **li**bros (*books*)

■ If a word ends in any consonant other than "n" or "s", stress falls upon the last syllable.

es**tar** (*to be*)          espa**ñol** (*Spanish*)          us**ted** (*you*)

■ Any exception to the previous rules has a written accent mark on the stressed vowel.

ca**fé** (*coffee*)          situa**ción** (*situation*)          es**tás** (*you are*)
**ár**bol (*tree*)          **lá**piz (*pencil*)          di**fí**cil (*difficult*)
gra**má**tica (*grammar*)          **mé**dico (*doctor*)          te**lé**fono (*telephone*)

Written accent marks are also used to distinguish between two words that are pronounced the same but have different meanings.

| **sí** | *yes* | vs. | **si** | *if* |
| **él** | *he* | vs. | **el** | *the* |
| **tú** | *you* | vs. | **tu** | *your* |

All questioning words are always written with accent marks.

**¿Qué?**     *What?*               **¿Dónde?**     *Where?*

## c  Dipthongs

A dipthong is the combination of a weak vowel ("i", "u") with each other or with a strong vowel ("a", "e", "o"). Both vowels belong to a single syllable.

famil**ia**     b**ie**n     rad**io**     s**ua**ve     **Eu**ropa     c**ui**dado
**ai**re     r**ey**     h**oy**     **au**to     h**ue**vo     c**iu**dad
h**ay**

When the stress of the word falls on the weak vowel ("i" or "u"), they are written with an accent mark. In these cases the two vowels do not form a diphthong but they are pronounced in two different syllables. That's what we call a hiatus.

**rí**o     d**ú**o     pa**ís**     ba**úl**     re**ír**

**a** How do you ask about someone's country or city of origin?

1 ¿Dónde estás?
2 ¿De dónde eres?
3 ¿Cuál es tu nacionalidad?
4 ¿Dónde está tu país?

**b** What question do you use when you need a word repeated?

1 ¿Cómo se dice esa palabra?
2 ¿Puedes repetir esa palabra?
3 ¿Puedes deletrear esa palabra?
4 ¿Puedes hablar más despacio?

**c** Use an accent mark where necessary.

1 frances
2 numero
3 mañana
4 conversación
5 arbol

**d** Fill in the gaps with the suitable word or expression.

| Perdona | Soy de | se dice | puedes repetir | soy |
|---------|--------|---------|----------------|-----|

— ¿De dónde eres?
— _____ 1 Alemania. _____ 2 alemán.
— ¿Cómo _____ 3 "Alemania" en alemán?
— _____ 4 , no entiendo. ¿_____ 5 ?

**Key**

**a:** 2.
**b:** 2
**c:** 1.- francés; 2.- número; 3.- mañana; 4.- conversación; 5.- árbol.
**d:** 1.- Soy de; 2.- soy; 3.- se dice; 4.- Perdona; 5.- Puedes repetir.

Spanish: Easy and Fun

**U5** ● 61

# Unidad 6
## Cartagena

**En esta unidad estudiaremos:**

◉ **Diálogo**

◉ **Hablemos español:**
**a)** Spelling. **b)** Indicating one's age. **c)** Telephone numbers.
**d)** Vocabulario: Habitaciones, muebles y objetos de casa (Rooms, pieces of furniture and household objects).

◉ **Gramática fácil:**
**a)** The verb "tener" (to have). Present indicative. **b)** Position of descriptive adjectives (I). **c)** Cardinal numbers [0-99].

◉ **Ejercicios**

*Ramón y Carmen se intercambian sus direcciones y números de teléfono antes de despedirse.*

Ramón: Y tú, Carmen, **¿qué edad tienes?**
Carmen: **Tengo 41 (cuarenta y un) años.** ¿Y tú? **¿Cuántos años tienes?**
R:   **Yo tengo 39 (treinta y nueve).** Y, ¿cuál es tu dirección?
C:   Avenida Bolívar, número **24 (veinticuatro).**
R:   ¿Cómo? **¿Puedes deletrear** el nombre de la avenida?
C:   B **de** Barcelona, O **de** Oregón, L **de** Londres, I **de** Italia, V **de** Venecia, A **de** Alemania, R **de** Roma.
R:   No la conozco. No soy de aquí.
C:   Es **una** avenida importante, pero vivo en **un** apartamento pequeño. Solo **tiene un dormitorio, una sala de estar, una cocina** pequeña y **un baño.** Pero es suficiente para **una** persona.
R:   **Tienes suerte.** Yo vivo con **dos** hermanos en **un** apartamento antiguo. Tengo que comprar **una lámpara** y **una cama.** Bueno, Carmen, ahora **tengo prisa** y también **tengo hambre.** Pero antes de irme... **¿Cuál es tu número de teléfono?** Te podría llamar esta semana.
C:   ¡De acuerdo! **Mi número de teléfono es el 769 853001 (siete-seis-nueve-ocho-cinco-tres-cero-cero-uno).**
R:   Yo **tengo un número de teléfono** nuevo.
C:   ¿Sí? ¿Cuál es?
R:   **Es el 769 120458 (siete-seis-nueve-doce-cero-cuatro-cincuenta y ocho).**
C:   ...**458.** De acuerdo. Ya lo **tengo.**
R:   Entonces, ¡hasta pronto, Carmen!
C:   ¡Hasta pronto, Ramón!

Centro histórico de Cartagena, Colombia.

*Ramón and Carmen are exchanging addresses and telephone numbers before saying good-bye.*

Ramón: And, Carmen, how old are you?
Carmen: I am 41 (forty-one) years old. And you? How old are you?
R:  I am 39 (thirty-nine). And, what's your address?
C:  Avenida Bolívar, 24 (twenty-four).
R:  What? Can you spell the name of the avenue?
C:  B for Barcelona, O for Oregon, L for London, I for Italy, V for Venice, A for Alabama, R for Rome.
R:  I don't know it. I am not from here.
C:  It is a prestigious avenue but I live in a small apartment. It only has a bedroom, a living-room, a small kitchen and a bathroom. But it's enough for one person.
R:  You are lucky. I am living with two brothers in an old apartment. I have to buy a lamp and a bed. Well, Carmen, I'm in a hurry now and I'm also hungry. But before I leave... What's your telephone number? I could call you this week.

C:  Okay! My telephone number is 769-853-001.

R:  I have a new phone number.
C:  Yes? What is it?
R:  It's 769-120-458.

C:  ...458. That's it.
R:  Then, see you soon, Carmen!
C:  See you soon, Ramón!

# Hablemos español

## a Spelling

[**deletrear**: *to spell*]

When we want someone to spell a word, we can ask:

| | | |
|---|---|---|
| **¿Cómo se deletrea...?** | > | *How do you spell...?* |
| **¿Puedes deletrear...?** | > | *Can you spell...?* |

Or even:

| | | |
|---|---|---|
| **¿Cómo se escribe...?** | > | *How do you spell...?* |
| | | |
| **¿Cómo se deletrea** tu nombre**?** | > | *How do you spell your name?* |
| **¿Puedes deletrear** tu apellido**?** | > | *Can you spell your last name?* |
| **¿Cómo se escribe** "casa"**?** C-A-S-A. | > | *How do you spell "casa"? C-A-S-A (ce-a-ese-a).* |

When answering, we will say each letter, even though there may be two of the same letters together in the word:

¿Cómo se deletrea "acción"? **A-C-C-I-O-N (a-ce-ce-i-o-ene)**.

The only case when we have two options is with the letters "ch" (ce-hache / che), "ll" (ele-ele / elle) and "rr" (ere-ere / erre).

When spelling (especially on the phone) we can emphasize the letters to avoid any confusion by means of expressions like:

D-A-N-I-E-L: "D" **de** "Dinamarca", "A" **de** "Alemania", "N" **de** "Navarra", "I" **de** "Italia", "E" **de** "España", "L" **de** "Londres".

*D-A-N-I-E-L: "D" for "Dakota", "A" for "Alabama", "N" for "Nebraska", "I" for "Italy", "E" for "Elephant", "L" for "London".* *

⭐ Obviously, you can choose the reference words you prefer.

## b Indicating one's age

In Spanish, the verb "tener" is used when talking about someone's age.

| | | |
|---|---|---|
| **¿Qué edad tienes?** | > | *How old are you?* |
| **Tengo** quince años. | > | *I am fifteen years old.* |

SpanishEasyAndFun.com

| ¿Cuántos años tiene usted? | > | How old are you? |
| Tengo cincuenta y dos años. | > | I am fifty-two years old. |

## c Telephone numbers

Telephone numbers in Spanish are frequently read in pairs although they can also be expressed digit by digit (or even combining single numbers and pairs of numbers). [See "Gramática Fácil"].

958283412: nueve – cinco – ocho – veintiocho – treinta y cuatro – doce

To ask for a telephone number we say:

| **¿Cuál es tu número de teléfono?** | > | What's your (tele)phone number? |

And to answer:

| **Mi número de teléfono** | > | My phone number is 509274831. |
| **es** (el) 509274831. | | |

## d Vocabulario: Habitaciones, muebles y objetos de casa (Rooms, pieces of furniture and household objects)

| HABITACIONES (rooms) | MUEBLES (PIECES OF FURNITURE) | OBJETOS DE CASA (HOUSEHOLD OBJECTS) |
| --- | --- | --- |
| **cocina**: kitchen | **mesa**: table | **lámpara\***: lamp |
| **comedor**: dining room | **silla**: chair | **cajón, gaveta**: drawer |
| **salón, sala de estar**: living room | **sillón**: armchair | **cortinas**: drapes |
| **dormitorio**: bedroom | **sofá**: couch, sofa | **cojín**: cushion |
| **baño**: bathroom | **cómoda**: chest of drawers, bureau | **cuadro**: picture |
| **aseo**: toilet | **armario**: closet | **alfombra\***: carpet |
| **pasillo**: hallway | **estante, repisa**: shelf | **televisor, televisión**: television set |
| **recibidor**: foyer | **estantería, librero**: bookcase | **puerta**: door |
| **lavadero**: laundry room | **cama**: bed | **ventana**: window |
| | **mesita de noche**: night table | **reloj de pared**: clock |
| | | **despertador**: alarm clock |

 Orthographic rule: before a "p" or a "b" we can never use an "n" but we use an "**m**":

lá**mp**ara (lamp) sie**mp**re (always) ca**mp**o (country)
a**mb**os (both) alfo**mb**ra (carpet) ca**mb**io (change)

# Gramática fácil

## a The verb "tener" (to have). Present indicative

| | | | |
|---|---|---|---|
| yo | **tengo** | nosotros/nosotras | **tenemos** |
| tú | **tienes** | vosotros/as | **tenéis** |
| usted | **tiene** | ustedes | **tienen** |
| él | **tiene** | | |
| ella | **tiene** | ellos/ellas | **tienen** |

The verb "tener" is used to express possession and , in most cases, its equivalent in English is *"to have (got)"*.

| | | |
|---|---|---|
| **Tengo** tres amigos en California. | > | *I have (got) three friends in California.* |
| ¿**Tienes** hermanos? | > | *Do you have any brothers?* |
| Usted no **tiene** auto. | > | *You don't have a car.* |
| Ella **tiene** dos lámparas en su salón. | > | *She has two lamps in her living room.* |
| Su apartamento **tiene** dos dormitorios. | > | *His apartment has two bedrooms.* |
| No **tenemos** trabajo. | > | *We don't have a job.* |
| ¿Dónde **tienen** ustedes sus boletos? | > | *Where do you have your tickets?* |
| Ellos **tienen** la nacionalidad americana. | > | *They have an American nationality.* |

The verb "tener" is also used in other cases, such as:

- To express age:

| | | |
|---|---|---|
| —¿Cuántos años **tienes**? / ¿Qué edad **tienes**? | > | —How old are you? |
| —**Tengo** diecinueve años. | > | —I am nineteen years old. |

- To express sensations:

| | | | |
|---|---|---|---|
| **tener calor** (to be hot) | Mi hija **tiene** calor. | > | My daughter is hot. |
| **tener frío** (to be cold) | No **tengo** frío. | > | I am not cold. |
| **tener hambre** (to be hungry) | ¿**Tienes** hambre? | > | Are you hungry? |
| **tener sed** (to be thirsty) | Ellos **tienen** sed. | > | They are thirsty. |
| **tener suerte** (to be lucky) | No **tenemos** suerte. | > | We aren't lucky. |
| **tener miedo** (to be afraid) | ¿**Tiene** él miedo? | > | Is he afraid? |
| **tener cuidado** (to be careful) | No **tienes** cuidado. | > | You aren't careful. |
| **tener** éxito (to be successful) | Madonna **tiene** éxito. | > | Madonna is successful. |
| **tener prisa** (to be in a hurry) | ¿**Tienes** prisa? | > | Are you in a hurry? |
| **tener razón** (to be right) | Ustedes **tienen** razón. | > | You are right. |
| **tener sueño** (to be sleepy) | ¿**Tienen** sueño? | > | Are they sleepy? |

In these expressions, the English equivalent of "tener" is not "to have (got)" but "to be". There are more uses of the verb "tener" that will be covered in upcoming units.

## b Position of descriptive adjectives (I)

These adjectives are usually placed after the noun they describe. When they precede the noun, these adjectives can change the nouns meaning, or be used to create a special emphasis or stylistic effect.

| | | |
|---|---|---|
| Ella es una <u>mujer</u> **pobre**. | > | She is a poor woman. |
| Ella es una **pobre** <u>mujer</u>. | > | She is a pitiable woman. |
| | | |
| Tengo <u>amigos</u> **viejos**. | > | I have some elderly friends. |
| Tengo **viejos** <u>amigos</u>. | > | I have some old (longtime) friends. |

# Cardinal numbers [0-99]

| | | |
|---|---|---|
| 0 – cero | 10 – diez | 20 – veinte |
| 1 – uno | 11 – once | 21 – veintiuno |
| 2 – dos | 12 – doce | 22 – veintidós |
| 3 – tres | 13 – trece | 30 – treinta, treinta y uno... |
| 4 – cuatro | 14 – catorce | 40 – cuarenta, cuarenta y uno... |
| 5 – cinco | 15 – quince | 50 – cincuenta, cincuenta y uno... |
| 6 – seis | 16 – dieciséis | 60 – sesenta, sesenta y uno... |
| 7 – siete | 17 – diecisiete | 70 – setenta, setenta y uno... |
| 8 – ocho | 18 – dieciocho | 80 – ochenta, ochenta y uno... |
| 9 – nueve | 9 – diecinueve | 90 – noventa, noventa y uno... |

We can see that:

- All numbers from 11 to 15 end in "-ce".
- All numbers from 16 to 19 start with "dieci-".
- All numbers from 16 to 29 are spelled as one word and those ending in "s" have a written accent mark (16, 22, 23 and 26).
- All compound numbers from 31 to 99 are written with three words.

The number "**uno**" (1) changes into "**un**" when it precedes a noun:

Tengo **un** hermano y tres hermanas.   >   *I have one brother and three sisters.*

"**Uno**" and "**un**" have a feminine form: "**una**".

Ella tiene **una** hija y **un** hijo.   >   *She has a daughter and a son.*
  *(one daughter and one son)*

All numbers ending in "**un/una**" have to agree with the gender of the noun they go with:

Tengo **treinta y un** años.   >   *I am thirty-one years old.*
Hay **veintiuna** niñas en la clase.   >   *There are twenty-one girls in the classroom.*

SpanishEasyAndFun.com

# Ejercicios de la **Unidad 6**

**a** What question do you use to ask someone's age?

**1** ¿Cómo eres de viejo?
**2** ¿Cuántos años eres?
**3** ¿Qué edad tienes?
**4** ¿Qué edad eres?

**b** Match the words and their meanings.

**1** sillón
**2** alfombra
**3** comedor
**4** cocina
**5** cama

**a** kitchen
**b** armchair
**c** dining room
**d** bed
**e** carpet

**c** Match the questions and the answers.

**1** ¿Puedes deletrear tu nombre?
**2** ¿Cuántos años tienes?
**3** ¿Cómo se deletrea tu nombre?
**4** ¿Qué edad tiene?

**a** C-A-R-M-E-N
**b** Tiene 23 años
**c** Tengo 23 años
**d** Sí, C-A-R-M-E-N

**d** Write these numbers:

**1** 48 _____
**2** 76 _____
**3** 14 _____
**4** 29 _____
**5** 35 _____

**e** Fill in the gaps with the correct form of the verb "tener".

**1** Ellos _____ una casa bonita.
**2** ¿Qué edad _____ vosotros?
**3** ¿Dónde _____ tú el auto?
**4** Yo no _____ quince años.
**5** El perro _____ sed.

**Key**

**a:** 3.
**b:** 1.- b; 2.- e; 3.- c; 4.- a; 5.- d.
**c:** 1-d; 2 - c; 3 - a; 4 - b.
**d:** 1.- cuarenta y ocho; 2.- setenta y seis; 3.- catorce; 4.- veintinueve; 5.- treinta y cinco.
**e:** 1.- tienen; 2.- tenéis; 3.- tienes; 4.- tengo; 5.- tiene.

Spanish: Easy and Fun **U6** 69

# Unidad 7
## Salamanca

### En esta unidad estudiaremos:

● **Diálogo**

● **Hablemos español:**
  **a)** Question words. **b)** Vocabulario: Los colores (The colors).

● **Gramática fácil:**
  **a)** The verb "ser" vs. the verb "estar". **b)** Agreement of adjectives and nouns.

● **Ejercicios**

---

*Gustavo ha comprado un sofá y la vendedora le pide datos personales para rellenar el formulario y llevárselo a su casa.*

Gustavo: Ya **estoy** decidido. Quiero ese sofá **verde oscuro. Es pequeño**, pero me gusta. El sofá que tengo en mi casa **es antiguo** y este **es más moderno.**

Vendedora: **Es muy bonito**, y también lo tenemos en **azul celeste** y en **amarillo.**

G: No, gracias. Me gusta en **verde oscuro.**

V: **Está bien. Es** una buena decisión.

G: Sí, creo que **es** una buena decisión. **Estoy contento.**

V: Bueno, necesito algunos datos suyos para llevar el sofá a su casa. **¿Cómo** se llama usted**?**

G: Me llamo Gustavo.

V: **¿Cuáles son** sus apellidos**?**

G: Gómez López.

V: **¿Cuál es** su dirección**?**

G: **¿Cómo?**

V: **¿Dónde** vive**?**

G: ¡Ah! Calle Nueva, número 159.

V: **¿Cuál es** su número de teléfono, Gustavo**?**

G: Mi teléfono **es** el 761039845.

V: ¿Tiene dirección de correo electrónico?

G: ¡Sí, claro! guigo@pitimail.com

V: Muy bien. Ya **está** todo. ¿Puede firmar aquí, por favor?

G: **¿Dónde?**

V: Aquí. Pues ya está todo. Pasado mañana lo tendrá en su casa.

G: ¡Estupendo! Gracias por todo.

SpanishEasyAndFun.com

Catedral vieja y Catedral nueva, Salamanca, España.

Gustavo has bought a couch and the salesperson asks him for personal information to fill out a form so that he may have the couch delivered to his house.

Gustavo: I've made up my mind. I want that dark green couch. It is small but I like it. The couch I have at home is old and this one is more modern.

Shop A.: It's very nice. We also have it in sky blue and yellow.

G:   No, thank you. I like it in dark green.
S:   That's fine. It's a good decision.
G:   Yes, I think it's a good decision. I'm happy.
S:   Well, I need some personal information to have the couch delivered to your house. What is your name?
G:   My name is Gustavo.
S:   What's your last name?
G:   Gómez López.
S:   What's your address?
G:   Pardon?
S:   Where do you live?
G:   Ah! Calle Nueva, 159.
S:   What's your telephone number, Gustavo?
G:   My telephone number is 761-039-845.
S:   Do you have an email address?
G:   Yes, of course! guigo@pitimail.com
S:   Okay, that's all. Can you sign here, please?
G:   Where?
S:   Here. That's all. You will have it at home the day after tomorrow.
G:   Great! Thank you for everything.

# Hablemos español

Information questions begin with question words. Here are some of them:

| | | |
|---|---|---|
| **¿Qué?** | > | *What?* |
| **¿Cuál?/¿Cuáles?** | > | *What?, Which (one)?/ Which (ones)?* |
| **¿Quién?/¿Quiénes?** | > | *Who?* |
| **¿Cuándo?** | > | *When?* |
| **¿Dónde?** | > | *Where?* |
| **¿Cómo?** | > | *How?* |

These question words or interrogative pronouns are always written with an accent mark on the stressed syllable.

When we use interrogative pronouns, the subject (if necessary) is placed after the verb.

### ¿Qué? *(What?)*

| | | |
|---|---|---|
| **¿Qué** es eso**?** | > | *What is that?* |
| **¿Qué** son los virus**?** | > | *What are the viruses?* |
| **¿Qué** tienes en el auto**?** | > | *What do you have in the car?* |

### ¿Cuál? *(Which one?)*/¿Cuáles? *(Which ones?)*

The pronoun "**¿Cuál?**" is used if the subject of the question is a singular noun and "**¿Cuáles?**" if it is a plural noun. Both are the equivalent to *"What?"* in English.

| | | |
|---|---|---|
| **¿Cuál** es su nombre**?** | > | *What is her name?* |
| **¿Cuáles** son tus libros**?** | > | *Which are your books?* |

### ¿Quién?/¿Quiénes? *(Who?)*

To ask about people we use "**¿Quién?**" with a singular subject and "**¿Quiénes?**" with a plural one.

| | | |
|---|---|---|
| **¿Quién** es tu prima**?** | > | *Who is your cousin?* |
| **¿Quiénes** son ellos**?** | > | *Who are they?* |

### ¿Cuándo? *(When?)*

We use "**¿Cuándo?**" when we ask about the time, a date, etc.

| | | |
|---|---|---|
| **¿Cuándo** es su cumpleaños**?** | > | *When is his birthday?* |
| **¿Cuándo** estás en la escuela**?** | > | *When are you at school?* |

SpanishEasyAndFun.com

### ¿Dónde? *(Where?)*

"**¿Dónde?**" is used to ask where people or things are located.

**¿Dónde** están nuestros hijos**?**  >  *Where are our children?*
**¿Dónde** está mi diccionario**?**  >  *Where is my dictionary?*

There is a similar pronoun "**¿Adónde?**" *(To where?)* that asks for a destination:

**¿Adónde** vas**?**  >  *Where are you going to?*

### ¿Cómo? *(How?)*

**¿Cómo** estás**?**  >  *How are you?*
**¿Cómo** se escribe tu nombre**?**  >  *How do you spell your name?*

[There are more question words that will be studied in other units].

---

## b  Vocabulario: Los colores (The colors)

**rojo**: *red*
**amarillo**: *yellow*
**verde**: *green*
**blanco**: *white*
**rosa**: *pink*
**celeste**: *sky blue*
**gris**: *gray*
**verde claro\***: *light green*
**verde oscuro**\*: *dark green*
**turquesa**: *turquoise*
**azul marino**: *navy blue*
**morado**: *purple*
**negro**: *black*
**marrón**: *brown*
**anaranjado**: *orange*
**azul**: *blue*

✳ To indicate the shades of a color we use "**claro**" *(light)* and "**oscuro**" *(dark)*.

El sofá es **gris claro**.
*The couch is light gray.*

All colors have a plural form and those ending in "o" have a feminine form ending in "a" (rojo – roja). They all have to agree with the noun they modify in gender and number.

La <u>bandera</u> es **blanca** y **verde**.
*The flag is white and green.*

Ellos tienen un <u>auto</u> **negro**.
*They have a black car.*

Las <u>flores</u> son **rojas, amarillas** y **blancas**.
*The flowers are red, yellow and white.*

# Gramática fácil

## a The verb "ser" vs. the verb "estar"

The verbs "**ser**" and "**estar**" are both equivalent to *"to be"* in English, but have very different meanings in Spanish.

In units 1 and 2 we saw the most common uses of these verbs, but the most important difference is that:

 The verb "**ser**" is used to describe one's being, that is, what someone or something is like or looks like. We use "**ser**" when giving physical descriptions or describing someone's personality traits.

| | | |
|---|---|---|
| ¿Cómo **es** Laura? | > | *What is Laura like?/What does Laura look like?* |
| Yo **soy** alta y rubia. | > | *I am tall and blonde.* |
| Tú **eres** extrovertido y hablador. | > | *You are extroverted and talkative.* |
| Ustedes **son** simpáticos. | > | *You are friendly.* |

■ Adjectives used after the verb "ser":

| | | | | |
|---|---|---|---|---|
| **grande** | *big, large* | **hablador/a** | *talkative* |
| **pequeño/a** | *small* | **extrovertido/a** | *extroverted* |
| **largo/a** | *long* | **tímido/a** | *shy* |
| **corto/a** | *short (in length)* | **optimista** | *optimistic* |
| **alto/a** | *tall* | **pesimista** | *pessimistic* |
| **bajo/a** | *short* | **simpático/a** | *nice, friendly* |
| **guapo/a, lindo/a** | *good-looking* | **antipático/a** | *unpleasant,* |
| **feo/a** | *uglydisagreeable* | **inteligente** | *intelligent* |
| **joven** | *young* | **tonto/a** | *stupid* |
| **mayor** | *old, biggest* | **agotador/a** | *tiring* |
| **viejo/a** | *old* | **responsable** | *responsible* |
| **rubio/a** | *blonde* | **moderno/a** | *modern* |
| **antiguo/a** | *old, antique* | **moreno/a** | *brunette* |

 The verb "**estar**" describes a current state of being, and is used when expressing someone's feelings, as well as how people or things are in that moment.

| | | |
|---|---|---|
| ¿Cómo **están** tus padres? | > | *How are your parents?* |
| Mis hermanos **están** enfadados. | > | *My brothers are angry.* |
| Yo no **estoy** enfermo. | > | *I am not ill.* |
| La ventana **está** cerrada. | > | *The window is closed.* |

SpanishEasyAndFun.com

● Adjectives used after the verb "estar":

| | | | |
|---|---|---|---|
| **contento/a** | happy | **cansado/a** | tired |
| **enamorado/a** | in love | **loco/a** | crazy |
| **enfermo/a** | ill, sick | **solo/a** | alone |
| **sano/a** | sane | **vivo/a** | alive |
| **enojado/a** | upset | **muerto/a** | dead |
| **enfadado/a** | angry | **ocupado/a** | busy |
| **preocupado/a** | worried | **avergonzado/a** | embarrassed |

● And there are adjectives with different meanings, depending on the verb they go with:

| | | | |
|---|---|---|---|
| **ser abierto/a** | to be extroverted | **estar abierto/a** | not to be closed |
| **ser aburrido/a** | to be boring | **estar aburrido/a** | to be bored |
| **ser nervioso/a** | to be a nervous person | **estar nervioso/a** | to be nervous |
| **ser listo/a** | to be clever | **estar listo/a** | to be ready |
| **ser triste** | to be a sad person | **estar triste** | to be sad |
| **ser alegre** | to be a happy person | **estar alegre** | to be happy |
| **ser gordo/a** | to be a fat person | **estar gordo/a** | to be fat |
| **ser delgado/a** | to be a thin person | **estar delgado/a** | to be thin |

Juan **es** nervioso. > Juan is a nervous person.
Juan **está** nervioso ahora. > Juan is nervous now.

Gloria **es** delgada. > Gloria is a thin person.
Gloria **está** delgada ahora. > Gloria is thin now.

Some of the most common and confusing expressions with the verbs "ser" y "estar":

**ser bueno**
to be good (or a good person)
**estar bueno**
to be tasty or to be in good health

El té **es bueno**.
Tea is good.

El té **está bueno**.
The tea tastes good.

The verb "estar" is used with the adverbs "bien" or "mal" ("ser" can never be used with these adverbs):

**estar bien**
to feel fine or to be correct (fine, okay...)
**estar mal**
to feel lousy or to be incorrect

El ejercicio **está bien**.
The exercise is okay.

Ellos no **están mal**.
They don't feel bad.

## b  Agreement of adjectives and nouns

Descriptive adjectives are used to describe a noun and always agree in gender (masculine/feminine) and number (singular/plural) with the noun they modify.

- Adjectives ending in "o" are masculine and can be changed into the feminine form by substituting an "a" for the "o" ending. Simply add an "s" to make it plural.

|  | SINGULAR | PLURAL |
|---|---|---|
| **masculine** | content**o** | content**os** |
| **feminine** | content**a** | content**as** |

Él está **cansado** y ellas están **aburridas**. >    *He is tired and they are bored.*

- Adjectives ending in "e" are both masculine and feminine, and can be made plural by adding an "s" on the end.

El director es un hombre **responsable** y trabaja con personas **inteligentes**.
*The director is a responsible man and works with intelligent people.*

- Most singular adjectives ending in a consonant can be both masculine and feminine, and to make them plural you add "es" to the end.

Lidia y Virginia son profesoras **jóvenes**.    >    *Lidia and Virginia are young professors.*

- When an adjective ending in "z" is made plural, the "z" changes into "c" before the "es" plural ending.

Soy **feliz**. Ellos son **felices**.    >    *I am happy. They are happy.*

- Adjetives ending in "r" in the masculine singular add "a" in the feminine and "es/as" in plural. [Exception: "mayor" is both a masculine and feminine adjective. Its plural form is "mayores"].

|  | SINGULAR | PLURAL |
|---|---|---|
| masculine | agotador | agotador**es** |
| feminine | agotador**a** | agotador**as** |

Los vuelos largos son **agotadores**.    >    *Long flights are tiring.*

- Adjectives ending in "ista" can be both masculine and feminine. In the plural they add an "s".

Sus padres no son personas **pesimistas.**    >    *Her parents aren't pessimistic people.*

SpanishEasyAndFun.com

**a** Fill in the gaps with the correct form of the verbs "ser" or "estar".

1 Juan _____ tranquilo, pero hoy _____ nervioso.
2 Mis amigos _____ alemanes. Ahora _____ en España.
3 Tu hermana _____ enfadada. Ella _____ alta y morena.
4 ¿_____ ustedes cansados? No, _____ aburridos.
5 El bar _____ abierto.

**b** Complete the phrase with the suitable question word.

1 ¿_____ es su número de teléfono?
2 ¿_____ está tu hermano? Está bien, gracias.
3 ¿_____ se dice "gracias" en inglés?
4 ¿_____ es esa mujer? Es mi prima.
5 ¿_____ son sus apellidos?

**c** Fill in the gaps with the missing letters (hint: colors).

1 M __ R__O __
2 __ M __ R __ L __ O
3 __ R __ S
4 __ E __ D __

**d** Identify and correct the mistake in the following sentences (there is one mistake per sentence).

1 Los muchachos están feliz.
2 Los libros interesantes son caro.
3 Ese estudiante inglesa es simpática y alegre.
4 Las mesas son grande y cómodas.
5 ¿Son difícil estos ejercicios?

· · · · · · · · · · · · · · · · · · · · · · · · · · · · · · · · · · · · · · · · · · · · · · · · · · · · · · · · · · · · · ·

# Unidad 8
## Machu Picchu

**En esta unidad estudiaremos:**

◉ **Diálogo**

◉ **Hablemos español:**
  **a)** Asking and answering about jobs and occupations.
  **b)** Vocabulario: Trabajos (Jobs).

◉ **Gramática fácil:**
  **a)** Spanish verbs. **b)** Present indicative of regular verbs: "-ar" verbs.
  **c)** Present indicative of regular verbs: "-er" verbs.
  **d)** Present indicative of regular verbs: "-ir" verbs.

◉ **Ejercicios**

*Ernesto y Mercedes se acaban de conocer y hablan sobre sus trabajos.*

Ernesto: **¿Cuál es su trabajo,** Mercedes**?**
Mercedes: Soy **agente de viajes**.
E:   ¡Qué interesante!
M:   Y usted, ¿a qué se dedica?
E:   Yo soy **profesor**.
M:   ¿Sí? ¿Y qué **enseña**?
E:   **Enseño** español.
M:   **¿Habla** otros idiomas?
E:   Sí, **hablo** inglés y un poco de ruso. ¿Y usted? ¿Qué idiomas **habla**?
M:   Inglés y francés. Bueno, también **estudio** alemán, pero no lo **hablo** muy
     bien. Solo algunas palabras.
E:   Entonces usted **vende** billetes de viaje.
M:   Sí, **vendo** billetes, **informo** a la gente sobre destinos, **leo** las cartas que
     **escriben** nuestros clientes...
E:   ¿Dónde **trabaja**?
M:   En una oficina en el centro de la ciudad. Allí **trabajamos** muchas personas.
     ¿Y usted?
E:   Yo **trabajo** en una escuela de idiomas. Está lejos de aquí y **tomo** el autobús
     para ir allí todos los días. De hecho, ya me tengo que ir. **Llego** tarde a clase.
M:   De acuerdo. ¡Que tenga un buen día!
E:   Gracias. Igualmente. ¡Adiós!

SpanishEasyAndFun.com

Santuario Histórico de Machu Picchu, Cusco, Perú.

*Ernesto and Mercedes have just met and are talking about their jobs.*

Ernesto: What do you do, Mercedes?
Mercedes: I am a travel agent.
E:   How interesting!
M:   And you? What do you do?
E:   I am a teacher.
M:   Are you? What do you teach?
E:   I teach Spanish.
M:   Do you speak other languages?
E:   Yes, I speak English and a little Russian. And you? What languages do you
     speak?
M:   English and French. Well, I am also studying German, but I don't speak it very
     well. Just some words.
E:   So you sell travel tickets.
M:   Yes, I sell tickets, inform people about destinations, read the letters that our
     clients write...
E:   Where do you work?
M:   In an office downtown. There are many of us working there. And you?
E:   I work in a language school. It's far from here and I take the bus to go there
     everyday. In fact, I have to go now. I'm late for class.
M:   Okay. Have a nice day!
E:   Thanks. Same to you. Goodbye!

# Hablemos español

## a Asking and answering about jobs and occupations

To ask about someones job, we can say:

| | | |
|---|---|---|
| **¿Cuál es tu trabajo?** | > | *What's your job?* |
| **¿Qué haces?** | > | *What do you do?* |
| **¿A qué te dedicas?** | > | *What's your job? / What do you do?* |

When answering, we only need the subject (if necessary), the verb "ser" and the profession. When the subject is singular no article is needed before the profession.

| | | |
|---|---|---|
| **—¿Cuál es tu trabajo?** | > | *—What's your job?* |
| **—Soy** empresario. | > | *— I'm a businessman.* |
| | | |
| **—¿Qué hacen ellos?** | > | *— What do they do?* |
| **—Son** escritores. | > | *— They are writers.* |
| | | |
| **—¿Cuál es su trabajo** (de ella)**?** | > | *— What's her job?* |
| **—Ella es** dentista. | > | *— She's a dentist.* |
| | | |
| **—¿A qué se dedica él?** | > | *— What's his job?* |
| **—Es** electricista. | > | *— He's an electrician.* |

But we can also say:

**Trabajar de / como** + profession

| | | |
|---|---|---|
| **Trabajo como** profesor. | > | *I work as a teacher.* |

## b Vocabulario: Trabajos (Jobs)

| | |
|---|---|
| **profesor / maestro:** *teacher* | **electricista:** *electrician* |
| **estudiante:** *student* | **artista:** *artist* |
| **médico:** *doctor* | **ama de casa:** *housewife* |
| **enfermera:** *nurse* | **conductor de bus:** *bus driver* |
| **panadero:** *baker* | **taxista:** *taxi driver* |
| **arquitecto:** *architect* | **futbolista:** *soccer player* |
| **vendedor:** *salesperson* | **secretario:** *secretary* |
| **dependiente:** *store clerk* | **escritor:** *writer* |
| **dentista:** *dentist* | **periodista:** *journalist* |

Remember that these nouns also have feminine forms (see unit 4).

SpanishEasyAndFun.com

# Gramática fácil

## a Spanish verbs

When we refer to a verb in Spanish we use the infinitive, which is how we will look it up in a dictionary. Infinitives have three endings ("-ar", "-er", "-ir") and all the verbs are classified according to these endings.

| -AR | -ER | -IR |
|---|---|---|
| **hablar** to speak | **comer** to eat | **vivir** to live |
| **trabajar** to work | **beber** to drink | **salir** to go out |
| **cantar** to sing | **leer** to read | **escribir** to write |
| **estudiar** to study | **aprender** to learn | **abrir** to open |

All verbs in Spanish are either regular or irregular. A **regular verb** follow a predictable pattern when it is conjugated, and an **irregular verb** does not follow a pattern or has other changes when conjugated.

To conjugate a regular verb, we have to take off the infinitive ending (-ar, -er, -ir) and replace it with the correct ending for each pronoun or subject. The Spanish verbal system has a set of endings that indicate the subject of the sentence, as well as the tense.

The infinitive without the "-ar", "-er", "-ir" ending is called the verb stem.

| hablar – ar = **habl-** | comer – er = **com-** | vivir – ir = **viv-** |
|---|---|---|

(yo) **habl**o    (I speak)
(yo) **habl**é    (I spoke)
(yo) **habl**aré  (I will speak)

Irregular verbs don't follow standard rules of conjugation in the different verb tenses and we will have to practice them to learn them.

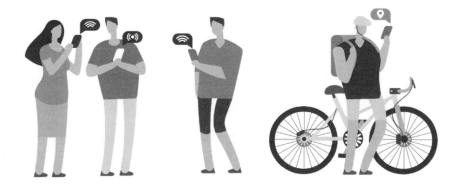

# Present indicative of regular verbs: "-ar" verbs

Ex: **hablar** *(to speak)*     stem  **>**  **habl**

|  | ENDING | VERB FORM |  |
|---|---|---|---|
| yo | **-o** | habl**o** | *I speak, I am speaking, I do speak* |
| tú | **-as** | habl**as** | *you speak, you are speaking, you do speak* |
| usted | **-a** | habl**a** | *you speak, you are speaking, you do speak* |
| él | **-a** | habl**a** | *he speaks, he is speaking, he does speak* |
| ella | **-a** | habl**a** | *she speaks, she is speaking, she does speak* |
| nosotros/as | **-amos** | habl**amos** | *we speak, we are speaking, we do speak* |
| vosotros/as | **-áis** | habl**áis** | *you (all) speak, you are speaking, you do speak* |
| ustedes | **-an** | habl**an** | *you (all) speak, you are speaking, you do speak* |
| ellos/as | **-an** | habl**an** | *they speak, they are speaking, they do speak* |

There are many verbs that follow the same pattern. Some of them are:

**ayudar** *(to help)*                    **llegar** *(to arrive)*
**comprar** *(to buy)*                 **enseñar** *(to teach, to show)*
**estudiar** *(to study)*                **cantar** *(to sing)*
**preguntar** *(to ask)*               **trabajar** *(to work)*
**visitar** *(to visit)*                    **amar** *(to love)*
**pagar** *(to pay)*                      **bailar** *(to dance)*
**caminar** *(to walk)*                **lavar** *(to wash)*
**limpiar** *(to clean)*                 **escuchar** *(to listen)*
**necesitar** *(to need)*              **tomar** *(to take)*
**desayunar** *(to have breakfast)*     **cenar** *(to have supper/dinner)*

Ella **estudia** geografía.                      **>**  *She studies geography.*
**Compramos** el periódico todos los días.  **>**  *We buy the newspaper everyday.*
Ellos **enseñan** inglés.                            **>**  *They teach English.*
Usted **pregunta** muchas cosas.          **>**  *You ask about a lot of things.*

## c  Present indicative of regular verbs: "-er" verbs

Ex: **comer** *(to eat)*       stem  >  **com**

|  | ENDING | VERB FORM | |
|---|---|---|---|
| yo | **-o** | com**o** | *I eat, I am eating, I do eat* |
| tú | **-es** | com**es** | *you eat, you are eating, you do eat* |
| usted | **-e** | com**e** | *you eat, you are eating, you do eat* |
| él | **-e** | com**e** | *he eats, he is eating, he does eat* |
| ella | **-e** | com**e** | *she eats, she is eating, she does eat* |
| | | | |
| nosotros/as | **-emos** | com**emos** | *we eat, we are eating, we do eat* |
| vosotros/as | **-éis** | com**éis** | *you (all) eat, you are eating, you do eat* |
| ustedes | **-en** | com**en** | *you (all) eat, you are eating, you do eat* |
| ellos/as | **-en** | com**en** | *they eat, they are eating, they do eat* |

Some of the verbs that follow this pattern are:

| | |
|---|---|
| **beber** *(to drink)* | **aprender** *(to learn)* |
| **correr** *(to run)* | **ver** *(to see, to watch)* |
| **vender** *(to sell)* | **comprender** *(to understand)* |
| **romper** *(to break)* | **responder** *(to answer)* |
| **leer** *(to read)* | **creer** *(to believe)* |
| **poseer** *(to possess)* | **temer** *(to fear)* |

| | | |
|---|---|---|
| **Vendo** autos. | > | *I sell cars.* |
| Él **come** carne. | > | *He eats meat.* |
| **Vemos** la televisión. | > | *We watch television.* |
| Tú **aprendes** español. | > | *You are learning Spanish.* |

## d  Present indicative of regular verbs: "-ir" verbs

Ex: **vivir** *(to live)*       stem  >  **viv**

|  | ENDING | VERB FORM | |
|---|---|---|---|
| yo | **-o** | viv**o** | *I live, I am living, I do live* |
| tú | **-es** | viv**es** | *you live, you are living, you do live* |
| usted | **-e** | viv**e** | *you live, you are living, you do live* |
| é | **-e** | viv**e** | *he lives, he is living, he does live* |
| ella | **-e** | viv**e** | *she lives, she is living, she does live* |
| | | | |
| nosotros/as | **-imos** | viv**imos** | *we live, we are living, we do live* |
| vosotros/as | **-ís** | viv**ís** | *you (all) live, you are living, you do live* |
| ustedes | **-en** | viv**en** | *you (all) live, you are living, you do live* |
| ellos/as | **-en** | viv**en** | *they live, they are living, they do live* |

Some verbs that follow this pattern are:

**escribir** *(to write)*          **decidir** *(to decide)*
**recibir** *(to receive)*         **descubrir** *(to discover)*
**asistir** *(to attend)*          **abrir** *(to open)*
**subir** *(to go up, climb)*      **partir** *(to leave, to split up)*
**discutir** *(to discuss)*        **cubrir** *(to cover)*
**existir** *(to exist)*           **insistir** *(to insist)*
**permitir** *(to allow)*          **repartir** *(to distribute)*

Él **escribe** novelas.              >   *He writes novels.*
Mis padres **asisten** a la reunión. >   *My parents are attending the meeting.*
Nosotras **vivimos en** Nueva York.  >   *We live in New York.*
Los científicos **descubren** medicinas. >   *Scientists discover medicines.*
Yo **abro** las ventanas.            >   *I open the windows.*
Vosotros **recibís** muchas cartas.  >   *You receive a lot of letters.*

## e   Present indicative endings for "–ar", "–er", "–ir" verbs

To sum up:

|                    | -AR    | -ER    | -IR    |
|--------------------|--------|--------|--------|
| yo                 | –o     | –o     | –o     |
| tú                 | –as    | –es    | –es    |
| usted, él, ella    | –a     | –e     | –e     |
| nosotros/as        | –amos  | –emos  | –imos  |
| vosotros/as        | –áis   | –éis   | –ís    |
| ustedes, ellos/as  | –an    | –en    | –en    |

SpanishEasyAndFun.com

# Ejercicios de la **Unidad 8**

**a**  Which of these questions is not used to ask about jobs?

**1** ¿A qué te dedicas?
**2** ¿Qué haces?
**3** ¿Cuál es tu trabajo?
**4** ¿Cuál es tu costumbre?

**b**  Fill in the gaps with the correct verb form.

**1** ¿A qué hora (abrir) _____ los bancos por la mañana?
**2** Fernando (amar) _____ a la familia de Luisa.
**3** ¿Qué (comer) _____. vosotros ahora?
**4** ¿Cuándo (partir) _____. nosotros para Granada?
**5** Él (tocar) _____ el piano en una banda de jazz.
**6** Nosotros (beber) _____ dos litros de agua al día.
**7** Mis padres (vivir) _____. en Madrid y mi hermana (vivir) _____. en París.
**8** Ellos (bailar) _____. en la discoteca.
**9** ¿Qué (leer) _____ tú? (Leer) _____. el periódico.
**10** Su tía (escribir) _____ novelas de terror.

**c**  Match the words with their meaning.

**1** dependiente
**2** ama de casa
**3** agricultor
**4** panadero
**5** enfermera
**6** abogado
**7** periodista
**8** peluquero

**a** journalist
**b** farmer
**c** housewife
**d** lawyer
**e** hairdresser
**f** store clerk
**g** nurse
**h** baker

# Unidad 9
## Santiago de Compostela

### En esta unidad estudiaremos:

- **Diálogo**
- **Hablemos español:**
  **a)** Structuring sentences. **b)** The verb "llevar puesto" (to be wearing).
  **c)** Vocabulario: La ropa (Clothes).
- **Gramática fácil:**
  **a)** Uses of the present indicative. **b)** Questions beginning with a preposition. **c)** Asking about reasons. **d)** Position of descriptive adjectives (II): «bueno/buen»; «malo/mal»; «grande/gran».
- **Ejercicios**

*Sonia y Manuel hablan sobre una fiesta a la que les han invitado.*

Sonia: Tengo **una camisa** muy elegante para la fiesta. ¡Mírala!

Manuel: Yo no **quiero** ir. ¿**Por qué tenemos** que hacerlo?

S: **Porque** es importante para Julia. Ella es una **buena** amiga y **celebra** su cumpleaños. Además, **viaja** mucho y no **pasa** mucho tiempo en la ciudad. No la **podemos** ver a menudo.

M: No es un **buen** momento para ir. Está lloviendo.

S: ¡Venga, Manuel!

M: De acuerdo, de acuerdo.

S: ¿**En qué** piensas ahora?

M: ¿Qué **ropa** me pongo?

S: Aquí **tienes** estos **pantalones** y **un cinturón**. Te puedes poner la **chaqueta** nueva y los **zapatos** negros.

M: ¡Uff! Ahora no **tengo** ganas de cambiarme de **ropa**. [Silvia lo mira desafiante]. Está bien, está bien... ¿Y tú? ¿**Qué ropa llevas**?

S: Yo **llevo una camisa**, **una falda** azul y **unos zapatos** rojos.

M: ¿**Para quién** es ese regalo?

S: Para Julia. Es una **bufanda**. Manuel, **tenemos** que darnos prisa.

M: ¿**Vamos** en autobús?

S: No, es mejor en taxi. No **tenemos** mucho tiempo. Además, está lloviendo.

M: Sí, **tienes** razón.

Plaza del Obradoiro y Catedral de Santiago de Compostela, Galicia, España.

Sonia and Manuel are talking about a party they have been invited to.

Sonia: I have a very elegant shirt for the party. Look!

Manuel: I don't want to go. Why do we have to go?

S: Because it's important for Julia. She is a good friend and is celebrating her birthday. Besides, she travels a lot and doesn't spend much time in the city. We don't see her often.

M: It isn't a good time to go. It's raining.

S: Come on, Manuel!

M: Okay, okay.

S: What are you thinking about now?

M: What should I wear?

S: Here are these trousers and a belt. You can put on the new jacket and the black shoes.

M: Ugh! I don't feel like changing clothes now. [Silvia looks at him defiantly]. Alright, alright... And you? What are you wearing?

S: I am going to wear a shirt, a blue skirt and red shoes.

M: Who is this gift for?

S: For Julia. It's a scarf. Manuel, we have to hurry up.

M: Are we going by bus?

S: No, it's better by taxi. We don't have much time. And it's raining.

M: Yes, you are right.

# Hablemos español

## a Structuring sentences

Now that we have learned some Spanish verbs, let's review some rules in order to begin to structure sentences:

🔹 Since the verb endings reveal the subject, it is not necessary to use the subject pronouns except for emphasis, contrast or clarification:

| | | |
|---|---|---|
| Hablo español. | > | I speak Spanish. |
| Trabajamos como fontaneros. | > | We work as plumbers. |
| | | |
| **Él** canta ópera. | > | He sings opera. |
| **Usted** canta ópera. | > | You sing opera. |

🔹 When referring to animals, things, etc., no pronoun is used, but the verb alone is conjugated for the masculine "él" or the feminine "ella".

| | | |
|---|---|---|
| El perro salta con la pelota. | ········➤ | **Salta** con la pelota. |
| The dog jumps with the ball. | ········➤ | It jumps with the ball. |
| | | |
| El gato bebe agua. | ········➤ | **Bebe** agua. |
| The cat drinks water. | ········➤ | It drinks water. |

🔹 To structure negative sentences in the present, "**no**" is placed just before the verb.

| | | |
|---|---|---|
| Ella **no** habla ruso. | > | She doesn't speak Russian. |
| **No** estudio en la universidad. | > | I'm not studying at university. |
| Ellos **no** compran leche. | > | They don't buy any milk. |
| **No** comes fruta. | > | You don't eat any fruit. |
| Nosotras **no** escribimos en francés. | > | We don't write in French. |
| **No** comprendo. | > | I don't understand. |
| **No** sé. | > | I don't know. |

🔹 In asking questions intonation changes, and we can invert the order of the subject (if necessary) and the verb.

| | | |
|---|---|---|
| ¿Ustedes **estudian** español? | > | Are you studying Spanish? |
| ¿**Estudian** ustedes español? | > | Are you studying Spanish? |
| | | |
| ¿**Trabajas** en casa? | > | Do you work at home? |
| ¿**Venden** ellos su casa? | > | Are they selling their house? |
| ¿**Comprendes**?/¿**Entiendes**? | > | Do you understand? |

 SpanishEasyAndFun.com

🔖 When the question starts with an interrogative pronoun, the subject (if necessary) is most commonly placed after the verb.

¿Cuándo **estudian** <u>ustedes</u> español?   ➤   *When do you study Spanish?*
¿Dónde **trabaja** (<u>él</u>)?   ➤   *Where does he work?*
¿Qué **bebes**?   ➤   *What are you drinking? / What do you drink?*

## b   The verb "llevar puesto" (to be wearing)

When referring to clothes, we frequently use the verb "**llevar (puesto)**" *(to be wearing).*

**¿Qué llevas puesto**? **Llevo (puestos)\*** unos **pantalones tejanos**, una **camiseta** blanca y una **camisa** azul.
*What are you wearing? I'm wearing a pair of jeans, a white T-shirt and a blue shirt.*

**¿Qué lleva puesto** tu madre? **Lleva (puesto)\*** <u>un</u> **vestido** y <u>una</u> **chaqueta**.
*What is your mother wearing? She's wearing a dress and a jacket.*

🔧 Sometimes there is no need to say "puesto", as it is understood, but when we use that word, it has to agree in gender and number with the noun it goes before:

¿Quién lleva **puesto** <u>un suéter</u>?   ➤   *Who is wearing a sweater?*
Él lleva **puesta** <u>una gorra</u>.   ➤   *He is wearing a cap.*
Yo no llevo **puestos** <u>unos calcetines</u> rojos.   ➤   *I am not wearing red socks.*

## c   Vocabulario: La ropa (Clothes)

| | |
|---|---|
| **camisa**: *shirt* | **camiseta**: *T-shirt* |
| **blusa**: *blouse* | **suéter**: *sweater* |
| **jersey**: *jersey* | **vestido**: *dress* |
| **falda**: *skirt* | **chaqueta**: *jacket* |
| **traje**: *suit* | **abrigo**: *coat* |
| **sombrero**: *hat* | **gorra**: *cap* |
| **pantalón**: *pants, trousers* | **jeans, tejanos**: *jeans* |
| **pantalones cortos**: *shorts* | **impermeable**: *raincoat* |
| **zapatos**: *shoes* | **botas**: *boots* |
| **zapatillas deportivas**: *sneakers* | **sandalias**: *sandals* |
| **calcetines, medias**: *socks* | **ropa interior**: *underwear, underpants* |
| **pijama**: *pajamas* | **cinturón**: *belt* |
| **corbata**: *tie* | **guantes**: *gloves* |
| **bufanda**: *scarf* | **pañuelo**: handkerchief |

# Gramática fácil

## a  Uses of the present indicative

The present indicative is used:

- To express habitual actions at present:

  Ella **compra** el periódico todos los días.  ➤  *She buys the newspaper everyday.*

- To express temporary situations at present:

  Mi madre **está** enferma ahora.  ➤  *My mother is ill now.*

- To describe an action that is taking place at the time the word is spoken:

  ¿Qué **hacen** los niños ahora?  ➤  *What are the children doing now?\**

  ⭐ The present progressive also exists in Spanish but it is used less frequently than in English.

- To express general truths:

  Los gatos **comen** ratones.  ➤  *Cats eat mice.*

- To express planned actions in the near future. In this case, the moment when the action is going to happen has to be shown:

  El sábado ella **canta** en el auditorio.  ➤  *She's singing in the auditorium next Saturday.*

- To make the present action more emphatic:

  **Trabajo** todos los días.  ➤  *I (do) work everyday.*

## b  Questions beginning with a preposition

In unit 7 we learned how to ask questions with interrogative pronouns.

In Spanish, when a preposition modifies an interrogative it is placed at the beginning of the question, before the interrogative pronoun. In other languages, like English, these prepositions are placed at the end.

¿**Con** quién ?  ➤  *Who with?*      ¿**Para** qué?  ➤  *What for?*

Let's review some of the most common prepositions:

**a**: *to*                           **en**:  *in, on, at, about*
**con**: *with*                       **para**: *for*
**de**: *of, from*

¿**A** <u>quién</u> esperas? Espero **a** Juan.       >       *Who are you waiting for? I'm waiting for Juan.*

¿**Con** <u>quién</u> vives? Vivo **con** mi madre.   >       *Who are you living with? I'm living with my mother.*

¿**De** <u>dónde</u> eres? **De** México.             >       *Where are you from? From Mexico.*

¿**En** <u>qué</u> estás pensando?                    >       *What are you thinking about?*
Estoy pensando **en** mis vacaciones.                 >       *I'm thinking about my vacation.*

¿**Para** <u>quién</u> es el regalo? **Para** su padre. >      *Who is the gift for? For his father.*

There are some cases in which we use prepositions in Spanish but not in English:

¿**Por** qué?                         >       *Why?*
¿**De** quién?                        >       *Whose?*

## c   Asking about reasons

When asking about a reason we need the following interrogative:
¿**Por qué?** (*Why?*)

¿**Por qué** están las llaves en la cocina?   >   *Why are the keys in the kitchen?*
¿**Por qué** tienes frío?                     >   *Why are you cold?*

Do not confuse **"¿Por qué?"** *(why?)* and **"Porque"** *(because)*. "Porque" is the answer to "¿Por qué?".

¿**Por qué** no vienes con nosotros? **Porque** no tengo tiempo.
*Why don't you come with us? Because I don't have time.*

¿**Por qué** están preocupados? **Porque** tienen problemas.
*Why are they worried? Because they have problems.*

The adjectives "**bueno**" (*good*) and "**malo**" (*bad*) always follow the noun they modify. If they precede it they have to change into "**buen**" and "**mal**", respectively (with no change in meaning). This change only happens with singular masculine nouns.

| | | |
|---|---|---|
| Es un <u>auto</u> **bueno**. | = Es un **buen** <u>auto</u>. | *t's a good car.* |
| Tengo un <u>día</u> **malo**. | = Tengo un **mal** <u>día</u>. | *I am having a bad day.* |
| Es una <u>oportunidad</u> **buena**. | = Es una **buena** <u>oportunidad</u>. | *It's a good opportunity.* |

The adjectives "**bueno/buen**" (*good*) and "**malo/mal**" (*bad*) can be mistaken for the adverbs "**bien**" (*well*) and "**mal**" (*badly*). In order to avoid confusion, remember that adverbs do not modify nouns.

The adverbs "**bien**" and "**mal**" may be the answer to the question "*How?*" and have no masculine, feminine, singular or plural forms. They are invariable.

The use of the adjectives "**grande**" and "**gran**" may also be confusing.
"**Grande**" is used after a singular noun and means "big, large". "**Gran**" is its shortened form and is placed before singular nouns. It means "great, excellent".

| | |
|---|---|
| El presidente es un <u>hombre</u> **grande**. | *The president is a big/large man.* |
| El presidente es un **gran** <u>hombre</u>. | *The president is a great man.* |

SpanishEasyAndFun.com

**a** Choose the correct answer.

1. Ella lleva puestos unos pantalones, un corbata, una camisa y un chaqueta.
2. Ella lleva puesto un pantalones, una corbata, una camisa y un chaqueta.
3. Ella lleva puestas una corbata, unos pantalones, un camisa y una chaqueta.
4. Ella lleva puestos unos pantalones, una corbata, una camisa y una chaqueta.

**b** Fill in the gaps with the correct expression (por qué, porque, para quién, en qué, de dónde, con quién).

1. ¿_____ trabajas? Trabajo con mi hermana.
2. ¿_____ es este pastel? Es para ellos.
3. ¿_____ es tu profesor? Es de Madrid.
4. ¿_____ ciudad está la torre Eiffel?
5. ¿_____ estás triste? _____ tengo problemas.

**c** Match the words with their meanings.

| | | |
|---|---|---|
| 1 vestido | | a pants, trousers |
| 2 traje | | b tie |
| 3 camisa | | c shirt |
| 4 pantalones | | d dress |
| 5 botas | | e jacket |
| 6 corbata | | f skirt |
| 7 chaqueta | | g coat |
| 8 falda | | h gloves |
| 9 chaqueta | | i boots |
| 10 abrigo | | j suit |

**d** Choose the correct answer.

1. Ella tiene una casa _____ (gran / grande / buena)
2. Él es un _____ hombre (grande / bueno / buen)
3. Ella es una estudiante _____. (gran / mal / buena)

•••••••••••••••••••••••••••••••••••••••••••••••••••••••••••••••••

**Key**

**a:** 4.

**b:** 1.- Con quién; 2.- Para quién; 3.- De dónde; 4.- En qué; 5.- Por qué, Porque.

**c:** 1- d; 2 - j; 3 - c; 4 - a; 5.- i; 6.- b; 7.- e; 8.- f; 9.- h; 10.- g.

**d:** 1.- grande; 2.- buen; 3.- buena.

# Unidad 10
## Santiago de Chile

**En esta unidad estudiaremos:**

● **Diálogo**

● **Hablemos español:**
  **a)** The present tense: time markers. **b)** Vocabulario: Los días de la semana (The days of the week); Los meses del año (The months).

● **Gramática fácil:**
  **a)** Irregular verbs. **b)** Present indicative of irregular verbs (I).
  **c)** The conjunctions "o", "u", "o... o...", "ni... ni...".

● **Ejercicios**

---

*Santos tiene algunos problemas en su casa y pide ayuda a Miriam, una vecina.*

Santos: ¡Hola! Me llamo Santos. Soy su vecino. Compré el apartamento de la segunda planta en **abril**, pero no paso mucho tiempo en él.

Miriam: ¡Hola, Santos! Encantada de conocerle. Yo soy Miriam. Usted no tiene acento de aquí. ¿De dónde es?

S: Soy dominicano. **Actualmente** estoy en la ciudad porque **juego** en el equipo de béisbol local.

M: ¡Qué interesante! ¿**Quiere** pasar?

S: Gracias, pero solo **quiero** hacerle una pregunta. La puerta de mi cocina no **cierra** y el grifo **pierde** agua. ¿Podría recomendarme algún **fontanero**? No conozco a nadie en el barrio.

M: Me temo que yo **no** soy fontanera **ni** carpintera. **Pienso** que otro vecino **puede** ayudarle, pero no está en casa **en este momento**. Hoy es **miércoles** y él no **vuelve** hasta el **viernes por la noche**. No **recuerdo** dónde está **ahora**, pero tengo su número de teléfono.

S: Bueno, después **puedo** llamarlo. **Ahora** es hora de comer. Yo siempre **almuerzo** pronto y luego **duermo** la siesta. Más tarde hablaré con él. Muchas gracias.

M: No hay de qué. Recuerde que **puede** verlo el **sábado o** el **domingo**.

S: Sí, pero **prefiero** hablar con él antes.

M: De acuerdo. Su número de teléfono es el...

SpanishEasyAndFun.com

Providencia, ciudad de Santiago, Chile.

*Santos has some problems at home and is asking his neighbor Miriam for help.*

Santos: Hello! My name is Santos. I am your neighbor. I bought the apartment on the second floor in April but I don't spend much time in it.

Miriam: Hello, Santos! Pleased to meet you. I am Miriam. You don't have the local accent. Where are you from?

S: I am Dominican. At present I am in this city because I play for the local baseball team.

M: How interesting! Would you like to come in?

S: Thank you but I only want to ask you a question. My kitchen door doesn't close and the faucet is leaking. Could you recommend a plumber? I don't know anyone in the neighborhood.

M: I'm afraid I'm neither a plumber nor a carpenter. I think that another neighbor can help you but he is not at home at the moment. Today is Wednesday and he won't be back until Friday evening. I don't remember where he is now but I have his telephone number.

S: Well, I can call him later. Now it's time to have lunch. I always have lunch early and then I have a siesta. I'll talk to him later. Thank you very much.

M: Don't mention it. Remember that you can see him on Saturday or Sunday.

S: Yes, but I prefer to talk to him before.

M: Okay. His phone number is...

# Hablemos español

## a The present tense: time markers

Time markers are those words or expressions that are used to show the time when the action takes place (adverbs of time). For the present tense, some of them are:

| | | | |
|---|---|---|---|
| **ahora** | *now* | **en este momento** | *in this moment* |
| **hoy** | *today* | **siempre** | *always* |
| **esta semana** | *this week* | **de vez en cuando** | *from time to time* |
| **este año** | *this year* | **todos los días** | *everyday* |
| **este mes** | *this month* | **actualmente** | *currently, at present* |

And the different parts of the day:

| | |
|---|---|
| **por la mañana** | *in the morning* |
| **por la tarde** | *in the afternoon* |
| **por la noche** | *in the evening, at night* |

If these expressions are used with a particular day, then the day is placed just before the phrase:

| | | | |
|---|---|---|---|
| **mañana** | *tomorrow* | **lunes** | *Monday* |

Mañana **por la mañana** veo a Luis.   >   *I'm meeting Luis tomorrow morning.*
Los lunes **por la tarde** estudiamos.   >   *We study on Monday afternoons.*

All these markers are usually placed at the beginning or end of a sentence:

| | | |
|---|---|---|
| **Ahora** vivo en Monterrey. | > | *I'm living in Monterrey now.* |
| **De vez en cuando** comen paella. | > | *They eat paella from time to time.* |
| Escribo **todos los días**. | > | *I write everyday.* |
| Ella trabaja **por la mañana**. | > | *She works in the morning.* |
| **Esta semana** no trabajas. | > | *You are not working this week.* |

## b Vocabulario

**Los días de la semana (The days of the week)**

| | |
|---|---|
| **lunes**: *Monday* | **viernes**: *Friday* |
| **martes**: *Tuesday* | **sábado**: *Saturday* |
| **miércoles**: *Wednesday* | **domingo**: *Sunday* |
| **jueves**: *Thursday* | |

SpanishEasyAndFun.com

The days of the week are not capitalized in Spanish.

| | | |
|---|---|---|
| Hoy es **martes**. | > | *Today is Tuesday.* |
| El partido es el **sábado**. | > | *The match is on Saturday.* |

The days of the week are preceded by **"el"** (except when referring to the day today, yesterday, tomorrow, etc.).

| | | |
|---|---|---|
| Tengo una cita **el** <u>jueves</u>. | > | *I have a date on/next Thursday.* |
| Él vino **el** <u>domingo</u>. | > | *He came on/last Sunday.* |
| Hoy es <u>martes</u>. | > | *Today is Tuesday.* |
| Ayer fue <u>lunes</u>. | > | *Yesterday was Monday.* |

When using the days of the week in plural we only change the article **"el"** for **"los"**, except for **"sábado"** and **"domingo"**, which have plural forms (**sábados, domingos**).

| | | |
|---|---|---|
| No me gustan **los** <u>lunes</u>. | > | *I don't like Mondays.* |
| Ellos tienen clases de español **los** <u>miércoles</u> y <u>viernes</u>. | > | *They have Spanish lessons on Wednesdays and Fridays.* |
| Ella va al teatro **los** <u>sábados</u> <u>por la noche</u>. | > | *She goes to the theater on Saturday evenings.* |

### Los meses del año (The months)

| | |
|---|---|
| **enero**: *January* | **julio**: *July* |
| **febrero**: *February* | **agosto**: *August* |
| **marzo**: *March* | **septiembre**: *September* |
| **abril** : *April* | **octubre**: *October* |
| **mayo**: *May* | **noviembre**: *November* |
| **junio**: *June* | **diciembre**: *December* |

Remember that the months are written in lower case letters in Spanish.

The preposition that almost always precedes the months is **"en"** *(in)*.

| | | |
|---|---|---|
| Mi cumpleaños es **en** <u>septiembre</u>. | > | *My birthday is in September.* |
| El curso comienza **en** <u>marzo</u>. | > | *The course starts in March.* |

# Gramática fácil

### a  Irregular verbs

Irregular verbs also end with "-ar", "-er" or "-ir", but they do not follow the patterns we have studied when they are conjugated. They change in ways that may affect either the stem of the verb or the ending (or even both).

### b  Present indicative of irregular verbs (I)

As the present indicative is one of the most irregular tenses, we recommend to study it by comparing the conjugation of the three main types of verb endings (-ar, -er and –ir), and always remembering the conjugation of regular verbs.

There are some verbs that <u>change a vowel for a diphthong in the verb stem</u>:

▪ Change of the vowel "**e**" for the diphthong "**ie**" (**e>ie**):

Ex: p**e**nsar *(to think)*, ent**e**nder *(to understand)*, s**e**ntir *(to feel)*.

|  | **PENSAR** | **ENTENDER** | **SENTIR** |
|---|---|---|---|
| yo | p**ie**ns**o** | ent**ie**nd**o** | s**ie**nt**o** |
| tú | p**ie**ns**as** | ent**ie**nd**es** | s**ie**nt**es** |
| usted-él-ella | p**ie**ns**a** | ent**ie**nd**e** | s**ie**nt**e** |
| | | | |
| nosotros/as * | pens**amos** | entend**emos** | sent**imos** |
| vosotros/as * | pens**áis** | entend**éis** | ent**ís** |
| ustedes-ellos/as | p**ie**ns**an** | ent**ie**nd**en** | s**ie**nt**en** |

✱ The stem doesn't change when the subject is "nosotros/as" or "vosotros/as".

More examples of verbs that follow this pattern are:

**comenzar** *(to start/begin)*　　**empezar** *(to start/begin)*
**cerrar** *(to close)*　　**recomendar** *(to recommend)*
**perder** *(to lose)*　　**querer** *(to want/love)*
**preferir** *(to prefer)*　　**despertar** *(to wake someone up)*

| | | |
|---|---|---|
| Pedro no **entiende** los verbos irregulares. | > | Pedro doesn't understand the irregular verbs. |
| El chef **recomienda** la sopa. | > | The chef recommends the soup. |
| ¿Cuándo **comienza** el partido? | > | When does the match start? |

SpanishEasyAndFun.com

● Change of the vowel "**o**" for the diphthong "**ue**" (o>ue):

Ex: rec**o**rdar *(to remember)*, v**o**lver *(to come back)*, d**o**rmir *(to sleep)*.

|  | RECORDAR | VOLVER | DORMIR |
|---|---|---|---|
| yo | rec**ue**rdo | v**ue**lvo | d**ue**rmo |
| tú | rec**ue**rdas | v**ue**lves | d**ue**rmes |
| usted-él-ella | rec**ue**rda | v**ue**lve | d**ue**rme |
| nosotros/as * | record**amos** | volv**emos** | dorm**imos** |
| vosotros/as * | record**áis** | volv**éis** | dorm**ís** |
| ustedes-ellos/as | rec**ue**rd**an** | v**ue**lven | d**ue**rmen |

✪ The stem doesn't change when the subject is "nosotros/as" or "vosotros/as". Other verbs that follow this pattern are:

**encontrar** *(to find)*
**mostrar** *(to show)*
**contar** *(to count/to tell)*
**volar** *(to fly)*
**doler** *(to hurt/pain)*
**poder** *(can, be able, may)*

**almorzar** *(to have lunch)*
**costar** *(to cost)*
**soñar** *(to dream)*
**mover** *(to move)*
**llover** *(to rain)*
**morir** *(to die)*

| Ellos **vuelven** por la noche. | > | *They come back in the evening.* |
|---|---|---|
| No **recuerdo** eso. | > | *I don't remember that.* |
| ¿Cuánto **cuesta** este libro? | > | *How much is this book?* |
| ¿Cuándo **almorzamos**? | > | *When do we have lunch?* |

● Change of the vowel "**u**" for the diphthong "**ue**" (u>ue):

The only example is the verb "**jugar**" (to play).

|  | JUGAR |
|---|---|
| yo | j**ue**go |
| tú | j**ue**gas |
| usted-él-ella | j**ue**ga |
| nosotros/as * | jug**amos** |
| vosotros/as * | jug**áis** |
| ustedes-ellos/as | j**ue**gan |

✪ The stem doesn't change when the subject is "nosotros/as" or "vosotros/as".

| Nosotros **jugamos** al tenis los fines de semana. | > | *We play tennis on weekends.* |
|---|---|---|
| El no **juega** al dominó. | > | *He doesn't play dominoes.* |

## c The conjunctions "o", "u", "o... o...", "ni... ni..."

- The conjunction "**o**" *(or)* is used to indicate an alternative.

  ¿Quieres azúcar **o** miel?  > *Would you like sugar or honey?*

  Él vuelve el martes **o** el miércoles.  > *He is coming back on Tuesday or on Wednesday.*

- When the conjunction "**o**" precedes a word that begins with "o-" or "ho-", it becomes "**u**".

  Yo duermo siete **u** ocho horas.  > *I sleep for seven or eight hours.*

  ¿Son aquellas personas mujeres **u** hombres?  > *Are those people women or men?*

- The expression "**o... o...**" *(either... or...)* indicates an alternative between two elements that are related.

  Puedo comprar **o** el anillo **o** el collar.  > *I can buy either the ring or the necklace.*

  Ella puede tomar **o** vino **o** cerveza.  > *She may have either wine or beer.*

- When a negative element is added to another negative element we use "**ni (no)... ni...**" *("neither... nor...")*.

  No es **ni** barato **ni** bonito.  > *It is neither cheap nor nice.*

  Luisa **no** ha venido **ni** ha llamado por teléfono.  > *Luisa has neither come nor phoned.*

🖐 SpanishEasyAndFun.com

# Ejercicios de la **Unidad 10**

**a** Fill in the gaps with the correct form of the verb in the present indicative.

1 Mi abuela (dormir) _____ por la tarde.
2 La secretaria no (poder) _____ venir ahora.
3 ¿A qué hora (almorzar) _____ ellos?
4 El curso (empezar) _____ en abril.
5 ¿Cuándo (jugar) _____ mi equipo?
6 Yo hablo pero ella no (entender) _____
7 ¿Qué (pensar) _____ tú de Miguel?
8 ¿Ellos (preferir) _____ el fútbol o el baloncesto?
9 Yo no (encontrar) _____ mi diccionario.
10 Ese auto (costar) _____ mucho dinero.

**b** Choose the correct answer: What is the chronological order?

1 jueves – viernes – sábado
2 viernes – domingo – lunes
3 martes- jueves- viernes
4 lunes – martes – jueves
5 martes – miércoles - viernes

**c** Word search: find the seven months

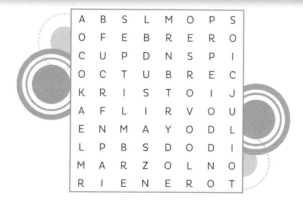

| A | B | S | L | M | O | P | S |
| O | F | E | B | R | E | R | O |
| C | U | P | D | N | S | P | I |
| O | C | T | U | B | R | E | C |
| K | R | I | S | T | O | I | J |
| A | F | L | I | R | V | O | U |
| E | N | M | A | Y | O | D | L |
| L | P | B | S | D | O | D | I |
| M | A | R | Z | O | L | N | O |
| R | I | E | N | E | R | O | T |

**Key**

**a:** 1.- duerme; 2.- puede; 3.- almuerzan; 4.- empieza; 5.- juega; 6.- entiende; 7.- piensas; 8.- prefieren; 9.- encuentro; 10.- cuesta.

**b:** 1

**c:** enero, febrero, marzo, mayo, julio, septiembre, octubre.

# Unidad 11
## San Sebastián

**En esta unidad estudiaremos:**

● **Diálogo**

● **Hablemos español:**
   **a)** Demonstrative adjectives and pronouns.

● **Gramática fácil:**
   **a)** Present indicative of irregular verbs (II). **b)** Changes in spelling to maintain the pronunciation of some verbs.

● **Ejercicios**

*Ana y Bernardo se encuentran en la calle.*

Ana: ¿Dónde **vas**, Bernardo?

Bernardo: **Voy** al supermercado. Hoy **vienen** unos amigos a almorzar y necesito algunas cosas.

A:  ¿Quiénes **van**?

B:  Paula y Daniel.

A:  ¿Paula? ¿La arquitecta?

B:  Sí, bueno, ahora ella **dirige** una empresa. **Construyen** puentes.

A:  Lo sé. La **conozco**. ¿Y qué harás de comida?

B:  **Estos** amigos siempre me **piden** paella y **eso** es lo que yo les **hago**.

A:  Suena muy bien pero, ¿no es mucho trabajo? ¿No prefieres comer fuera?

B:  No, no es mucho trabajo. A veces **salgo** a comer, pero prefiero almorzar en casa con los amigos.

A:  ¿A qué supermercado **vas**? ¿A **este** de aquí o a **aquel** de la esquina?

B:  **Voy** a **aquel**.

A:  ¿Y **vas** allí a pie?

B:  Sí. No **traigo** muchas cosas y nunca **conduzco** cuando **voy** allí. Está muy cerca.

A:  ¿Cómo? Perdona, pero no **oigo** nada con este viento.

B:  **Digo** que el supermercado está muy cerca de casa y **voy** andando.

A:  Bueno, pues te acompaño. Yo también **voy** en **esa** dirección.

San Sebastián (Donostia), Vizcaya, España.

*Ana and Bernardo run into each other on the street.*

Ana: Where are you going, Bernardo?
Bernardo: I am going to the supermarket. Today some friends are coming for lunch and I need some things.
A: Who is coming?
B: Paula and Daniel.
A: Paula? The architect?
B: Yes, well, she runs an architectural firm now. They build bridges.
A: I know. I know her. And what will you make for lunch?
B: These friends always ask me for a paella and that is what I make for them.
A: It sounds very good but, isn't it too much work? Don't you prefer to eat out?
B: No, it isn't much work. I sometimes eat out, but I prefer to have lunch with my friends at home.
A: Which supermarket are you going to? This one here or that one on the corner?
B: I'm going to that one.
A: And are you going there on foot?
B: Yes. I don't bring many things and I never drive when I go there. It is very close.
A: What? Sorry, but I can't hear anything with this wind.
B: I said that the supermarket is very near my house and I go walking.
A: Well, I'll go with you. I am also going that way.

# Hablemos español

## Demonstrative adjectives and pronouns

■ **Demonstrative adjectives** are used to indicate whether the object, people or period of time they refer to are near to or far from the speaker. They are always placed before a noun with which they have to agree in gender and number.

■ If the object is near the speaker:

|           | SINGULAR | PLURAL |
|-----------|----------|--------|
| masculine | **este** | **estos** |
| feminine  | **esta** | **estas** |
|           | ↓ *this* | ↓ *these* |

| | | |
|---|---|---|
| Ellos vienen **este** <u>mes</u>. | > | *They're coming this month.* |
| **Estas** <u>flores</u> son bonitas. | > | *These flowers are nice.* |

■ If the object is relatively near the speaker:

|           | SINGULAR | PLURAL |
|-----------|----------|--------|
| masculine | **ese**  | **esos** |
| feminine  | **esa**  | **esas** |
|           | ↓ *that* | ↓ *those* |

| | | |
|---|---|---|
| Ella vive en **ese** <u>apartamento</u>. | > | *She lives in that apartment.* |
| Tengo **esa** <u>computadora</u> en mi casa. | > | *I have that computer in my house.* |

SpanishEasyAndFun.com

If the object is far from the speaker (and the listener):

|  | SINGULAR | PLURAL |
|---|---|---|
| masculine | **aquel** | **aquellos** |
| feminine | **aquella** | **aquellas** |
|  | ↓ | ↓ |
|  | *that* | *those* |

| | | |
|---|---|---|
| **Aquella** <u>mujer</u> es enfermera. | > | *That woman is a nurse.* |
| **Aquellos** <u>hombres</u> son mis tíos. | > | *Those men are my uncles.* |

We can omit the noun after the demonstrative adjective, but then we will have to use a demonstrative pronoun instead.

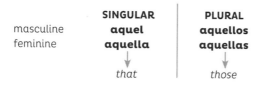 **Demonstrative pronouns** replace both the demonstrative adjective and the noun. Their masculine, feminine, singular and plural forms are exactly the same as those for demonstrative adjectives.

<u>Esta casa</u> es grande pero **esa** es pequeña. (esa = esa casa)
*This house is big but that (one) is small.*

<u>Ese diccionario</u> es caro. **Este** es barato. (Este = Este diccionario)
*That dictionary is expensive. This one is cheap.*

No quiero <u>esos zapatos</u>. Quiero **aquellos**. (aquellos = aquellos zapatos)
*I don't want those shoes. I want those ones over there.*

There are also neuter forms that do not change for gender or number: **esto**, **eso** and **aquello**. They are used when referring to abstract ideas, an unknown object or something non-specific.

| | | |
|---|---|---|
| **esto** *(this matter, this thing)* | ¿Qué es **esto**? | *What is this?* |
| **eso** *(that matter, that thing)* | No entiendo **eso** | *I don't understand that.* |
| **aquello** *(that matter, that thing)* | ¿Recuerdas **aquello**? | *Do you remember that?* |

# Gramática fácil

## a Present indicative of irregular verbs (II)

There are some verbs that change the ending of the first person singular (yo):

💧 Ending with **"-oy"**.

The first person changes, but the other subjects are conjugated as regular verbs ending with "-ar".

Ex: **dar** *(to give)*, **ir** *(to go)*.

|  | DAR | IR* |
|---|---|---|
| yo | d**oy** | **v**oy |
| tú | d**as** | **v**as |
| usted-él-ella | d**a** | **v**a |
| nosotros/as | d**amos** | **v**amos |
| vosotros/as | d**ais** | **v**ais |
| ustedes-ellos/as | d**an** | **v**an |

✪ The verb "ir" is very irregular, and we use the letter "v" for each person.

**Voy** al trabajo en auto.　　　　　　> 　*I go to work by car.*

Another example that follows this pattern is the verb "estar" (see unit 2).

No **estoy** contento.　　　　　　> 　*I am not happy.*

💧 Ending with **"-go"**.

The first person changes, but the other subjects are conjugated as regular verbs ending with "-er" or "-ir".

Ex: **suponer** *(to suppose)*, **oír** *(to hear)*.

|  | SUPONER | OÍR* |
|---|---|---|
| yo | supon**go** | oi**go** |
| tú | supon**es** | oy**es** |
| usted-él-ella | supon**e** | oy**e** |
| nosotros/as | supon**emos** | o**ímos** |
| vosotros/as | supon**éis** | o**ís** |
| ustedes-ellos/as | supon**en** | oy**en** |

　　　　　　　🖑 SpanishEasyAndFun.com

✪ The verb "oír" follows the same rule for the endings, but it also uses an "i" in the first person in singular (yo) and a "y" for the second and third persons in singular and plural.

Some other verbs that follow this pattern are:

**obtener** *(to get)*          **tener** *(to have)*
**hacer** *(to do/make)*        **traer** *(to bring)*
**venir** *(to come)*           **decir** *(to say/tell)*
**salir** *(to go out)*

Hoy no **traigo** el periódico.          >          *I'm not bringing the newspaper today.*
Nunca **salgo** por la noche.            >          *I never go out at night.*
**Hago** los deberes todos los días.     >          *I do my homework everyday.*

With some of these verbs we may see other changes, such as a vowel for a diphthong or an "e" for an "i" in the verb stem.

O<u>í</u>r      No **oi**go nada.                  >          *I can't hear anything.*
V<u>e</u>nir    Ella v**ie**ne de la escuela.      >          *She is coming from school.*

◍ Ending with "**-zco**".

▪ There are many verbs ending with "**-acer**", "**-ecer**" and "**-ocer**", whose first person in singular (yo) ends with "**-zco**". The other persons are conjugated with the endings of regular "-er" verbs.

Ex: **ofrecer** *(to offer)*, **parecer** *(to seem/look/look like)*, **conocer** *(to know)*.

|                    | OFRECER            | CONOCER          |
|--------------------|--------------------|------------------|
| yo                 | ofre**zco**        | cono**zco**      |
| tú                 | ofrec**es**        | conoc**es**      |
| usted-él-ella      | ofrec**e**         | conoc**e**       |
|                    |                    |                  |
| nosotros/as        | ofrec**emos**      | conoc**emos**    |
| vosotros/as        | ofrec**éis**       | conoc**éis**     |
| ustedes-ellos/as   | ofrec**en**        | conoc**en**      |

Other verbs that follow this pattern are:

**crecer** *(to grow)*       **(des)aparecer** *(to [dis]appear)*
**obedecer** *(to obey)*      **nacer** *(to be born)*
**reconocer** *(to recognize)*      **parecer** *(to seem/look/look like)*

No **conozco** a esa persona.    **>**    *I don't know that person.*
Yo **ofrezco** lo que tengo.    **>**    *I offer what I have.*

■ When the verb ends with "**-ucir**", the first person in singular ends with "**-zco**", but the rest are conjugated as a regular "-ir" verb.

Ex: **producir** *(to produce/make).*

|  | **PRODUCIR** |
|---|---|
| yo | produ**zco** |
| tú | produc**es** |
| usted-él-ella | produc**e** |
|  |  |
| nosotros/as | produc**imos** |
| vosotros/as | produc**ís** |
| ustedes-ellos/as | produc**en** |

Additional examples of these type of verbs are:

**conducir** *(to drive)*    **traducir** *(to translate)*    **reducir** *(to reduce)*

No **traduzco** documentos.    **>**    *I don't translate documents.*
**Traduzco** libros.    **>**    *I translate books.*

● Verbs ending with "**-uir**".

These verbs are conjugated as regular "-ir" verbs but they add "y" just before the ending, except for "nosotros/as" and "vosotros/as". Ex: **construir** *(to build).*

|  | **CONSTRUIR** |
|---|---|
| yo | constru**yo** |
| tú | constru**yes** |
| usted-él-ella | constru**ye** |
|  |  |
| nosotros/as | constru**imos** |
| vosotros/as | constru**ís** |
| ustedes-ellos/as | constru**yen** |

More examples include:

**incluir** *(to include)*　　　　　　**destruir** *(to destroy)*
**distribuir** *(to distribute)*　　　　**contribuir** *(to contribute)*

Soy albañil y **construyo** casas.　　　> 　*I am a bricklayer and I build houses.*

🔲 Change of the vowel "**e**" for "**i**" in the verb stem **(e>i)**.

There are verbs that change an "e" for an "i" in the verb stem, except for "nosotros/as" and "vosotros/as". Ex: **pedir** *(to ask for)*.

|  | **PEDIR** |
|---|---|
| yo | p**i**d**o** |
| tú | p**i**d**es** |
| usted-él-ella | p**i**d**e** |
| | |
| nosotros/as | ped**imos** |
| vosotros/as | ped**ís** |
| ustedes-ellos/as | p**i**d**en** |

Additional verbs that follow this pattern are:

**decir** *(to say/tell)*　　　　　　**corregir** *(to correct)*
**reír** *(to laugh)*　　　　　　　　**sonreír** *(to smile)*
**repetir** *(to repeat)*　　　　　　**conseguir** *(to get)*
**servir** *(to serve)*　　　　　　　**vestir[se]** *(to get dressed)*
**elegir** *(to choose)*

Yo siempre **pido** la factura.　　　> 　*I always ask for the bill.*
Ellos **corrigen** sus errores.　　　> 　*They correct their mistakes.*

🔲 Very irregular verbs.

There are some verbs that are very irregular, and when conjugated have changes in the verb stem and endings. An example is the verb "**haber**" *(to have)*, which is the auxiliary verb used to form the perfect tenses.

|  | **HABER** |
|---|---|
| yo | **he** |
| tú | **has** |
| usted-él-ella | **ha** |
| | |
| nosotros/as | **hemos** |
| vosotros/as | **habéis** |
| ustedes-ellos/as | **han** |

In addition to these irregular verbs, there are some others that undergo certain **changes in spelling to maintain the pronunciation of the verb**. In most cases, these changes affect the first person in singular (yo). The most common changes are:

🍃 **"g" a "j"**:

There are some verbs that change the "g" into "j". Ex: **dirigir** *(to lead/direct)*.

yo **dirijo**      ~~yo dirigo~~

The "g" is maintained for the rest of the subjects: diriges, dirige, dirigimos, dirigís, dirigen.
Additional examples: **elegir/escoger** *(to choose)*, **proteger** *(to protect)*, **recoger** *(to pick up)*, **coger** *(to take/catch)*.

🍃 **"c" a "z"**:

Other verbs change the "c" into "z". Ex: **vencer** *(to win)*.

yo **venzo**      ~~yo venco~~

Another example: **convencer** *(to convince/persuade)*.

🍃 **"gu" a "g"**:

To preserve the original pronunciation of the verb, some verbs change "gu" into "g" in the first person (yo). Ex: **seguir** *(to go on/continue)*.

Yo **sigo**      ~~yo siguo.~~

Other verbs that follow this pattern are: **perseguir** *[to pursue/chase (after)]*, **distinguir** *(to distinguish/discern)*.

**a** Choose the suitable demonstrative.

**1** _____ lápiz es negro. (Aquello/ Esto / Este)

**2** ¿Dónde está _____ gata? (esa / estas / ese)

**3** ¿Qué es _____ ? (este / esa/ aquello)

**4** _____ niños son mis sobrinos. (Estas / Aquellos / Esas)

**5** _____ es mi profesor (Este / Esa / Eso)

**6** _____ son sus botas. (Aquellas / Estos / Aquellos)

**7** Mi reloj es _____ (esto / este)

**8** ¿Es _____ tu camisa? (aquello / esta)

**9** Ricardo es _____ estudiante. (aquella / ese / esto)

**10** Su casa es _____ (aquella / este / eso)

**b** Fill in the gaps with the correct form of the verbs in the present indicative.

**1** Yo (decir) _____ la verdad.

**2** Ella (repetir) _____ el nombre de los alumnos.

**3** Esta tarde yo no (salir) _____ con ellos.

**4** Yo no (oír) _____ la canción.

**5** Mañana nosotros (ir) _____ al cine.

**6** Yo (traer) _____ una maleta pesada.

**7** Yo (hacer) _____ mis deberes todos los días.

**8** Ellos (construir) _____ edificios en muchas zonas.

**9** No (conocer) _____ a nadie en esta ciudad.

**10** Yo (dar)_____ caramelos a mis sobrinos.

• • • • • • • • • • • • • • • • • • • • • • • • • • • • • • • • • • • • • • • • • • • • • • • • • •

**b:** 1.- digo; 2.- repite; 3.- salgo; 4.- oigo; 5.- vamos; 6.- traigo; 7.- hago; 8.-
construyen; 9.- conozco; 10.- doy.

9.- ese; 10.- aquella.

**a:** 1.- Este; 2.- esa; 3.- aquello; 4.- aquellos; 5.- Este; 6.- Aquellas; 7.- este; 8.- esta;

**Key**

# Unidad 12
## La Habana

**En esta unidad estudiaremos:**

⦿ **Diálogo**

⦿ **Hablemos español:**
   **a)** Expressing likes and dislikes: the verb "gustar". **b)** The time (La hora).

⦿ **Gramática fácil:**
   **a)** Indirect object pronouns. **b)** The verbs "saber" and "conocer".

⦿ **Ejercicios**

---

*Camilo y Ángela están en una floristería.*

Camilo: ¿**Te gustan** esas flores?

Ángela:  ¿Estas o aquellas?

C:   Esas de ahí.

Á:   Sí, son bonitas, ¿por qué?

C:   Hoy es el cumpleaños de Brenda y quiero hacer**le** un regalo.

Á:   ¡Es verdad! Hoy es 30 de junio. No me acordaba. Bueno, esas flores son lindas, pero **le** puedes comprar esto, también.

C:   ¿Este jarrón? Mmm... no **sé**. Prefiero ese. ¿No **te gusta**?

Á:   ¡Oh, sí! **Ese me encanta**. Es muy colorido. Es un buen regalo para Brenda. A ella **le gustan** mucho los colores.

C:   ¿**Te apetece** acompañarme a su casa? **Le** llevamos el regalo, **le** damos un beso y nos vamos. Yo tengo un poco de prisa y ella no **sabe** que vamos.

Á:   Bueno. ¿**A qué hora?**

C:   Ahora **son las cinco menos diez**. Podemos llegar a su casa **a las cinco y media.**

Á:   Sí, **me gusta** el plan. Bueno, entonces, tú **le** puedes comprar esas flores y yo **le** compro el jarrón. También **le** podemos escribir una nota.

C:   Buena idea.

Á:   [A la florista] ¿**Nos** envuelve este jarrón y esas flores, por favor? Son un regalo.

C:   ¿Y puede dar**nos** también una tarjeta, por favor?

El Capitolio, La Habana, Cuba.

Camilo and Ángela are at the florist's.

Camilo: Do you like those flowers?
Ángela: These ones or those ones?
C:  Those ones over there.
Á:  Yes, they are nice, why?
C:  Today is Brenda's birthday and I want to give her a gift.
Á:  It's true! Today is June 30th. I didn't remember. Well, those flowers are
    beautiful, but you can also buy this for her.
C:  This vase? Mmm... I don't know. I prefer that one. Don't you like it?
Á:  Oh, yes! I love that one. It's colorful. It's a good present for Brenda. She likes
    colors a lot.
C:  Do you feel like going to her house with me? We'll take her the
    present, give her a kiss and leave. I'm in a bit of a hurry and she doesn't know
    we are coming.
Á:  Alright. What time?
C:  It's ten to five now. We can get to her house at half past five.
Á:  Yes, I like the plan. Well, then, you can buy those flowers and I'll buy the vase
    for her. We can also write a note to her.
C:  Good idea.
Á:  [To the florist] Could you wrap up this vase and those flowers, please? They
    are a gift.
C:  And could you also give us a card, please?

# Hablemos español

## a    Expressing likes and dislikes: the verb "gustar"

The verb "**gustar**" *(to like, to be pleasant to)* is unique in Spanish because what is used before the verb is an indirect object pronoun repesenting the person who likes. After the verb comes the object that is liked, which is the real subject of the sentence.

**Me** gusta el baloncesto.    >    Basketball *is pleasant to me. (I like basketball).*
**Nos** gusta el arroz.    >    Rice *is pleasant to us. (We like rice).*

🔹 In order to express what people like and dislike we use the following sentence construction:

| | | | | |
|---|---|---|---|---|
| (A mí) | **me** | | | el arte |
| (A ti) | **te** | **gusta** + singular noun* | | Bárbara |
| (A usted / A él / A ella) | **le** | | | cantar |
| (A nosotros-as) | **nos** | | | Pablo y Miguel |
| (A vosotros-as) | **os** | **gustan** + plural noun** | | ellos |
| (A ustedes / A ellos-as) | **les** | | | los perros |

The words in parentheses are optional and are used for clarification or emphasis.

✪    It can be a singular noun, a singular pronoun, a name or an infinitive.
✪✪    It can be a plural noun, a plural pronoun or more than one name.

🔹 The preposition "A" can be followed by a noun, a pronoun or a name:

(A mí) **Me gusta** el vino.    >    *I like wine.*
A mi amiga **le gustan** esos zapatos.    >    *My friend likes those shoes.*
A Juan **le gusta** tocar el piano.    >    *Juan likes playing the piano.*
¿A ellos **les gusta** el café?    >    *Do they like coffee?*

🔹 In negative sentences, "no" is placed just before the pronoun (me, te, le...):

**No** me gusta fumar.    >    *I don't like smoking.*
A ustedes **no** les gusta bailar.    >    *You don't like dancing.*
(A ti) **No** te gustan ellos.    >    *You don't like them.*

🔹 Other verbs that follow this pattern are:

**apetecer** [apetece/apetecen]    *(to feel like)*
**encantar** [encanta/encantan]    *(to love/like very much)*

**¿Te apetece** un helado?    >    *Do you feel like an ice cream?*
**A Luisa le encanta** jugar al tenis.    >    *Luisa loves playing tennis.*

🖐 SpanishEasyAndFun.com

With the verbs "**gustar**" and "**apetecer**" we can use adverbs to intensify the action.

| | | |
|---|---|---|
| Me gusta **muchísimo** esa película. | > | I like that movie very much. |
| Me gusta **mucho** esa película. | > | I like that movie a lot. |
| <u>No</u> me gusta **nada** esa película.* | > | I don't like that movie at all. |

✪ When using "nada" the sentence has to be negative.

## b   The time

Menos
*To*

Y
*After*

To tell the time in Spanish, first we say the hours and then the minutes. The hours are preceded by "**Son las...**" * *(It's...).*

✪ "**Es la...**" *(It's...)* is used when the hour is "one".

🔖 After the hour we say **"y"** *(after)* or **"menos"** *(to)*, followed by the minutes:

| | | | |
|---|---|---|---|
| 10:05 | Son las diez **y** cinco. | > | It's five after ten/It's ten oh five. |
| 8:20 | Son las ocho **y** veinte. | > | It's twenty after eight/ It's eight twenty. |
| 1:10 | Es la una **y** diez. | > | It's ten after one/ It's one ten. |
| 6: 35 | Son las siete **menos** veinticinco. | > | It's twenty-five to seven/It's six thirty five. |
| 11:50 | Son las doce **menos** diez. | > | It's ten to twelve/ It's eleven fifty. |

To say "o'clock" we use "**en punto**":

| 4:00 | Son las cuatro **en punto**. | > | *It's four o'clock.* |
| 1:00 | Es la una **en punto**. | > | *It's one o'clock.* |

"**Y media**" is the equivalent to *"half past"* and "**cuarto**" means *"a quarter"*:

| 7:30 | Son las siete **y media**. | > | *It's half past seven/It's seven thirty.* |
| 5:45 | Son las seis **menos cuarto**. | > | *It's a quarter to six/It's five forty-five.* |
| 3:15 | Son las tres **y cuarto**. | > | *It's a quarter after three/It's three fifteen.* |

In order to avoid ambiguity, after telling the time we can add:

**de la mañana**: *in the morning*

**de la tarde**: *in the afternoon*

**de la noche**: *in the evening*

Or simply: **a.m.** /a eme/: *am* , **p.m.** / pe eme/: *pm*

Son las diez **de la noche** =
Son las diez **p.m.**    *It's ten p.m.*

Son las cinco **de la mañana** =
Son las cinco **a.m.**  *It's five a.m.*

When asking the time we say:

| —**¿Qué hora es?** | > | —*What time is it?* |
| —Son las nueve menos cuarto. | > | —*It's a quarter to nine.* |

And to ask at what time something happens, we say:

| ¿A qué hora...? | > | *(At) What time...?* |
| **¿A qué hora** es el concierto? | > | *What time is the concert?* |

To answer this question or to say when an event takes place we use "**a la(s)**" *(at)* and then the time.

| —¿A qué hora es la clase de español? | > | —*What time is the Spanish class?* |
| —Es **a las** siete y media. | > | —*It's at half past seven.* |
| El programa acaba **a la** una. | > | *The program ends at one.* |

"**A mediodía**" *(at noon)* and "**a medianoche**" *(at midnight)* are also expressions we can use when telling the time, but then the article "la(s)" is omitted.

| | | | |
|---|---|---|---|
| —¿A qué hora almuerzan ustedes? | > | —What time do you have lunch? | |
| **—A mediodía**. | > | —At noon. | |

Vuelvo a casa **a medianoche**. > I get back home at midnight.

● The word "**hora**" is found in other expressions, such as:

| | | |
|---|---|---|
| Es **hora** de + infinitive | > | It's time to + infinitive |
| ¡Es la **hora**! | > | Time's up! |
| ¡Ya era **hora**! | > | And about time too! |
| **Hora** punta / pico | > | Rush hour |

# Gramática fácil

## a Indirect object pronouns

The indirect object tells us "to whom" or "for whom" the action is directed.

| SUBJECT PRONOUNS | INDIRECT OBJECT PRONOUNS | |
|---|---|---|
| yo | **me** | me |
| tú | **te** | you |
| usted | **le** | you |
| él | **le** | him, it |
| ella | **le** | her, it |
| nosotros/as | **nos** | us |
| vosotros/as | **os** | you |
| ustedes | **les** | you |
| ellos/as | **les** | them |

These pronouns either precede a conjugated verb, or follow attached to an infinitive or gerund.

**Les** está escribiendo una carta. = Está escribiéndo**les** una carta.
*He is writing them a letter.*

| | |
|---|---|
| Mi hija **me** da su amor. | *My daughter gives me her love.* |
| Quiero decir**te** algo. | *I want to tell you something..* |

To emphasize or clarify who the receiver of the action is, we can use the preposition "a" and a name, a noun or a pronoun. When using pronouns, we have to use subject pronouns, except for "yo" and "tú", that change into "mí" and "ti", respectively.

Mi hija **me** da su amor **a mí**.
Quiero dar**le** un regalo **a él. (a Juan, a mi padre)**

## b | The verbs "saber" and "conocer"

"**Saber**" is used when we mean *"to know"* *(to have knowledge)*:

**PRESENT INDICATIVE**

| | |
|---|---|
| yo | **sé** |
| tú | **sabes** |
| usted-él-ella | **sabe** |
| | |
| nosotros/as | **sabemos** |
| vosotros/as | **sabéis** |
| ustedes-ellos/as | **saben** |

| | | |
|---|---|---|
| No **sé** la respuesta. | > | *I don't know the answer.* |
| ¿**Sabe** él mi dirección? | > | *Does he know my address?* |
| ¿Qué **sabes** de mi país? | > | *What do you know about my country?* |

It also means *"to know how to do something"* *(can)*. In this case, the verb "**saber**" precedes an infinitive.

| | | |
|---|---|---|
| Ellos **saben** <u>hablar</u> inglés. | > | *They can speak English.* |
| No **sabemos** <u>nadar</u>. | > | *We can't swim.* |
| Él **sabe** <u>jugar</u> al tenis. | > | *He can play tennis.* |

The verbs "**saber**" and "**conocer**" (see unit 11) are synonyms; both mean *"to have knowledge"*, but there are some differences:

- "conocer" is also used to mean *"to know"*, or *"to be acquainted with"*.
- "conocer" can be followed by a person. In this case we need the preposition "a" in between.
- with places, the verb "saber" is never used.

| | | |
|---|---|---|
| **Conozco** <u>a</u> tu padre. | > | *I know your father.* |
| El taxista **conoce** la ciudad. | > | *The taxi driver knows the city.* |

🖐 SpanishEasyAndFun.com

**a** Match the time.

1 2:35
2 5:10
3 4:50
4 3:25
5 6:45

a Son las siete menos cuarto p.m.
b Son las cinco y diez p.m.
c Son las tres y veinticinco a.m.
d Son las cinco menos diez a.m.
e Son las dos y treinta y cinco a.m.

**b** Complete the dialogues with the correct indirect object pronoun: **me, te, le, nos, os, les**.

1 ¿Puedes dar_____ este paquete a Silvia?
2 El profesor _____ enseña español (a ellos).
3 Yo _____ escribo cartas (a él), pero no _____ responde.
4 No _____ dice su nombre (a nosotros).
5 Ellos _____ preguntan cosas (a ellos).

**c** Complete the sentences with the correct form of the verb **"gustar"**:

1 A mí no _____ el chocolate.
2 A ellos _____ bailar.
3 ¿A ti _____ la paella?
4 A nosotros _____ los animales.
5 A Berta _____ Juan.

**d** Choose the correct verb.

1 ¿_____ Nueva York? (Sabes / Conoces)
2 Ellos no _____ a mis hermanas. (saben / conocen)
3 Pablo no _____ jugar al tenis. (sabe / conoce)
4 ¿_____ qué hora es? (Sabes / Conoces)
5 Yo no _____ dónde vives. (sé / conozco)

• • • • • • • • • • • • • • • • • • • • • • • • • • • • • • • • • • • • • • • • • • • • • • • •

**d:** 1.– Conoces; 2.– conocen; 3.– sabe; 4.– Sabes; 5.– sé.
**c:** 1.– me gusta; 2.– les gustar; 3.– te gusta; 4.– nos gustan; 5.– le gusta.
**b:** 1.– le; 2.– les; 3.– le, me; 4.– nos; 5.– les.
**a:** 1.– e; 2.– b; 3.– d; 4.– c; 5.– a.

**Key**

# Unidad 13
## Valencia

**En esta unidad estudiaremos:**

◉ **Diálogo**

◉ **Hablemos español:**
**a)** The verb "hacer" (to do / to make). **b)** Expressions with the verb "hacer". **c)** Vocabulario: El tiempo (The weather); Las estaciones (The seasons).

◉ **Gramática fácil:**
**a)** The impersonal form "hay". **b)** Indefinite pronouns.

◉ **Ejercicios**

---

*Esteban acaba de llegar a casa. Raquel está en la cocina.*

Esteban: ¿Qué **haces**?

Raquel: **Hago** la cena: sopa de cebolla y pollo frito. Espero que estén buenos.

E: ¡Estupendo! Tengo hambre. **Hace** mucho tiempo que no como sopa de cebolla. Es un buen plato para hoy porque **hace viento** y **frío**. ¡Brrr!

R: ¿Sí? ¿**Qué tiempo hace**?

E: **Hay tormenta**, como es normal en **otoño**.

R: ¿**Hay alguien** en la calle?

E: No, no **hay nadie** en la calle. No **hay mucho** que hacer ahí. Es un mal día para pasear.

R: ¿Y cuál es el **pronóstico del tiempo** para mañana?

E: No lo sé.

R: Espero que haga un buen día porque quiero ir a ver a mi madre. Por cierto, ¿has visto a Ricardo?

E: Sí.

R: ¿Cómo está? **Hace** semanas que no lo veo.

E: Está **bien**, pero un poco enfadado hoy.

R: ¿Qué **hace** ahora? ¿Por qué está enfadado?

E: Es conductor de camiones y trabaja **mucho**. Hoy está enojado porque se le ha averiado el camión y ha perdido el teléfono móvil.

R: Bueno, todos tenemos días buenos y días malos.

SpanishEasyAndFun.com

Fuente del Túria y Catedral de Santa María, Valencia, España.

*Esteban has just returned home. Raquel is in the kitchen.*

*Esteban: What are you doing?*
*Raquel: I am cooking dinner: onion soup and fried chicken. I hope they are good.*
E:   Great! I am hungry. I haven't had onion soup for a long time. It's a good meal
     for today because it is windy and cold. Brrr!
R:   Is it? What's the weather like?
E:   It is stormy, as usual in the fall.
R:   Is there anyone on the street?
E:   No, there is no one on the street. There isn't much to do there. It is a bad day
     to take a walk.
R:   And what is the weather forecast for tomorrow?
E:   I don't know.
R:   I hope it is good weather because I want to see my mother. By the way, have
     you seen Ricardo?
E:   Yes.
R:   How is he? I haven't seen him for weeks.
E:   He is fine, but a bit upset today.
R:   What is he doing now? Why is he annoyed?
E:   He is a truck driver and works a lot. Today he is upset because his truck is
     broken down and he lost his cell phone.
R:   Well, we all have good days and bad days.

# Hablemos español

## a  The verb "hacer" (to do / to make)

The verb "**hacer**" is used a lot in Spanish. Its equivalent are the verbs "*to do*" and "*to make*" (among some others) in English. In context, "**hacer**" can refer to almost any activity.

It is an irregular verb. When conjugated in the present indicative, there is a change in the first person singular (yo).

|  | HACER |
|---|---|
| yo | ha**go** |
| tú | hac**es** |
| usted-él-ella | hac**e** |
| | |
| nosotros/as | hac**emos** |
| vosotros/as | hac**éis** |
| ustedes-ellos/as | hac**en** |

| | | |
|---|---|---|
| Yo **hago** mi cama. | > | *I make my bed.* |
| ¿Qué **haces**? | > | *What are you doing?/ What are you making?* |

The verb "**hacer**" seldom stands alone. It is almost always followed by a noun:

**hacer** la comida *(to make the meal)*
**hacer** la limpieza *(to do the cleaning)*
**hacer** un favor *(to do a favor)*
**hacer** una película *(to make a film)*, etc.

| | | |
|---|---|---|
| Nosotros **hacemos** páginas web. | > | *We make web pages.* |
| Ellos **hacen** preguntas y yo contesto. | > | *They ask questions and I answer.* |
| ¿Dónde **hacen** ustedes la fiesta? | > | *Where will you have the party?* |

## b  Expressions with the verb "hacer"

The third person singular of the verb "**hacer**" (**hace**) is used in different expressions:

In weather terminology. Typically, weather terms use the third person singular (**hace**) followed by a noun:

| | | |
|---|---|---|
| **Hace** calor. | > | *It is hot.* |
| **Hace** frío. | > | *It is cold.* |

SpanishEasyAndFun.com

**Hace** viento.      >      *It is windy.*
**Hace** sol.      >      *It is sunny.*

🔲 In expressions with time. In this case **"hace"** is followed by a period of time:

   🔹 to indicate how long ago something happened.

Ella vivió en EEUU **hace** dos años.    >    *She lived in the USA two years ago.*

   🔹 to indicate how long ago an action or situation began. In this case we use the present indicative in Spanish (the present perfect continuous in English), the expression **"desde hace"** *(for)* and a period of time.

Estudio español **desde hace** un mes.    >    *I've been studying Spanish for a month.*
Él juega al béisbol **desde hace**    >    *He has been playing baseball for two*
dos años.      *years.*

These sentences can also be stated as follows:

**Hace** un mes **que** estudio español.   >   *I've been studying Spanish for a month.*
**Hace** dos años **que** él juega al béisbol.   >   *He has been playing baseball for two years.*

The verb **"hacer"** is also used in many other situations and idiomatic expressions, some of which will be studied further on.

🔲 El tiempo (The weather)

| | |
|---|---|
| **sol**: *sun* | **nube**: *cloud* |
| **lluvia**: *rain* | **llover**: *to rain* |
| **nieve**: *snow* | **nevar**: *to snow* |
| **viento**: *wind* | **tormenta**: *storm* |

**niebla**: *fog*
**brisa**: *breeze*
**trueno**: *thunder*
**pronóstico (previsión)**
**del tiempo**: *weather forecast*

**neblina**: *mist*
**huracán**: *hurricane*
**relámpago**: *lightning*

**Está soleado** = **Hace sol**: *It is sunny*
**Está nublado**: *It is cloudy*
**Está lluvioso**: *It is rainy*
**Hay niebla**: *It is foggy*
**Hay tormenta**: *It is stormy*
**Hace buen tiempo**: *It's good weather*

**Hace calor**: *It is hot*
**Hace frío**: *It is cold*
**Está templado**: *It is warm*
**Hace fresco**: *It is cool/chilly*
**Hace viento**: *It is windy*
**Hace mal tiempo**: *It's bad weather*

Hoy **hace calor** y **está nublado**.
**Hace frío** y **hay tormenta**.
El **pronóstico del tiempo** es terrible.

*Today it is hot and cloudy.*
*It is cold and stormy.*
*The weather forecast is terrible.*

## Las estaciones (The seasons)

| | |
|---|---|
| **primavera** | *spring* |
| **verano** | *summer* |
| **otoño** | *fall / autumn* |
| **invierno** | *winter* |

En **primavera** hace buen tiempo. > *The weather is good in Spring.*
Hace un poco de frío en **otoño**. > *It's a little cold in the Fall.*

SpanishEasyAndFun.com

# Gramática fácil

## a  The impersonal form "hay"

"**Hay**" *(there is / there are)* is an impersonal form of the verb "haber", which is used when we refer to the existence of something.

This form is invariable in Spanish and can be followed by a singular or plural noun.

| | | |
|---|---|---|
| **Hay** <u>un libro</u> en la mesa. | > | *There is a book on the table.* |
| **Hay** <u>tres libros</u> en la mesa. | > | *There are three books on the table.* |

| | | |
|---|---|---|
| ¿Qué **hay** en la caja? | > | *What is there in the box?* |
| No **hay** estudiantes en la clase. | > | *There aren't any students in the classroom.* |
| No **hay** leche en el refrigerador. | > | *There isn't any milk in the fridge.* |

## b  Indefinite pronouns

Indefinite pronouns are those pronouns that refer to no particular person or thing. Some of the indefinite pronouns have masculine, feminine, singular and plural forms, so <u>they must agree with the noun they refer to</u>.

The most common ones are:

| | |
|---|---|
| **alguien** | *somebody, anybody* |
| **algo** | *somenothing, anything* |
| **alguno, alguna,** | *none, some, (things or* |
| **algunos, algunas** | *people).* |

| | | |
|---|---|---|
| Hay **alguien** en la puerta. | > | *There is someone at the door.* |
| ¿Tienes **algo** para mí? | > | *Have you got something for me?* |
| **Algunos** (de ellos) van al cine esta tarde. | > | *Some (of them) are going to the movies this afternoon.* |

| | |
|---|---|
| **mucho, mucha** | *much* |
| **muchos, muchas** | *many* |

| | | |
|---|---|---|
| Hay **mucho** por hacer. | > | *There is much to do.* |
| ¿Hay galletas en la caja? Sí, hay **muchas**. | > | *Are there any cookies in the box?* |

| | |
|---|---|
| **(un) poco, (una) poca** | *(a) little* |
| **(unos) pocos, (unas) pocas** | *(a) few* |

These pronouns refer to a small quantity, but when we use "un, una, unos, unas" before them, we mean that there is a small but sufficient quantity.

| | | |
|---|---|---|
| Hay **poco** (pan). | > | *There is little (bread).* |
| Hay **un poco** (de pan). | > | *There is a little (bread).* |
| Hay unas **pocas** (fotos). | > | *There are a few (photos).* |
| ¿Te gusta el tenis? **Un poco**. | > | *Do you like tennis? A little.* |

| | |
|---|---|
| **nadie** | *nobody, anybody* |
| **nada** | *nothing* |
| **ninguno, ninguna,** | *none, nobody, no one* |
| **ningunos, ningunas** | |

If these pronouns are placed before the verb, it has to be affirmative. If they go after it, the verb has to be negative.

| | | |
|---|---|---|
| **Nadie** <u>es</u> perfecto. | > | *Nobody is perfect.* |
| <u>No hay</u> **nadie** en la puerta. | > | *Nobody is at the door.* |
| No tengo **nada** en los bolsillos. | > | *I don't have anything in my pockets.* |
| **Ninguna** (de ellas) va al parque. | > | *None of them are going to the park.* |
| No conozco a **ninguno** de ellos. | > | *I don't know any/either of them.* |

| | |
|---|---|
| **todo, toda** | *everything* |
| **todos, todas** | *everybody, all* |

| | | |
|---|---|---|
| Me gusta **todo**. | > | *I like everything.* |
| **Todas** (ellas) saben tocar el violín. | > | *All (of them) can play the violin.* |
| Vienen **todos** a mi fiesta. | > | *Everybody is coming to my party.* |

| | |
|---|---|
| **otro, otra** | *another (one)* |
| **otros, otras** | *others* |

| | | |
|---|---|---|
| Esta no me gusta. Quiero **otra**. | > | *I don't like this one. I want another one.* |
| Algunos estudiantes están aquí. | > | *Some students are here. The others* |
| Los **otros** están fuera. | > | *are outside.* |

SpanishEasyAndFun.com

**a** Fill in the gaps with the correct form: **hacen, hacemos, hago, haces, hace, hacer**.

1 ¿Qué _____? _____ la limpieza.
2 Me puedes _____ un favor?
3 Sus padres viven allí desde _____ dos meses.
4 Los niños no _____ sus deberes.
5 Nosotros no _____ nunca la comida.

**b** Choose the correct answer: **invierno, verano, otoño, primavera**.

Which season is the transition period between...?
1 Winter and Summer          _____
2 Summer and Winter          _____
3 Spring and Fall            _____
4 Fall and Spring            _____

**c** Choose the correct verb.

1 ¿En España _____ muchos bares. (hay / están)
2 La gente _____. en la calle. (hay / está)
3 ¿_____ agua en el refrigerador? (Hay /Está)
4 No _____ flores en el jardín. (hay / están)
5 Los niños _____ en la escuela. (hay / están)

**d** Complete the sentences with: **nada, nadie, ninguna, otra, alguien**.

1 ¿Tienen la solución? No, _____ tiene la solución.
2 ¿Quieres esta manzana? Esa no, quiero _____.
3 ¿Vives con _____? Sí, vivo con mi madre.
4 Le gusta Sara o Miriam? No le gusta _____.
5 No hay _____. en este armario.

# Unidad 14
## Costa Rica

**En esta unidad estudiaremos:**

◉ **Diálogo**

◉ **Hablemos español:**
   **a)** The verb "poder". Present indicative. **b)** Making requests, asking for and borrowing things. **c)** Asking for a favor. **d)** Expressions to confirm and excuse.

◉ **Gramática fácil:**
   **a)** The verb "venir". **b)** The adverbs "también" and "tampoco".

◉ **Ejercicios**

*Luis y su esposa, María, están en casa.*

María: ¡Eh! Pareces preocupado. ¿Qué te pasa?

Luis: Quiero recoger un paquete en la oficina de correos, pero no **puedo** ir. No tengo tiempo. ¿**Podrías ayudarme**?

M: Yo **tampoco** tengo mucho tiempo libre y no sé dónde está la oficina de correos. Pero si **vienes** conmigo me **puedes** decir cómo llegar.

L: **Lo siento pero no puedo. Puedes** ir en mi auto, pero no tiene combustible. ¿**Puedes** ir **también** a la gasolinera, por favor?

M: **De acuerdo.**

L: Aquí tienes 2.500 pesos para el combustible y para pagar el paquete. Bueno, ¿**puedes hacerme** otro favor?

M: ¿Qué quieres ahora?

L: Ese paquete es para mi tía Laura. ¿**Puedes llevarlo** a su casa?

M: Mmmm... **Me temo que no voy a poder.** Sabes que estoy muy enfadada con tu tía Laura. ¿Por qué no vas tú?

L: Yo **tampoco** quiero ver a mi tía Laura. Además, ahora empieza mi programa favorito.

M: Entonces **podemos** dejarlo para mañana y así **vienes** conmigo a ver a tu tía.

SpanishEasyAndFun.com

Iglesia San Rafael Arcángel, Zarcero, Costa Rica.

*Luis and his wife María are at home.*

María: Hey! You look worried. What's the matter?

Luis: I want to pick up a package from the post office, but I can't go. I have no time. You have some free time now. Could you help me?

M: I don't have a lot of time either and I don't know where the post office is. But if you come with me you can show me the way.

L: I'm sorry but I can't. You can take my car, but it has no gas. Can you go to the gas station too, please?

M: Sure!

L: Here are 2,500 pesos for gas and to pick up the package. Can you do me another favor?

M: What do you want now?

L: That package is for my aunt Laura. Can you take it to her house?

M: Mmmm... I'm afraid not. You know I am very angry with your aunt Laura. Why don't you go yourself?

L: I don't want to see my aunt either. And it's time for my favorite TV show now.

M: Then we can go and see your aunt tomorrow and you can come with me.

# Hablemos español

## a The verb "poder". Present indicative

The verb "**poder**" is commonly used in Spanish. Its equivalents in English are "*can*", "*be able*" or "*may*".

In the present indicative it is conjugated as follows:

| | |
|---|---|
| yo | **puedo** |
| tú | **puedes** |
| usted-él-ella | **puede** |
| | |
| nosotros/as | **podemos** |
| vosotros/as | **podéis** |
| ustedes-ellos/as | **pueden** |

"**Poder**" is almost always followed an infinitive and is used:

🔹 to express ability.

    **Puedo** resolver este problema.    **>**    *I can solve this problem.*

🔹 to show options.

    **Puedes** ir al teatro o al cine.    **>**    *You can go to the theater or to the movies.*

🔹 to express permission and prohibition.

    Ella **puede** llegar tarde.    **>**    *She can be late.*
    Ellos no **pueden** fumar aquí.    **>**    *They can't smoke here.*

🔹 to express future possibility.

    **Puede** que llueva mañana.    **>**    *It may rain tomorrow.*

🔹 to make requests.

    ¿**Puede** usted decirme la hora?    **>**    *Can you tell me the time?*
    ¿**Pueden** ayudarme?    **>**    *Can you help me?*

🔹 in questions, to know if we can do something or not.

    ¿**Puedo** pasar?    **>**    *May I come in?*
    ¿**Podemos** venir mañana?    **>**    *Can we come tomorrow?*

SpanishEasyAndFun.com

The most common structures that we use when asking someone to do something are:

**¿Puedes + infinitive…?**
**¿Puede usted + infinitive…?** ⟩ *Can you + infinitive…?*
**¿Pueden ustedes + infinitive…?**

| | | |
|---|---|---|
| **¿Puedes pasar**me la sal? | **>** | *Can you pass me the salt?* |
| **¿Puede usted apagar** la luz, por favor? | **>** | *Can you turn off the light, please?* |
| **¿Pueden ustedes cerrar** la puerta? | **>** | *Can you close the door?* |

When making polite requests we use the conditional: **podrías** (tú), **podría** (usted) and **podrían** (ustedes). In English we would use *"could"*.

| | | |
|---|---|---|
| **¿Podría** usted venir mañana? | **>** | *Could you come tomorrow?* |

And when asking for or borrowing things we use:

**¿Me das** + (determinant) + noun?     *Can you give me + noun?*

**¿Me prestas** + (determinant) + noun?
**¿Me dejas** + (determinant) + noun? ⟩ *May/Can I borrow your + noun?*

| | | |
|---|---|---|
| **¿Me das** un pastel? | **>** | *Can you give (pass) me the cake?* |
| **¿Me prestas** tu bicicleta? | **>** | *May I borrow your bicycle?* |
| **¿Me dejas** tu diccionario? | **>** | *Can I borrow your dictionary?* |

In Spanish, the verbs **"prestar"** / **"dejar"** *(to lend)* are used instead of **"pedir prestado"** *(to borrow).*

Remember that in some Latin American countries, the verb "prestar" means *"to give"*, instead of *"to lend"*.

## c  Asking for a favor

When we ask for a favor we can use several phrases:

| | | |
|---|---|---|
| **¿Puedes hacerme un favor?** | > | *Can you do me a favor?* |
| **¿Me haces un favor?** | > | *Can you do me a favor?* |
| **¿Puedes hacer algo por mí?** | > | *Can you do something for me?* |
| **¿Puedes ayudarme?** | > | *Can you help me?* |
| **¿Puedes echarme una mano?** | > | *Can you lend me a hand?* |

We can emphasize the receiver of the action by adding "a + noun/pronoun/name" to these sentences.

| | | |
|---|---|---|
| ¿Puedes prestar(le) la bicicleta **a** Ana? | > | *Can Ana borrow your bicycle?* |
| ¿Puedes hacer(les) un favor **a** mis padres? | > | *Can you do my parents a favor?* |
| ¿Puedes ayudarle **a** él? | > | *Can you help him?* |

## d  Expressions to confirm and excuse

In order to answer affirmatively when someone asks a question, asks for a favor or makes a request, we can use any of the following expressions:

| | | |
|---|---|---|
| **¡Claro!** | > | *Sure!* |
| **¡Claro que sí!** | > | *Yes of course!* |
| **¡Por supuesto!** | > | *Of course!* |

¿Puede usted hacerme un favor? **¡Claro que sí!**
*Can you do me a favor? Yes, of course!*

But if the answer is negative, or we want to give an excuse we can use:

| | | |
|---|---|---|
| **¡Claro que no!** | > | *Of course not!* |
| **¡Por supuesto que no!** | > | *Of course not!* |
| **Lo siento pero...** | > | *I am sorry but...* |
| **Me temo que...** | > | *I am afraid that...* |

| | | |
|---|---|---|
| —¿Puedes dejarme el coche? | > | *—May I borrow your car?* |
| —**Lo siento pero** lo necesito yo. | > | *—I'm sorry but I need it myself.* |

| | | |
|---|---|---|
| —¿Puedes prestarme algo de dinero? | > | *—Can you lend me some money?* |
| —**Me temo que** no puedo. | > | *—I'm afraid I can't.* |

| | | |
|---|---|---|
| —¿Quieres manejar tú el auto? | > | *—Would you like to drive the car?* |
| —**¡Por supuesto que no!** | > | *—Of course not!* |

SpanishEasyAndFun.com

# Gramática fácil

## a · The verb "venir"

The verb "**venir**" means *"to come"*.

It is an irregular verb that is conjugated in the same way as the verb "sentir" (see unit 10) in the present indicative, but the first person singular (yo) is "vengo".

"**Venir**" is commonly used with certain prepositions:

🔹 **Venir a** + noun *(to come to + noun)*:

| | | |
|---|---|---|
| **Vengo a** este hospital todas las semanas. | > | *I come to this hospital every week.* |
| Ellos nunca **vienen a** mi casa. | > | *They never come to my house.* |

🔹 **Venir a** + infinitive *(to come to + infinitive)*:

| | | |
|---|---|---|
| ¿**Vienes a** hacer la compra conmigo? | > | *Will you come and do the shopping with me?* |

🔹 **Venir de** + noun *(to come from + noun)*:

| | | |
|---|---|---|
| ¿**Vienen** ustedes **del** cine? | > | *Are you coming from the movies?* |
| Mi hermana **viene de** la tienda. | > | *My sister is coming from the store.* |

🔹 **Venir de** + infinitive *(to come from + gerund)*:

| | | |
|---|---|---|
| Él **viene de** pasear al perro. | > | *He is coming from walking the dog.* |

## b · The adverbs "también" and "tampoco"

These two adverbs are used to show agreement with something that has just been said. When the sentence is affirmative, we show agreement with "**también**" *(also/too)* and, when it is negative, with "**tampoco**" *(neither/not... either)*.

| | | |
|---|---|---|
| —Vivo en Los Ángeles. | > | *—I live in Los Angeles.* |
| —Yo **también** (vivo en Los Ángeles). | > | *—Me, too. (I also live in Los Angeles).* |

| | | |
|---|---|---|
| —Ellos no tienen frío. | > | *—They aren't cold.* |
| —Nosotros **tampoco** (tenemos frío). | > | *—Neither are we. (We aren't cold, either).* |

As we can see in these examples, both expressions can be part of a smaller structure (Yo también) or a longer one (Yo también vivo en Los Ángeles).

The Spanish language is very flexible, and sometimes the position of an element does not change the meaning of the sentence. This is also the case with "también" and "tampoco". Keep in mind:

🔹 **"También"** can be placed before the verb or at the end of the sentence.

| | | |
|---|---|---|
| **También** tengo tres hijos. | > | *I also have three children.* |
| Tengo tres hijos, **también**. | > | *I have three children, too.* |

🔹 **"Tampoco"** can precede the verb in affirmative sentences or be placed at the end in negative sentences.

| | | |
|---|---|---|
| **Tampoco** estudiamos geografía. | > | *We don't study geography, either.* |
| <u>No</u> estudiamos geografía **tampoco**. | > | *We don't study geography, either.* |

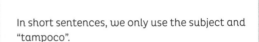

In short sentences, we only use the subject and "también".

Ella sabe la respuesta. **Yo, también**.
*She knows the answer. Me, too.*

In short sentences, we only use the subject and "tampoco".

Usted no sabe manejar camiones. **Yo, tampoco**.
*You don't know how to drive trucks. Me, neither.*

🖐 SpanishEasyAndFun.com

**a** Fill in the gaps with the correct form: **puedo, vienes, podemos, puedes, viene, puedo, venimos, vengo,  puede, vienen.**

**1** Ellos no _____ de la fiesta.
**2** ¿Nosotros _____ comer algo ahora?
**3** Luis _____ enseñarnos a tocar el piano.
**4** Yo _____ a comprar una computadora.
**5** Me temo que yo no _____ ayudarte.
**6** ¿De dónde viene él? _____ de estudiar en la biblioteca.
**7** ¿_____ tú encender la luz?
**8** Nosotros _____ a decirte algo importante.
**9** ¿Qué _____ yo hacer ahora?
**10** ¿Tú _____ a la fiesta con nosotros?

**b** Choose the correct answer. Which of the following questions would you use to ask a favor?

**1** ¿Tienes una bicicleta?
**2** ¿Me prestas tu bicicleta?
**3** ¿Puedes venir en bicicleta?
**4** ¿Puedes romper tu bicicleta?

**c** "**También**" or "**tampoco**"?

**1** Yo no estudio ruso. Ellos, _____.
**2** Ellas hacen ejercicio y sus novios _____.
**3** A ella le gusta cantar y _____ bailar.
**4** Miguel no viene a la fiesta. ¿Tú _____?
**5** No tiene amigos _____.

· · · · · · · · · · · · · · · · · · · · · · · · · · · · · · · · · · · · · · · · · · · · · · · · · · · · · · · ·

**c:** 1.- tampoco; 2.- también; 3.- también; 4.- tampoco; 5.- tampoco.

**b:** 2.

8.- venimos; 9.- puedo; 10.- vienes.

**a:** 1.- vienen; 2.- podemos; 3.- puede; 4.- vengo; 5.- puedo; 6.- viene; 7.- puedes;

**Key**

# Unidad 15
## Islas Canarias

**En esta unidad estudiaremos:**

◉ **Diálogo**

◉ **Hablemos español:**
 **a)** Expressing how often an action occurs: adverbs of frequency.
 **b)** The verb "soler". **c)** Vocabulario: Hábitos y rutinas (Habits and routines).

◉ **Gramática fácil:**
 **a)** Reflexive verbs. **b)** The conjunctions "pero" and "sino".

◉ **Ejercicios**


*José y Dolores hablan sobre sus hábitos.*

Dolores: ¿Qué **sueles** hacer por la mañana, José?

José: **Suelo despertarme** temprano, **me levanto**, **me ducho**, **desayuno**, **me visto** y **me voy** al trabajo. ¿Y tú? ¿Qué **sueles** hacer?

D: Yo **siempre me levanto** tarde porque trabajo por las noches. **Me lavo** la cara y **desayuno**. **Suelo desayunar** café con leche y tostadas.

J: Yo **nunca** tomo café. **Me pongo** nervioso.

D: Y cuando terminas de trabajar, ¿qué haces?

J: **Me voy al gimnasio** con un amigo y hacemos ejercicio. **Nos cansamos** un poco, **pero** luego **nos sentimos** mejor.

D: Yo **voy al gimnasio dos o tres veces a la semana, pero normalmente** no voy por la tarde, **sino** por la mañana o después de **almorzar**.

J: Después **suelo irme** a casa, **me quito** la ropa, **me pongo** el pijama, **ceno**, **veo la televisión** y **me voy a la cama**. Ese es un día típico en mi vida.

D: Por la tarde yo **ordeno** el apartamento, **voy al supermercado**, **paseo** durante un rato o voy a **ver a los amigos**. Y **siempre me voy** al hospital antes de las 8. **Empiezo a trabajar** a las 8:30.

J: ¿Y cómo vas al hospital?

D: **A veces** voy en autobús, pero, si tengo prisa, **manejo** mi auto.

J: Yo **nunca manejo**. No me gusta.

D: Bueno, Juan, ahora **me voy** a ver a Luisa. ¿**Te acuerdas** de ella?

SpanishEasyAndFun.com

Puerto de la Cruz, Tenerife, Islas Canarias, España.

*José and Dolores are talking about their habits.*

Dolores: What do you usually do in the morning, José?
José: I usually wake up early, get up, take a shower, have breakfast, get dressed and go to work. And you? What do you usually do?
D: I always get up late because I work at night. Then I wash my face and have breakfast. I usually have coffee with milk, and toast for breakfast.
J: I never have coffee. It makes me nervous.
D: And when you finish work, what do you do?
J: I go to the gym with a friend and we work out. It wears us out a little, but we feel better later.
D: I go to the gym two or three times a week, but I usually don't go there in the evening but in the morning or after lunch.

J: Then I usually go home, take off my clothes, put on my pajamas, have dinner, watch television and go to bed. That is a typical day in my life.
D: In the afternoon I straighten up the apartment, go to the supermarket, walk for a while or see my friends. And I always go to the hospital before 8:00 p.m. I start work at 8:30 p.m.
J: And how do you get to the hospital?
D: I sometimes go by bus but, if I am in a hurry, I drive my car.
J: I never drive. I don't like to drive.
D: Well, Juan, I have to go and see Luisa now. Do you remember her?

# Hablemos español

## a  Expressing how often an action occurs: adverbs of frequency

Adverbs of frequency indicate how often an action occurs. They are the answer to the questions:

**"¿Con qué frecuencia...?"** *(How often...?)*
**"¿Cuántas veces...?"** *(How many times...?/How often...?)*

⬤ The most common adverbs of frequency are:

| | |
|---|---|
| **siempre** | *always* |
| **normalmente** | *usually* |
| **a menudo** | *often* |
| **con frecuencia** | *frequently, often* |
| **muchas veces** | *many times* |
| **a veces, algunas veces** | *sometimes* |
| **pocas veces, raras veces** | *seldom, rarely* |
| **de vez en cuando** | *from time to time* |
| **casi nunca** | *hardly ever* |
| **nunca, jamás** | *never* |

⬤ They can be placed anywhere in the sentence with no change in meaning, but they usually go either at the beginning or at the end of a sentence.

—¿**Con qué frecuencia** lees periódico?  >  *—How often do you read the el newspaper?*
—Leo el periódico **a menudo**.  >  *—I read the newspaper often.*

Mi madre **a veces** compra vino.  >  *My mother sometimes buys wine.*
Su padre usa la computadora **de vez en cuando**.  >  *Her father uses the computer from time to time.*
**Siempre** llegan tarde.  >  *They are always late.*

The verb is affirmative when "**casi nunca**", "**nunca**" or "**jamás**" is placed before it:
**Nunca** <u>como</u> carne porque soy vegetariano.
*I never eat meat because I am a vegetarian.*

The verb is negative when "**casi nunca**", "**nunca**" or "**jamás**" is placed after it:
<u>No juego</u> al tenis **casi nunca** porque no me gusta mucho.
*I hardly ever play tennis because I don't like it very much.*

🖐 SpanishEasyAndFun.com

● Another way to express how often an action takes place is:

una vez *(once)*

dos veces *(twice)*
muchas veces *(many times)*

+

al día / al mes / al año *(a day / a month / a year)*
a la semana *(a week)*

—¿**Cuántas veces** vas al gimnasio?  >  —*How many times do you go to the gym?*

—Voy al gimnasio **dos veces > a la semana**.  —*I go to the gym twice a week.*

Él se afeita **una vez al día**.  >  *He shaves once a day.*
Navegamos por internet **muchas > veces al mes**.  *We surf the internet many times a month.*

## b  The verb "soler"

The verb "**soler**" implies something that usually happens. When we use "<u>normalmente</u>" *(usually)* or "<u>a menudo</u>" *(often)*, we can almost always replace them and the verb form for the verb "**soler**" (see the conjugation in unit 11, present of irregular verbs, section b) and the infinitive of the main verb.

Ella **normalmente va** al trabajo en autobús = Ella **suele ir** al trabajo en autobús.
*She usually goes to work by bus.*

Pay attention to the position of the reflexive pronoun if we use a reflexive verb.

(Yo) **Suelo despertar**<u>me</u> a las 6. = (Yo) <u>me</u> **suelo despertar** a las 6.
*I usually wake up at 6:00.*

## c  Vocabulario: Hábitos y rutinas (Habits and routines)

**despertarse**: *to wake up*
**levantarse**: *to get up*
**ducharse**: *take a shower*
**vestirse**: *to get dressed*
**desayunar**: *to have breakfast*
**ir al trabajo**: *to go to work*

**almorzar**: *to have lunch*
**volver a casa**: *come back home*
**hacer ejercicio**: *to do exercise*
**ver la televisión**: *to watch television*
**cenar**: *to have dinner/supper*
**ir a la cama**: *to go to bed*

Suelo **desayunar** café y tostadas.  >  *I usually have some coffee and toast for breakfast.*

¿Con qué frecuencia **vas al > trabajo** a pie?  *How often do you go to work on foot?*

Nunca **veo la televisión** por la noche.  >  *I never watch television at night.*

# Gramática fácil

## a Reflexive verbs

Reflexive verbs are those that indicate an action in which the subject (doer) and the object (receiver) are the same person.

Yo **me lavo**.        *I wash myself.*

Reflexive verbs need reflexive pronouns to be expressed.

|  | REFLEXIVE PRONOUNS |  |
|---|---|---|
| yo | **me** | *myself* |
| tú | **te** | *yourself* |
| usted-él-ella | **se** | *yourself (usted), himself, herself, itself* |
| nosotros/as | **nos** | *ourselves* |
| vosotros/as | **os** | *yourselves* |
| ustedes-ellos/as | **se** | *yourselves (ustedes), themselves* |

Take note that, unlike in English, reflexive pronouns are placed just before the conjugated verb in Spanish.

**Me** levanto temprano.
*I get up early.*
Ella **se** ducha por la mañana.
*She takes a shower in the morning.*

A reflexive verb can be identified by the ending "**-se**" *(oneself)* attached to the infinitive:

callar**se** *(to shut up)*
poner**se** *(to put on clothes)*
vestir**se** *(to get dressed).*

Reflexive verbs are conjugated in the same way as non-reflexive verbs and they can be regular or irregular. When we drop the reflexive ending (-se), we see if the infinitive form ends with "-ar", "-er" or "-ir", and then we conjugate it.

|  | CALLAR(SE) | PONER(SE)* | VESTIR(SE)** |
|---|---|---|---|
| yo | **me** call**o** | **me** pon**go** | **me** vist**o** |
| tú | **te** call**as** | **te** pon**es** | **te** vist**es** |
| usted-él-ella | **se** call**a** | **se** pon**e** | **se** vist**e** |
| nosotros/as | **nos** call**amos** | **nos** pon**emos** | **nos** vest**imos** |
| vosotros/as | **os** call**áis** | **os** pon**éis** | **os** vest**ís** |
| ustedes-ellos/as | **se** call**an** | **se** pon**en** | **se** vist**en** |

🖐 SpanishEasyAndFun.com

✪ We have learned
that the verb "poner" has an irregular form for the first person in singular (yo).
✪ ✪ The verb "vestir" changes the "e" into an "i" in the verb stem, except for "nosotros/as" and "vosotros/as".

More examples of reflexive verbs are:

| | | | |
|---|---|---|---|
| **acordarse** | to remember | **lavarse** | to wash oneself |
| **afeitarse** | to shave oneself | **levantarse** | to get up |
| **cansarse** | to get tired | **llamarse** | to be named |
| **casarse** | to get married | **mirarse** | to look at oneself |
| **cortarse** | to cut oneself | **peinarse** | to comb one's hair |
| **despertarse** | to wake up | **preocuparse** | to worry |
| **dormirse** | to fall asleep | **quedarse** | to stay/remain |
| **ducharse** | to take a shower | **quitarse (ropa)** | to take off (clothes) |
| **enojarse** | to get angry | **sentarse** | to sit down |
| **irse** | to go away | **sentirse** | to feel |

| | | |
|---|---|---|
| Ella **se mira** en el espejo. | > | *She is looking at herself in the mirror.* |
| No **te preocupes**. | > | *Don't worry.* |
| Ellos no **se despiertan** tarde. | > | *They don't get up late.* |
| **Nos casamos** en marzo. | > | *We are getting married in March.* |
| **Me quedo** en un hotel. | > | *I'm staying at a hotel.* |
| Ustedes **se cansan**. | > | *You get tired.* |

Reflexive pronouns are placed either before a conjugated verb or attached to an infinitive or a gerund.

¿**Me** puedo poner esta camisa? = ¿Puedo poner**me** esta camisa?
*Can I put on this shirt?*

Ella **se** está vistiendo = Ella está vistiéndo**se**.
*She is getting dressed.*

## b  The conjunctions "pero" and "sino"

Both "**pero**" and "**sino**" are conjunctions that indicate <u>contrast</u>. They are equivalent to *"but"* in English.

● **Pero** introduces an idea that contrasts with the previous one:

| | | |
|---|---|---|
| Sé manejar **pero** no tengo auto. | > | *I can drive but I don't have a car.* |
| Tus padres no vienen **pero** tu hermano sí. | > | *Your parents are not coming but your brother is.* |
| No teníamos café, **pero** teníamos té. | > | *We didn't have any coffee but we had some tea.* |

● **Sino** introduces an idea that corrects something previously said. First an idea is negated and then it is replaced by another.

| | | |
|---|---|---|
| No hablo francés **sino** español. | > | *I don't speak French but Spanish.* |
| Él no tiene 42 años **sino** 48. | > | *He isn't 42 years old but 48.* |
| Ellos no venían de Argentina **sino** de Chile. | > | *They didn't come from Argentina but from Chile.* |

▪ There is a common mistake that English speakers make:

| | | |
|---|---|---|
|                sino<br>No soy Juan ~~pero~~ Pedro. | > | *I'm not Juan but Pedro.* |

▪ **Sino** can also precede an infinitive, a gerund or a conjugated verb. Before conjugated verbs, **sino** changes for **sino que**.

| | | |
|---|---|---|
| No quieren cantar **sino** <u>bailar</u>. | > | *They don't want to sing but to dance.* |
| No estamos leyendo **sino** <u>viendo</u> la TV. | > | *We aren't reading but watching TV.* |
| Ella no aprobó el examen **sino que** lo <u>suspendió</u>. | > | *She didn't pass the test: she failed it, instead.* |

# Ejercicios de la **Unidad 15**

**a** Choose the correct answer: What do these adverbs of frequency mean?

1 pocas veces      (always / seldom / usually)
2 jamás      (never / always / sometimes)
3 a veces      (hardly ever / seldom / sometimes)
4 nunca      (usually / never / from time to time)
5 dos veces al mes      (twice a week / once a month / twice a month)

**b** Fill in the gaps with the correct form (present indicative) of the following verbs.

1 Yo (soler) _____. ir al gimnasio.
2 Ella (levantarse) _____ a las 8 todos los días.
3 Mi hermano (ducharse) _____ por la mañana.
4 ¿Qué ropa (ponerse) _____ yo para la fiesta?
5 Nosotros (soler) _____ pasear por el parque.

**c** Complete the sentences with "pero" or "sino".

1 María es alta _____ no es fuerte.
2 Pablo no es alto _____ fuerte.
3 Ellos no hablan español _____ francés.
4 Tengo hambre _____ no puedo comer.
5 En el equipo no juega Miguel _____ Francisco.

**d** Choose the correct sentence.

1 Casi nunca bebo café porque no me pongo nervioso.
2 No bebo café casi nunca porque no me pongo nervioso.
3 Nunca bebo café porque no me pongo nervioso.
4 No bebo café casi nunca porque me pongo nervioso.
5 Bebo café nunca porque me pongo nervioso.

**d:** 4

**c:** 1.- pero; 2.- sino; 3.- sino; 4.- pero; 5.- sino.

**b:** 1.- suelo; 2.- se levanta; 3.- se ducha; 4.- me pongo; 5.- solemos.

**a:** 1.- seldom; 2.- never; 3.- sometimes; 4.- never; 5.- twice a month.

**Key**

Spanish: Easy and Fun                 **U15** 143

# Unidad 16
## La Patagonia

**En esta unidad estudiaremos:**

◉ **Diálogo**

◉ **Hablemos español:**
**a)** Prepositions and adverbs of place. **b)** Vocabulario: La ciudad (The city); Objetos de la calle (Objects on the street).

◉ **Gramática fácil:**
**a)** The present participle (the gerund). **b)** The present progressive: estar + present participle. **c)** The adverbs "todavía", "aún" and "ya".

◉ **Ejercicios**

*Martín y Blanca, su esposa, están hablando por teléfono.*

Martín: Son las 7 de la tarde, Blanca. ¿Todavía **estás trabajando**?
Blanca: Sí, **aún estoy trabajando**. ¿Qué haces tú?
M: **Estoy paseando** por la calle. Ahora estoy **enfrente de** la casa.
B: ¿Están los niños contigo?
M: No. Están en la casa.
B: ¿Qué **están haciendo**?
M: **Están haciendo** sus deberes **arriba**, en su dormitorio.
B: **¿Todavía están haciendo** sus deberes?
M: Creo que sí. Yo voy ahora al **banco** que hay **entre** la **oficina de correos** y la **biblioteca**. Necesito sacar dinero.
B: Muy bien. Yo **estoy escribiendo** unos correos electrónicos, pero acabaré pronto. Luego iré a la **librería** a comprar una revista. Está **cerca de** aquí.
M: ¿Sabes? **Estoy viendo** a Miguel. **Está paseando** a su perro. Ahora está **delante de** la **farmacia** y **está hablando** con un muchacho que está sentado en un **banco**.
B: Bueno, Martín, voy a seguir **trabajando** porque quiero acabar pronto. Si hablas con Miguel, dale recuerdos de mi parte.
M: De acuerdo, lo haré. Yo **ya estoy bajando** la calle hacia el **banco**. Ahora lo veré. ¡Hasta luego, Blanca!
B: ¡Hasta luego!

SpanishEasyAndFun.com

Glaciar Perito Moreno, Santa Cruz, Patagonia, Argentina.

*Martín and Blanca, his wife, are talking on the phone.*

Martín: It is 7:00 p.m. in the evening, Blanca. Are you still working?

Blanca: Yes, I am still working. What are you doing?

M: I am taking a walk along the street. I am across from the house now.

B: Are the kids with you?

M: No, they are in the house.

B: What are they doing?

M: They are doing their homework upstairs, in their bedroom.

B: They are still doing their homework?

M: I think so. Now I'm going to the bank that is between the post office and the library. I need to take out some money.

B: Okay. I'm writing some emails but I'll finish soon. Then I'm going to the bookstore to buy a magazine. It's close by.

M: You know what? I see Miguel. He's walking his dog. He is in front of the drugstore, talking to a boy who is sitting on a bench.

B: Well, Martín, I'm going to keep on working because I want to finish soon. If you speak to Miguel, give him my regards.

M: Alright; I will. I'm already walking down the street towards the bank. I'll see him right now. See you later, Blanca!

B: See you later!

# Hablemos español

## a Prepositions and adverbs of place

Prepositions and adverbs of place or location are the elements that will show us where something or somebody is, or where the action occurs.

In addition to those that we have already learned (aquí, allí,..., see unit 3), some of the most common ones are:

| | | | |
|---|---|---|---|
| **en** | in, on, at | **entre** | between, among |
| **encima (de)** | on, on top (of) | **debajo (de)** | under |
| **arriba** | above, upstairs | **abajo** | below, downstairs |
| **por encima de** | over, above | **por debajo de** | below |
| **dentro (de)** | in, inside | **fuera (de)** | out (of), outside |
| **lejos (de)** | far (from) | **cerca (de)** | near, nearby |
| **delante (de)** | in front of | **detrás (de)** | behind |
| **enfrente (de)** | across from | **al lado (de)** | next to |
| **a la derecha** | on/to the right | **a la izquierda** | on/to the left |

| | | |
|---|---|---|
| El teatro está **entre** el banco y la tienda. | > | The theater is between the bank and the store. |
| Hay un hotel **enfrente del** taller. | > | There is a hotel across from the garage. |
| Hay alguien **en** la puerta. | > | There is someone at the door. |
| La farmacia está **lejos del** parque. | > | The drugstore is far from the park. |
| No hay nada **detrás de** la puerta. | > | There is nothing behind the door. |
| El perro está **debajo de** la mesa. | > | The dog is under the table. |
| El supermercado está allí, **a la izquierda**. | > | The supermarket is there, on the left. |
| Hay un buzón **delante de** mi casa. | > | There is a mailbox in front of my house. |

## b Vocabulario

### La ciudad (The city)

**supermercado**: supermarket
**escuela**: school
**museo**: museum
**cine**: movie theater, cinema
**iglesia**: church
**agencia de viajes**: travel agency
**farmacia**: drugstore, pharmacy
**comisaría**: police station
**oficina de correos**: post office
**estación de autobuses**: bus station

**oficina**: office
**banco**: bank
**restaurante**: restaurant
**parque**: park
**teatro**: theater
**biblioteca**: library
**universidad**: university
**hospital**: hospital
**taller**: garage
**hotel**: hotel

SpanishEasyAndFun.com

**salón de belleza**: *beauty salon*
**centro comercial, plaza**: *department store, plaza*

**tienda**: *store, shop*
**librería**: *bookstore*

## Objetos de la calle (Objects on the street)

**banco**: *bench*
**fuente**: *fountain*
**semáforo**: *traffic light*
**valla publicitaria**: *billboard*
**farola**: *street light*
**monumento**: *monument*
**jardinera**: *flower bed*

**papelera**: *garbage can*
**buzón**: *mailbox*
**caseta del autobús**: *bus shelter/ bus stop*
**estatua**: *statue*
**acera**: *sidewalk*

Hay una **valla publicitaria** delante de la **fuente**.
No hay **papeleras** cerca de aquí.
El perro está al lado de la **caseta del autobús**.

> There is a billboard in front of the fountain.
> There are no garbage cans near here.
> The dog is next to the bus shelter.

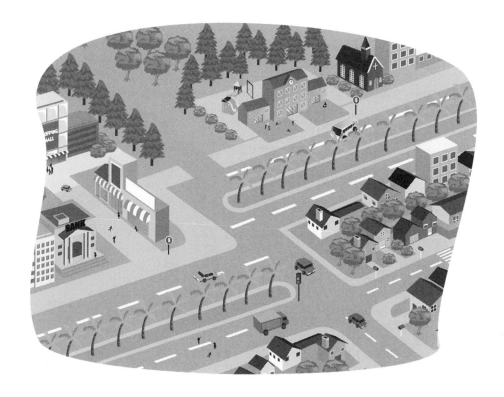

# Gramática fácil

## a The present participle (gerund)

The Spanish present participle is formed by adding "**-ando**" to the stem of "-ar" verbs and "**-iendo**" to the stems of "-er" and "-ir" verbs.

| habl**ar** ➔ | habl**ando** | com**er** ➔ | com**iendo** | part**ir** ➔ | part**iendo** |
|---|---|---|---|---|---|
| *speak* | *speaking* | *eat* | *eating* | *split* | *splitting* |

But when the verb is irregular:

- Verbs that change "**e**" into "**i**" in the verb stem keep this change in the gerund.

| d**e**cir ➔ | d**i**ciendo | p**e**dir ➔ | p**i**diendo | rep**e**tir ➔ | rep**i**tiendo |
|---|---|---|---|---|---|
| *say* | *saying* | *ask for* | *asking for* | *repeat* | *repeating* |

- Verbs ending in "-ir" with a stem change "**e>ie**" or "**o>ue**" in present, show "**i**" and "**u**" in the gerund.

| m**e**ntir ➔ | m**i**ntiendo | **e**ntir ➔ | s**i**ntiendo |
|---|---|---|---|
| *lie* | *lying* | *feel* | *feeling* |

| p**o**der ➔ | p**u**diendo | d**o**rmir ➔ | d**u**rmiendo |
|---|---|---|---|
| *can* | *being able* | *sleep* | *sleeping* |

- If the "i" in the ending "-iendo" is preceded by a vowel, it changes for "**y**".

| c**a**er ➔ | ca**y**endo | l**e**er ➔ | le**y**endo | o**í**r ➔ | o**y**endo |
|---|---|---|---|---|---|
| *fall* | *falling* | *read* | *reading* | *hear* | *hearing* |

The present participle of the verb "ir" is "**yendo**" (going).

🖐 SpanishEasyAndFun.com

Reflexive verbs add the pronoun (me, te, se,...) to the end, and change to the gerund form, which then requires a graphic accent on the stressed vowel of the gerund.

mirarse → mirándo**se**
*look at oneself*    *looking at oneself*

levantarse → levantándo**se**
*get up*    *getting up*

sentirse → sintiéndo**se**
*feel*    *feeling*

The most common use of the present participle or gerund is to be coupled with the verb "estar" (never "ser") to form progressive tenses:

Luis **está comiendo**.    >    *Luis is eating.*

## b  The present progressive: estar + present participle

The present progressive or continuous is formed by the present indicative of "estar" and the present participle of the main verb, and expresses an ongoing action.

Subject **+ present of "estar" + present participle (gerund) +** (complements)

(Yo) **Estoy estudiando** español.    >    *I am studying Spanish.*

This is the tense used when referring to an action that is taking place at the moment of speaking or near that moment.

Ella **está escribiendo** un correo electrónico.    >    *She is writing an email.*
**Estoy leyendo** un libro interesante.    >    *I am reading an interesting book.*

● Remember that sometimes the present indicative can also be used in these cases.

¿Qué **estás haciendo** ahora? = ¿Qué **haces** ahora? **>** *What are you doing now?*

● The present progressive is not used to express habits or repeated actions, except when using an adverb of frequency.

Juan **siempre** está sonriendo. **>** *Juan is always smiling.*

● With reflexive verbs, the reflexive pronoun can be placed either before the verb "estar" or attached to the end of the gerund form.

Ella **se** está lavando la cara ←——→ Ella está lavándo**se** la cara.
*She is washing her face.*

---

**C** **The adverbs "todavía", "aún" and "ya"**

In affirmative sentences, the adverbs "**todavía**" and "**aún**" mean *"still/yet"*. They can be placed before or after the verb.

**Todavía (aún)** tengo esos documentos. **>** *I still have those documents.*
Está nevando **todavía (aún)**. **>** *It's still snowing.*
¿**Todavía (aún)** sales con él? **>** *Are you still going out with him?*

● When used in the negative, "**todavía**"/ "**aún**" means *"not yet"*.

Ella no vive **todavía (aún)** en su **>** *She isn't living in her new house yet.*
casa nueva.

● "**Ya**" has several uses, but its most common meanings are *"already"* and *"now"* in affirmative sentences, and *"not anymore/no longer"* in negative sentences (**"ya no"**).

**Ya** tengo el celular nuevo. **>** *I already have the new cell phone.*
**Ya** vuelve la lluvia. **>** *The rain is back now.*
**Ya no** voy al gimnasio. **>** *I'm not going to the gym anymore.*
**Ya no** les gusta bailar. **>** *They don't like dancing anymore.*

**a**   What is the opposite of...?:

**1** delante          _____
**2** encima          _____
**3** a la derecha     _____
**4** cerca           _____
**5** fuera           _____

**b**   Fill in the gaps with the present progressive forms. What are these people doing?

**1** La camarera (servir) _____ el desayuno.
**2** El bebé (dormir) _____ en su habitación.
**3** El Sr. González (leer) _____ un correo electrónico.
**4** Mis hermanos (estudiar) _____ para el examen.
**5** ¿Quiénes (construir) _____ esa casa?
**6** ¿Ella (pasear) _____ al perro?
**7** Tus hermanas te (esperar) _____ en la parada del autobús.
**8** Ahora mis amigos y yo (jugar) _____ a las cartas.
**9** ¿Qué (hacer) _____ tú?
**10** Huele bien. ¿Qué (cocinar) _____ ellos?

**c**   Match the words with their meanings.

**1** buzón                  **a** waste basket
**2** papelera               **b** bench
**3** semáforo               **c** sidewalk
**4** banco                  **d** traffic light
**5** acera                  **e** mailbox

................................................................

**Key**

**a:** 1.- detrás; 2.- debajo; 3.- a la izquierda; 4.- lejos; 5.- dentro.

**b:** 1.- está sirviendo; 2.- está durmiendo; 3.- está leyendo; 4.- están estudiando; 5.- están construyendo; 6.- está paseando; 7.- están esperando; 8.- estamos jugando; 9.- estás haciendo; 10.- están cocinando.

**c:** 1- e; 2 - a; 3 - d; 4 - b; 5.- c.

# Unidad 17
## La Rioja

**En esta unidad estudiaremos:**

◉ **Diálogo**

◉ **Hablemos español:**
  **a)** Expressing opinions. **b)** Expressing quantity: adverbs of quantity.
  **c)** Vocabulario: La lista de la compra [I] (The shopping list [I]).

◉ **Gramática fácil:**
  **a)** Direct object pronouns. **b)** The personal "a". **c)** Cardinal numbers
  (100-999).

◉ **Ejercicios**

---

*Irene va al mercado a comprar vegetales y habla con el dependiente.*

Irene: ¡Hola! ¡Buenos días!
Dependiente: ¡Buenos días! ¿Qué le pongo?
I:   Quiero **un kilo de naranjas** y **medio kilo de fresas**.
D:   Las **fresas** pesan **550** gramos. ¿Está bien?
I:   Sí, está bien.
D:   Aquí tiene. ¿Algo más?
I:   Sí. ¿Tiene **pepinos**?
D:   Sí. Son muy buenos y están baratos. ¿**Los** quiere grandes?
I:   No, **creo que** son más sabrosos los pequeños. Póngame **algunos**. ¡Ah! Y
     quiero **una bolsa de cebollas**, también.
D:   Aquí **la** tiene. ¿Algo más?
I:   No sé...
D:   ¿**Lechugas, tomates, zanahorias**,...?
I:   ¿Están frescas las **zanahorias**?
D:   Sí, **las** tengo muy frescas.
I:   ¿Puedo ver**las**?
D:   Aquí **las** tiene.
I:   Pues me llevo **unas pocas**. ¿Cuánto es todo?
D:   Son **325** pesos.
I:   Aquí tiene. Voy a ver **a Ana**, la panadera, para pedirle el **pan** que tomo
     siempre. Muchas gracias.
D:   Gracias a usted.
I:   ¡Adiós!
D:   ¡Adiós!

SpanishEasyAndFun.com

Viñedos en Haro, La Rioja, España.

*Irene has gone to the market to buy some vegetables and is talking to the greengrocer.*

Irene: Hello! Good morning!
Greengrocer: Good morning! What can I get you?
I:   I'd like a kilo of oranges and half a kilo of strawberries.
G:   The strawberries come out to 550 grams. Is that okay?
I:   Yes, it's fine.
G:   Here you are. Anything else?
I:   Yes. Do you have any cucumbers?
G:   Yes. They are very good and inexpensive right now . Do you want them big?
I:   No, I think the small ones are tastier. I'll have a few. Oh! And I also want a bag of onions.
G:   Here you are. Anything else?
I:   I don't know…
G:   Lettuce, tomatoes, carrots…?
I:   Are the carrots fresh?
G:   Yes, very fresh.
I:   Can I see them?
G:   Here you are.
I:   I'll take a few. How much is everything?
G:   It's 325 pesos.
I:   Here you are. I'm going to see Ana, the baker, and ask her for the bread I always have. Thank you very much.
G:   Thank you.
I:   Goodbye!
G:   Goodbye!

# Hablemos español

## a Expressing opinions

When expressing an opinion, we frequently use the verbs "**creer (que)**" or "**pensar (que)**".

| | | |
|---|---|---|
| **Creo que** ella es mexicana. | > | *I think (that) she is Mexican.* |
| **Tú crees que** yo no tengo razón. | > | *You think (that) I'm wrong.* |
| **Ellos creen que** Silvia es mi hermana. | > | *They think (that) Silvia is my sister.* |

| | | |
|---|---|---|
| **Pienso que** esta reunión es aburrida. | > | *I think (that) this meeting is boring.* |
| Él **piensa que** hay demasiada gente aquí. | > | *He thinks there are too many people here.* |

And when asking for someone's opinion:

| | | |
|---|---|---|
| **¿Crees que...?** | > | *Do you think that...* |
| **¿Cree usted que...?** | > | *Do you think that...* |
| **¿Qué crees?** | > | *What do you think?* |
| **¿Qué cree usted?** | > | *What do you think?* |
| **¿Qué piensa(s) de/sobre/acerca de...?** | > | *What do you think about...?* |

| | | |
|---|---|---|
| **¿Crees que** puedo ganar la carrera? | > | *Do you think I can win the race?* |
| **¿Qué piensas de** Lucy? | > | *What do you think about Lucy?* |

## b Expressing quantity: adverbs of quantity

These adverbs express how much there is of something.

| | | | | |
|---|---|---|---|---|
| **demasiado/a** | *too much* | **tanto/a** | *as/so much* |
| **demasiados/as** | *too many* | **tantos/as** | *so many* |
| **bastante/s** | *quite, enough* | **muy** | *very* |
| **suficiente** | *enough* | **más** | *more* |
| **mucho/a** | *much, a lot (of)* | **menos** | *less, fewer* |
| **muchos/as** | *many, a lot (of)* | **nada de\*** | *no, any* |
| **(un/a) poco/a (de)** | *(a) little* | **ningún/a\*** | *no, any* |
| **(unos/as) pocos/as** | *(a) few* | | |

⭐ "Nada de" is used before uncountable nouns and "ningún, ninguna" before countable nouns.

| | | |
|---|---|---|
| Tenemos **demasiado** pan. | > | *We have too much bread.* |
| Hay **demasiadas** naranjas en el árbol. | > | *There are too many oranges in the tree.* |

| | | |
|---|---|---|
| ¿Tienes **bastante** leche? Sí, tengo **suficiente**. | > | *Do you have enough milk? Yes, I have enough.* |
| Hay **mucha** nieve en la calle. | > | *There is a lot of snow on the street.* |
| ¿Tiene ella **muchos** amigos? | > | *Does she have many friends?* |
| Necesitamos **un poco de** nata. | > | *We need a little cream.* |
| No necesito **tanto** azúcar. | > | *I don't need so much sugar.* |
| El auto es **muy** caro. | > | *The car is very expensive.* |
| ¿Quieres **más** vino? | > | *Would you like some more wine?* |
| Tenemos **menos** dinero. | > | *We have less money.* |
| No hay **nada de** café. | > | *There is no coffee.* |
| No tienen **ninguna** foto. | > | *They have no photos.* |

Commonly you will see the use of <u>plural and uncountable nouns with no quantifiers</u> before them:

| | | |
|---|---|---|
| Hay <u>niños</u> en la clase. | > | *There are children in the classroom.* |
| ¿Venden ustedes <u>libros</u>? | > | *Do you sell books?* |
| Quiero <u>pan</u>. | > | *I want some bread.* |
| No tienes <u>dinero</u>. | > | *You don't have any money.* |

## C  Vocabulario: La lista de la compra [I] (The shopping list [I])

**Productos de alimentación:** *groceries*

**Fruta:** *fruit*

| | | |
|---|---|---|
| **manzana** *apple* | **plátano, banana** *banana* | **naranja** *orange* |
| **coco** *coconut* | **piña, ananás** *pineapple* | **uva** *grape* |
| **limón** *lemon* | **mango** *mango* | **melón** *melon* |
| **fresa** *strawberry* | **pera** *pear* | **ciruela** *plum* |
| **sandía** *watermelon* | **melocotón/durazno** *peach* | |

**Verdura, vegetales:** *vegetables*

| | | |
|---|---|---|
| **tomate** *tomato* | **espinacas** *spinach* | **calabaza** *pumpkin* |
| **patata/papa** *potato* | **pepino** *cucumber* | **ají, pimiento** *pepper* |
| **cebolla** *onion* | **arvejas, guisantes** *peas* | **lechuga** *lettuce* |
| **ajo** *garlic* | **coliflor** *cauliflower* | **zanahoria** *carrot* |
| **col, repollo** *cabbage* | | |

**Otros:** *others*

| | | |
|---|---|---|
| **huevo** *egg* | **arroz** *rice* | **pan** *bread* |
| **pasta** *pasta* | **jam** *mermelada* | **cereales** *cereal* |
| **azúcar** *sugar* | **harina** *flour* | |

**Recipientes:** *containers*
**una bolsa de** limones: *a bag of lemons*
**un saco de** patatas/papas: *a sack of potatoes*
**un bote de** mermelada: *a jar of jam*
**una caja de** cereales: *a box of cereal*
**un frasco de** arvejas: *a jar of peas*
**un frasco de** aceitunas: *a jar of olives*

**But you can also ask for:**
**una docena de** huevos: *a dozen eggs*
**un racimo de** uvas: *a bunch of grapes*
**una barra de** pan: *a loaf of bread*
**un kilo de** tomates: *a kilo of tomatoes*
**una libra de** arroz: *a pound of rice*
**un litro de** zumo/jugo: *a litre of juice*

Necesito **una bolsa de naranjas, dos kilos de tomates** y **un racimo de uvas**.
*I need a bag of oranges, two kilos of tomatoes and a bunch of grapes.*

Ella quiere **un bote de mermelada** y **una docena de huevos**.
*She wants a jar of jam and a dozen eggs.*

# Gramática fácil

## a Direct object pronouns

Direct objects are the answer to the questions "*whom?*" or "*what?*".

¿**A quién** ves? Veo <u>a Miguel</u>.      >      *Whom do you see? I see Miguel.*
¿**Qué** quieren ellos? Ellos quieren      >      *What do they want? They want some*
<u>cebollas</u>.                                       *onions.*

In these examples, "Miguel" and "cebollas" are direct objects. We can substitute these direct objects for direct object pronouns.

Veo a **Miguel.**      ····➤   **Lo** veo.            *I see him.*
Ellos quieren **cebollas.**   ····➤   Ellos **las** quieren.   *They want them.*

| SUBJECT PRONOUNS | DIRECT OBJECT PRONOUNS | |
|---|---|---|
| yo | **me** | *me* |
| tú | **te** | *you* |
| usted | **lo, la** | *you* |
| él | **lo** | *him, it\** |
| ella | **la** | *her, it \** |
| nosotros/as | **nos** | *us* |
| vosotros/as | **os** | *you* |
| ustedes | **los, las** | *you* |
| ellos/as | **los, las** | *them\** |

⚙ The direct pronouns "it" and "them" have masculine and feminine forms, which have to agree with the gender and number of the noun they replace.

| Antonio compra **el periódico**. | Antonio **lo** compra. |
|---|---|
| *Antonio buys the mewspaper.* | *Antonio buys it.* |

| Mi padre come **carne**. | Mi padre **la** come. |
|---|---|
| *My father eats meat.* | *My father eats it.* |

| Tenemos **tres cuadros**. | **Los** tenemos. |
|---|---|
| *We have three pictures.* | *We have them.* |

These pronouns either precede a conjugated verb or follow attached to an infinitive or a present participle (gerund).

| Quiero comprar <u>un auto</u>. | > | *I want to buy a car.* |
|---|---|---|
| **Lo** quiero comprar. | > | *I want to buy it.* |
| Quiero comprar**lo**. | > | *I want to buy it.* |

| Ellos están visitando a <u>su madre</u>. | > | *They are visiting their mother.* |
|---|---|---|
| Ellos **la** están visitando. | > | *They are visiting her.* |
| Ellos están visitándo**la**. | > | *They are visiting her.* |

In negative sentences, "no" precedes the verb, but, if the pronoun is placed before the verb, "no" goes before the pronoun:

| Ellos **no** quieren ver<u>me</u>. | > | *They  don't want to see me.* |
|---|---|---|
| Ellos **no** <u>me</u> quieren ver. | > | *They don't want to see me.* |

## The personal "a"

When <u>a person</u> receives the action of the verb directly, that is, when he/she acts as a direct object, you need to use the personal "a".

| Berta mira **a** <u>Luis</u>. | > | *Berta is looking at Luis.* |
|---|---|---|
| Berta mira **a** <u>su padre</u>. | > | *Berta is looking at her father.* |
| Berta mira el cuadro. | > | *Berta is looking at the picture.* |

But the verb "tener" does not normally need the personal "a".

| **Tengo** <u>un pariente</u> en Cuba. | > | *I have a relative in Cuba.* |
|---|---|---|

100    cien

🔹 Between 101 and 199, "ciento" is used instead of "cien":

101    ciento uno
102    ciento dos
116    ciento dieciséis
145    ciento cuarenta y cinco
199    ciento noventa y nueve

🔹 The rest of the "hundreds" follow a fairly regular pattern:

| | | | | |
|---|---|---|---|---|
| 200 | doscientos | | 205 | doscientos cinco |
| 300 | trescientos | | 389 | trescientos ochenta y nueve |
| 400 | cuatrocientos | | 412 | cuatrocientos doce |
| 500 | quinientos | | 595 | quinientos noventa y cinco |
| 600 | seiscientos | | 633 | seiscientos treinta y tres |
| 700 | setecientos | | 721 | setecientos veintiuno |
| 800 | ochocientos | | 868 | ochocientos sesenta y ocho |
| 900 | novecientos | | 999 | novecientos noventa y nueve |

🔹 There are feminine forms for some numbers:

Up to number 199, the only figure with a feminine form is "una":

| | | |
|---|---|---|
| 31 | Treinta y **una** muchachas. | *Thirty-one girls.* |
| 101 | Ciento **una** flores. | *One hundred one flowers.* |
| 191 | Ciento noventa y **una** páginas. | *One hundred ninety-one pages.* |

🔹 From 200 on, the ending "-cientos" changes into "-cientas" before a feminine noun:

| | | |
|---|---|---|
| 200 | **Doscientas** botellas. | *wo hundred bottles.* |
| 301 | **Trescientas una** mesas. | *Three hundred one tables.* |
| 745 | **Setecientas** cuarenta y cinco mujeres. | *Seven hundred forty-five women.* |

SpanishEasyAndFun.com

**a** Match the sentences and their meanings.

**1** Tiene mucho dinero.
**2** Tiene demasiado dinero.
**3** Tiene suficiente dinero.
**4** Tiene poco dinero.
**5** Tiene más dinero.
**6** Tiene un poco de dinero.

**a** He has more money.
**b** He has a lot of money.
**c** He has a little money.
**d** He has enough money.
**e** He has too much money.
**f** He has little money.

**b** Fill in the dialogues with the correct direct object pronoun.

**1** Yo veo la televisión, pero Antonio no _____ ve.
**2** ¿Qué significa "istmo"? No _____ sé.
**3** Conozco a María y a Betty. ¿Y tú? ¿_____ conoces?
**4** ¿Dónde están los tomates? _____ tengo aquí.
**5** Este cuadro es barato. ¿Quieres comprar _____?
**6** ¿Hablas francés? Ni _____ hablo ni _____ entiendo.

**c** Find the one that doesn't belong:

**1** manzana – huevo – pera
**2** arroz – coliflor – lechuga
**3** pan – cereales – ajo
**4** pepino – calabaza – mango
**5** zanahoria – sandía – uva

**d** Choose the correct answer. Which of the following sentences is correct?

**1** El libro tiene doscientos diecinueve páginas.
**2** Ellos fabrican novecientas autos al mes.
**3** Pablo y Ricardo no tienen quinientas billetes.
**4** El boleto cuesta ochocientos veinte dólares.
**5** Hay cienta un participantes en la carrera.

• • • • • • • • • • • • • • • • • • • • • • • • • • • • • • • • • • • • • • • • • • • • • • • • • • •

**Key**

**a:** 1.– b; 2.– e; 3.– d; 4.– f; 5.– a; 6.–c.
**b:** 1.– la; 2.– lo; 3.– las; 4.– los; 5.– lo; 6.– lo, lo.
**c:** 1– huevo; 2 – arroz; 3 – ajo; 4 – mango; 5.– zanahoria.
**d:** 4.

# Unidad 18
## Potosí

### En esta unidad estudiaremos:

◉ **Diálogo**

◉ **Hablemos español:**
   **a)** Asking about quantity. **b)** Vocabulario: La lista de la compra [II]
   (The shopping list [II]).

◉ **Gramática fácil:**
   **a)** The adverbs "muy" and "mucho". **b)** Other expressions of quantity.
   **c)** The use of "lo". **d)** Cardinal numbers (1000-millions).

◉ **Ejercicios**

---

*Marina y Pablo están tomando un café y conversando.*

Pablo: ¿Quieres leche?
Marina: Sí, **un poco de** leche, por favor.
P:　¿Azúcar?
M:　Sí, gracias.
P:　¿**Cuánta**?
M:　Dos **cucharadas**.
P:　¡Eso es **mucho**!
M:　Sí, le pongo **bastante** azúcar al café. Siempre que voy al mercado compro
　　**dos paquetes de** azúcar.
P:　¡Ah! Ayer vi a tu hermana en el supermercado.
M:　¿Qué te dijo?
P:　Que había comprado **mil** cosas: **pescado, dos latas de mejillones,**
　　**carne y queso**.
M:　Eso no es **demasiado**. **Lo bueno** es que siempre tiene la casa llena de
　　comida.
P:　¿Tiene hijos?
M:　Sí.
P:　¿**Cuántos** hijos tiene?
M:　Dos. Y son **muy** fuertes, como su padre.
P:　No conozco a **mucha** gente así. En mi casa no comemos **mucho**. Pero
　　siempre tenemos **algo de** dulce.
M:　Bueno, hay **algo de** tarta. Hay **suficiente** para los dos. ¿Quieres?
P:　Sí, me encantan **todos** los pasteles.
M:　Aquí tienes.
P:　Gracias.

SpanishEasyAndFun.com

Centro histórico de Potosí y el Cerro Rico de fondo, Bolivia.

*Marina and Pablo are having a coffee and talking.*

Pablo: Would you like some milk?
Marina: Yes, a little milk, please.
P:   Sugar?
M:   Yes, thank you.
P:   How much?
M:   Two spoons.
P:   That is a lot!
M:   Yes, I put a lot of sugar in my coffee. When I go to the supermarket I always buy two bags of sugar.
P:   Oh! I saw your sister at the supermarket yesterday.
M:   What did she say?
P:   She said she bought loads of things: fish, two cans of mussels, meat and some cheese.
M:   That is not too much. The good thing is that her house is always full of food.

P:   Does she have any children?
M:   Yes.
P:   How many children does he have?
M:   Two. And they are very muscular, like their dad.
P:   I don't know many people like that. We don't eat so much at home, but we always have something sweet.
M:   Well, I have some cake. There's enough for both of us, would you like some?
P:   Sure! I love all kinds of cake.
M:   Here you are.
P:   Thank you.

# Hablemos español

## a   Asking about quantity

● When asking about quantity we have to use the interrogatives "**¿Cuánto?**", "**¿Cuánta?**", "**¿Cuántos?**" or "**¿Cuántas?**".

● **¿Cuánto?** *(how much?)* is used before uncountable masculine nouns.

¿**Cuánto** vino tienes en casa?   >   *How much wine do you have at home?*

● **¿Cuánta?** *(how much?)* is used before uncountable feminine nouns.

¿**Cuánta** mantequilla necesitas?   >   *How much butter do you need?*

● **¿Cuántos?** *(how many?)* is used before countable masculine nouns in plural.

¿**Cuántos** niños hay en el parque?   >   *How many children are there in the park?*

● **¿Cuántas?** *(how many?)* is used before countable feminine nouns in plural.

¿**Cuántas** naranjas hay?   >   *How many oranges are there?*

● When the subject is known the noun can be left out.

Tengo poco vino. ¿**Cuánto** tienes?   >   *I don't have much wine. How much (wine) do you have?*

Hay muchas naranjas. ¿**Cuántas** hay?   >   *There are a lot of oranges. How many (oranges) are there?*

● "**¿Cuánto?**" is also used when asking about prices. In this case the word "dinero" *(money)* is often left out as it is obvious that we are refering to it. In Spanish we use the verbs "**costar**" and "**valer**" *(to cost)* when talking about prices.

¿**Cuánto cuesta** esa chaqueta?   >   *How much is that jacket?*
¿**Cuánto valen** los tomates?   >   *How much are the tomatoes?*

● When asking for the total price:

¿**Cuánto es (todo)**?   >   *How much is it (all)?*

● But "**¿cuánto?**" can also appear together with the verbs "**medir**" *(to measure)* or "**pesar**" *(to weigh)* when we ask about measures or weights.

¿**Cuánto mide** tu hermano?   >   *How tall is your brother?*
¿**Cuánto pesas** (tú)?   >   *How much do you weigh?*

🖐 SpanishEasyAndFun.com

**Carne:** *meat*
**pollo**: *chicken*          **cordero**: *lamb*          **res, ternera**: *beef*
**cerdo**: *pork*          **filete**: *steak*          **chuleta**: *chop*
**salchicha**: *sausage*          **hamburger**: *hamburguesa*          **costillas**: *ribs*
**jamón**: *ham*          **tocineta, bacon**: *bacon*

**Pescado y mariscos:** *fish and seafood*
**sardina**: *sardine*          **salmón**: *salmon*          **lenguado**: *sole*
**trucha**: *trout*          **atún**: *tuna*          **cangrejo**: *crab*
**langosta**: *lobster*          **mejillones**: *mussels*          **calamar**: *squid*

**Productos lácteos:** *dairy products*
**leche**: *milk*          **mantequilla**: *butter*          **queso**: *cheese*
**nata, crema**: *cream*          **yogurt**: *yoghurt*

**Recipientes** *(containers)*
**una lata de** cola: *a can of coke*          **una botella de** vino: *a bottle of wine*
**una lata de** sardinas: *a tin of sardines*          **un cartón de** leche: *a carton of milk*

**But you can also ask for:**
**un trozo de** queso: *a piece of cheese*
**medio kilo de** carne: *half a kilo of meat*

Necesito **una lata de sardinas, dos kilos de chuletas** y **un trozo de queso**.
*I need a tin of sardines, two kilos of chops and a piece of cheese.*

Ella quiere **un cartón de leche** y **una botella de vino**.
*She wants a carton of milk and a bottle of wine.*

# Gramática fácil

## a   The adverbs "muy" and "mucho"

🔸 **"Muy"** *(very)* is used before adjectives and adverbs, and is never used alone:

Ese libro es **muy** <u>interesante</u>.    >    *That book is very interesting..*
Es **muy** <u>tarde</u>.    >    *It's very late.*

When an answer calls for a simple one-word "muy", it then becomes "mucho":

¿Es ella linda? Sí, **mucho.**    >    *Is she pretty? Yes, very.*

🔸 **"Mucho/a"** *(a lot, much)* is used before uncountable nouns, after a verb or alone.

Él compra **mucho** <u>pescado</u>.    >    *He buys a lot of fish.*
Ellos no corren **mucho**.    >    *They don't run much.*
¿Te gustan las sardinas? No, no **mucho**. >    *Do you like sardines? No, not much.*

## b   Other expressions of quantity

In unit 17 we studied some expressions of quantity. Here are some more:

🔸 **Demasiado** + <u>adjective</u> *(too + adjective)*

Esta maleta es **demasiado** <u>pesada</u>.    >    *This suitcase is too heavy.*

🔸 **Ambos/los dos, ambas/las dos**   *(both)*

**Ambos/Los dos** viven en San Francisco. >    *They both live in San Francisco.*

🔸 **Varios, varias** + <u>countable noun in plural</u> *(several + countable noun in plural)*

Hay **varios** <u>diccionarios</u> en la biblioteca.    >    *There are several dictionaries in the library.*

🔸 **Cada** + <u>countable noun</u> *(each /every + countable noun)*

**Cada** <u>libro</u> cuesta veinte dólares.    >    *Each book costs twenty dollars.*
Voy al gimnasio **cada** <u>tres días</u>.    >    *I go to the gym every three days.*

SpanishEasyAndFun.com

- **Todo, toda** + determinant + singular or uncountable noun *[the whole + singular noun// all + (det) + uncountable noun]*

Ella no lee **todo** el periódico.  >  *She doesn't read the whole newspaper.*
**Toda** la leche está en el refrigerador.  >  *All (the) milk is in the fridge.*

- **Todos, todas** + determinant + plural noun *[all (of) + det. + noun// every + noun in singular]*

Él se levanta temprano **todos** los días.  >  *He gets up early every day.*
**Todas** esas computadoras son japonesas. >  *All these computers are Japanese.*

- **Algo de** + uncountable noun  *(some + noun)*

Tenemos **algo de** dinero en el banco.  >  *We have some money in the bank.*

- **Nada de** + uncountable noun  *(no + noun)*

No hay **nada de** agua en la botella.  >  *There is no water in the bottle.*

- **Los demás / las demás** + noun in plural *[the rest of (the) + noun in plural]*

Tengo **las demás** fotos en casa.  >  *I have the rest of the pictures at home.*

## c  The use of "lo"

"**Lo**" can be used as a direct object pronoun (see unit 17).

- We also use **"lo"** as a complement to the verbs "ser", "estar" and "parecer" *(to seem)*:

Ella es alta. Sí, **lo** es.  >  *She is tall. Yes, she is.*

—Creo que tu hermano está aburrido.  >  *—I think that your brother is bored.*
—No, no **lo** está.  >  *—No, he isn't.*

Él es estudioso, pero no **lo** parece.  >  *He is studious but he doesn't look it.*

- **"Lo"** (as a neutral article) can be followed by a masculine singular adjective to express an abstract idea:

**lo bueno**   *the good part/thing*        **lo malo**   *the bad part/thing*
**lo mejor**   *the best part/thing*        **lo peor**   *the worst part/thing*
**lo** (más) **interesante**   *the (most) interesting part/thing*

| | | |
|---|---|---|
| Me gusta ese auto. **Lo malo** es que es muy caro. | > | *I like that car. The bad thing is that it is very expensive.* |
| Tuviste un accidente. **Lo bueno** es que estás bien. | > | *You had an accident. The good thing is that you are okay.* |
| **Lo** más **interesante** del viaje fue la gente. | > | *The most interesting part of the trip was the people.* |

## d Cardinal numbers (1000-millions)

| | |
|---|---|
| 1.000 | mil |
| 1.001 | mil uno/una |
| 1.348 | mil trescientos/as cuarenta y ocho |
| 2.000 | dos mil |
| 3.000 | tres mil |
| 15.000 | quince mil |
| 275.000 | doscientos/as setenta y cinco mil |
| 497.000 | cuatrocientos/as noventa y siete mil |
| 995.876 | novecientos/as noventa y cinco mil, ochocientos/as setenta y seis |
| | |
| 1.000.000 | un millón |
| 2.000.000 | dos millones |
| 33.000.000 | treinta y tres millones |

🔘 Remember that the words "ciento" and "millón" take the plural forms ("cientos/as" and "millones") when a number higher than one precedes them, but "mil" doesn't.

| | |
|---|---|
| 400 | cuatro<u>cientos/as</u> |
| 3.000 | tres <u>mil</u> |
| 5.000.000 | cinco <u>millones</u> |

🔘 The plural forms "cientos/as", "miles" and "millones" may be used when we can't determine an exact figure:

Hay **cientos** de hormigas.
*There are hundreds of ants.*

Hay **miles** de personas.
*There are thousands of people*

Ella tiene algunos **millones** de pesos.
*She has millions of pesos.*

Note that a dot (not a comma) is used to separate the thousands and millions in Spanish.
The comma is used to express decimals.

| | |
|---|---|
| 5,3 | cinco coma tres |
| 5.3 | *five point three* |
| 0,7 | cero coma siete |
| 0.7 | *zero point seven* |

🖑 SpanishEasyAndFun.com

# Ejercicios de la **Unidad 18**

**a** Fill in the gaps with "mucho" or "muy".

**1** El tiempo es _____ bueno.
**2** Ese auto es _____ caro.
**3** En mi país hace _____ frío.
**4** ¿Es este ejercicio _____ fácil?
**5** Ellos no tienen _____ dinero.

**b** Complete the sentences with: cuánto, cuánta, cuántos, cuántas, ambos, algo de, nada de, demasiado, varios, toda.

**1** ¿_____ revistas hay en la mesa?
**2** Quiero _____ mantequilla para el pastel.
**3** ¿_____ libros compraste el año pasado?
**4** Juan y Pedro pueden aprobar el examen. _____ son buenos estudiantes.
**5** ¿_____ carne hay en el refrigerador?
**6** El pescado es _____ caro y no puedo comprarlo.
**7** Estoy comiendo con _____ mi familia.
**8** No necesito _____ harina.
**9** Aquí hay _____ huevos.
**10** ¿_____ tiempo estuviste en Roma?

**c** Find the one that doesn't belong:

**1** cerdo – lenguado – cordero
**2** filete – atún – trucha
**3** mantequilla – queso – jamón
**4** chuleta – costillas – mejillones
**5** cangrejo – pollo - langosta

........................................................................

# Unidad 19
## Sevilla

**En esta unidad estudiaremos:**

◉ **Diálogo**

◉ **Hablemos español:**
   **a)** The preposition "de". **b)** The date. **c)** Vocabulario: La cara (The face).
   **d)** Tag questions: "¿no?", "¿verdad?".

◉ **Gramática fácil:**
   **a)** The past tense. **b)** The preterite. **c)** The preterite of regular verbs.
   **d)** The past tense: time markers.

◉ **Ejercicios**

---

*Jorge, el hermano de Antonio, y Rocío se encuentran en la calle.*

Rocío: ¡Hola, Jorge!
Jorge: ¡Hola! ¿Cómo estás**? Hace mucho tiempo** que no nos vemos, **¿verdad?**

R:  Estoy muy bien. **Llegué la semana pasada** a Madrid. ¿Cómo está tu hermano Antonio?

J:  Está muy bien, tuvo un hijo **el 20 de febrero**.

R:  ¡Qué bien! **Intenté** llamarlo **ayer**, pero no **contestó** al teléfono. ¿Cómo es el niño?

J:  Pues **anoche** estuve con ellos. El niño es muy guapo, tiene los **ojos** azules y el **pelo** rubio. Le **regalamos** una cadena **de oro** por su primer mes de vida.

R:  Pues voy a llamar otra vez a Antonio para felicitarle. Quiero regalarle un jersey **de lana** hecho por mí.

J:  ¡Muy bien! Tus hijos están bien, ¿no?

R:  Sí, los dos están ya muy altos. Juan **cumplió** 9 años **el 22 de septiembre**.

J:  ¡Qué bien! Me alegro mucho **de** verte, Rocío.

R:  Yo también me alegro mucho **de** verte. ¡Hasta luego!

J:  Hasta luego, espero verte de nuevo.

SpanishEasyAndFun.com

Metropol Parasol o las Setas, Sevilla, España.

Jorge, Antonio's brother, and Rocío run into each other on the street.

Rocío: Hello, Jorge!

Jorge: Hello! How are you? It's been a long time since we've seen each other, hasn't it?

R: I've been doing well. I arrived in Madrid last week. How is your brother Antonio?

J: He's fine; he had a baby on the 20th of February.

R: Great! I tried to call him yesterday, but he didn't answer. What does the baby look like?

J: I visited them yesterday. The baby is very handsome; he has blue eyes and blonde hair. We gave him a gold necklace to celebrate his first month.

R: I'll try to call him again to say congratulations. I want to give him a wool sweater I made.

J: Great! Your kids are fine, aren't they?

R: Yes! They are both very tall. Juan turned 9 on the 22nd of September.

J: Good! I'm very happy I saw you, Rocío.

R: I'm happy to see you too. Goodbye!

J: Bye! I hope to see you again soon.

# Hablemos español

## a  The preposition "de"

We know that the preposition "**de**" indicates a starting point or origin:

| | | |
|---|---|---|
| Ella es **de** Lima. | > | *She is from Lima.* |

| | | |
|---|---|---|
| —¿**De** dónde vienes? | > | *—Where are you coming from?* |
| —Vengo **de** mi casa. | > | *—I'm coming from my house.* |

But "**de**" also introduces an element to specify or identify another element. So "**de**" can also indicate:

🔹 Material, substance or content:

| | | |
|---|---|---|
| Un anillo **de** <u>oro</u>. | > | *A gold ring.* |
| Una gota **de** <u>agua</u>. | > | *A drop of water.* |

🔹 Possession. In Spanish the word order is:

<u>object possessed</u> + "**de**" + <u>possessor</u>

| | | |
|---|---|---|
| El <u>hermano</u> **de** <u>Juan</u> está ahí. | > | *Juan's brother is there.* |
| Una <u>pata</u> **de** <u>la mesa</u> está rota. | > | *One of the table legs is broken.* |

🔹 A reference to locate something.

| | | |
|---|---|---|
| Sus hijos están <u>lejos</u> **de** aquí. | > | *Her children are far from here.* |
| <u>Después</u> **de** la clase ella va a su casa. | > | *After the class she goes home.* |

🔹 A kind of object:

| | | |
|---|---|---|
| Un auto **de** carreras. | > | *A racing car.* |
| Un libro **de** español. | > | *A book of Spanish.* |

🔹 The starting point and the end of a period of time, or the distance from one place to another can be expressed with "**de**" and "**a**":

| | | |
|---|---|---|
| **De** mi casa **a** la estación hay 100 metros. | > | *There are 100 metres from my house to the station.* |
| Trabajo **de** lunes **a** viernes. | > | *I work from Monday to Friday.* |

Some common expressions with the preposition "**de**":

**¡De acuerdo!:** *Ok! All right!*
**de día**: *by day, in the daytime*

**¡De nada!:** *You're welcome!*
**de noche**: *by night, at night*

**de hoy en adelante**: *from today on*
**de buen/mal humor**: *in a good/bad mood*
**de pronto, de repente**: *suddenly*

**de nuevo**. *again*
**de memoria**: *by heart*
**de pie**: *standing*

🔵 Describing objects: materials

**cobre**: *copper*
**oro**: *gold*
**plata**: *silver*
**hierro**: *iron*
**acero**: *steel*
**madera**: *wood*
**cartón**: *cardboard*

**plástico**: *plastic*
**seda**: *silk*
**lana**: *wool*
**algodón**: *cotton*
**cuero, piel**: *leather*
**vidrio**: *glass*

To say what an object is made of we use the verb "<u>ser</u>" + **de** + <u>material</u>:

**Es** una mesa **de** madera.                    >     *It's a wooden table.*
La cuchara **es de** plástico.                     >     *The spoon is plastic.*
**Son** figuras **de** vidrio.                         >     *They are glass figures.*

## b    The date

In Spanish, the dates are expressed with cardinal numbers and the preposition "**de**" *(of)* introducing the month (and the year).

12 (doce) de febrero de 2003            >     *February 12, 2003*

- The years are always read as a quantity:

  2009: dos mil nueve    >    *two thousand nine*

  1966: mil novecientos sesenta y seis    (NOT diecinueve - sesenta y seis)

- To state the date when something occurs, the article **"el"** is placed before the number:

  Mi cumpleaños es **el** 15 (quince) de agosto.
  *My birthday is on August 15th.*
  El examen es **el** 3 (tres) de abril.
  *The exam is on April 3rd.*

  In Spanish we always follow this order: day / month / year.

---

## c    Vocabulario: La cara (The face)

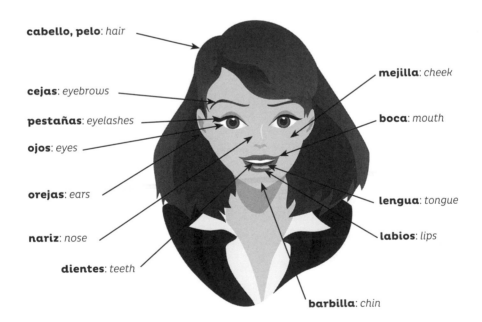

**cabello, pelo**: *hair*

**mejilla**: *cheek*

**cejas**: *eyebrows*

**pestañas**: *eyelashes*

**boca**: *mouth*

**ojos**: *eyes*

**orejas**: *ears*

**lengua**: *tongue*

**nariz**: *nose*

**labios**: *lips*

**dientes**: *teeth*

**barbilla**: *chin*

**cabello largo**: *long hair*
**cabello rizado**: *curly hair*
**cabello moreno**: *dark hair*
**cabello pelirrojo**: *red hair*

**cabello corto**: *short hair*
**cabello liso**: *straight hair*
**cabello rubio**: *blond/fair hair*

SpanishEasyAndFun.com

In Spanish, the questions "**¿no?**" or "**¿verdad?**" are used at the end of a sentence to confirm what has been said. They correspond to English question tags, such as "right?", "isn't it?", "don't they?", "aren't you?", etc.

| | | |
|---|---|---|
| Ese auto es caro, **¿verdad?** | > | *That car is expensive, isn't it?* |
| Ustedes no son franceses, **¿verdad?** | > | *You aren't French, are you?* |
| Él habla español, **¿no?** | > | *He speaks Spanish, doesn't he?* |
| Vives en esa casa, **¿no?** | > | *You live in that house, don't you?* |

# Gramática fácil

**a**   The past tense

In Spanish there are two past tenses with a simple form, known as the preterite and the imperfect. Although the English simple past can be conveyed in Spanish using the preterite or the imperfect, these two tenses are very different and not interchangeable.

**b**   The preterite (el pretérito indefinido)

The preterite is used when we refer to completed actions, that is, when the verb shows an action that has a clear end, which took place at a fixed time in the past.

| | | |
|---|---|---|
| Ayer **fui** al cine. | > | *Yesterday I went to the movies.* |
| Ella **compró** miel la semana pasada. | > | *She bought some honey last week.* |
| **Me levanté**, **me duché** y **salí** de mi casa. | > | *I got up, took a shower and left my house.* |

**c**   The preterite of regular verbs

The preterite forms are made by removing the infinitive ending of the verb (**"-ar"**, **"-er"** or **"-ir"**) and replacing it with an ending that indicates who is performing the action.

Ex: **hablar** *(to speak)*, **aprender** *(to learn)* and **escribir** *(to write)*.

The preterite is equivalent to "spoke", "learned" and "wrote", respectively.

|  | - AR<br>hablar | -ER<br>aprender | -IR<br>escribir |
|---|---|---|---|
| yo | hablé | aprendí | escribí |
| tú | hablaste | aprendiste | escribiste |
| usted-él-ella | habló | aprendió | escribió |
| | | | |
| nosotros/as | hablamos | aprendimos | escribimos |
| vosotros/as | hablásteis | aprendísteis | escribísteis |
| ustedes-ellos/as | hablaron | aprendieron | escribieron |

Nosotros **aprendimos** muchas cosas.  >   *We learned a lot of things.*
Cervantes **escribió** "Don Quijote".  >   *Cervantes wrote "Don Quixote".*
¿Con quién **hablaste**?  >   *Who did you speak to?*
Ellos no la **llamaron** la semana pasada.  >   *They didn't call her last week.*
**Viví** dos años en Santo Domingo.  >   *I lived in Santo Domingo for two years.*

Notice that "-er" and "-ir" verbs follow the same pattern in the preterite.

The "nosotros/as" form in the present indicative and the preterite is the same for "-ar" and "-ir" verbs. So "hablamos" can mean either *"we speak"* or *"we spoke"*, and "escribimos" can mean either *"we write"* or *"we wrote"*. The context will clarify the meaning.

Reflexive verbs conjugate the same way:
Ayer **me levanté** tarde  >   *I got up late yesterday.*

## d   The past tense: time markers

They are words and expressions that show the moment when the action occurred in the past. Although Spanish is a very flexible language, the common position of these expressions is either at the beginning or the end of the sentence.

**ayer**: *yesterday*
**ayer por la mañana**: *yesterday morning*
**ayer por la tarde**: *yesterday afternoon*
**ayer por la noche**: *yesterday evening*
**anoche**: *last night*
**anteayer**: *the day before yesterday*

**la semana pasada**: *last week*
**el mes pasado**: *last month*
**el año pasado**: *last year*
**el domingo pasado**: *last Sunday*
**el otro día**: *the other day*
**hace tres días**: *three days ago*

¿Trabajaste mucho **ayer**?  >   *Did you work a lot yesterday?*
**El otro día** compré un reloj.  >   *I bought a watch the other day.*
**Anoche** no vi la película de la televisión.  >   *I didn't watch the movie on television last night.*

Las clases comenzaron **hace dos meses** >   *The classes began two months ago.*
.Ellos me visitaron **el jueves pasado**.  >   *They visited me last Thursday.*

# Ejercicios de la **Unidad 19**

**a** Fill in the gaps with the correct form of the verbs in the preterite.

**1** El mes pasado le (comprar) _____ un reloj a mi hijo.

**2** ¿Te (gustar) _____ la tarta de chocolate?

**3** Juan y yo (temer) _____ por su salud.

**4** Ellos (bailar) _____ toda la noche.

**5** Esta tarde yo (llamar) _____ a mi madre por teléfono.

**6** ¿Ustedes (comer) _____ en el restaurante de la estación?

**7** Yo (beber) _____ un jugo de fruta delicioso.

**8** Víctor y Carmen (partir) _____ para México.

**9** Nosotros (escribir) _____ esa carta pero no la (enviar) _____.

**10** Él (casarse) _____ hace dos años.

**b** Match the expressions with their meanings:

**1** de repente          **a** again
**2** de pie             **b** from now on
**3** de nuevo           **c** suddenly
**4** de memoria         **d** by heart
**5** de hoy en adelante  **e** standing

**c** Word search: find six nouns related to the face.

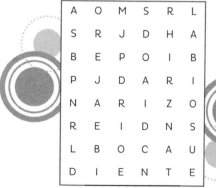

| A | O | M | S | R | L |
|---|---|---|---|---|---|
| S | R | J | D | H | A |
| B | E | P | O | I | B |
| P | J | D | A | R | I |
| N | A | R | I | Z | O |
| R | E | I | D | N | S |
| L | B | O | C | A | U |
| D | I | E | N | T | E |

**Key**

**a:** 1.- compré; 2.- gustó; 3.- temimos; 4.- bailaron; 5.- llamé; 6.- comieron; 7.- bebí; 8.- partieron; 9.- escribimos, enviamos; 10.- se casó.

**b:** 1.- c; 2.- e; 3.- a; 4.- d; 5.- b.

**c:** boca, diente, labio, nariz, ojo, oreja.

# Unidad 20
## Quito

### En esta unidad estudiaremos:

⦿ **Diálogo**

⦿ **Hablemos español:**
   **a)** "Desde", "hasta" and "durante". **b)** Adverbs of time: "antes", "después" / "más tarde" / "luego". **c)** Vocabulario: La computadora/el ordenador (The computer).

⦿ **Gramática fácil:**
   **a)** The preterite of irregular verbs. **b)** The verb "dar" (to give). **c)** The verb "tener" (to have).

⦿ **Ejercicios**

---

*Verónica ve a Ricardo un poco cansado y le pregunta si todo va bien.*

Verónica: Ricardo, pareces cansado. ¿Estás bien?
Ricardo:  Sí, estoy bien, gracias. Muy cansado, pero bien.
V:   ¿Por qué estás cansado? ¿Qué hiciste ayer?
R:   Ayer me **levanté** temprano y **estuve** todo el día trabajando con el ordenador.
V:   ¿Qué hiciste?
R:   La semana pasada **se rompió el teclado y tuve** que llevarlo a reparar. **Hasta** ayer no lo **tuve** en mi casa y **tuve** que acabar mi trabajo **durante** todo el día.
V:   ¿Y no te **sirvió** el teclado que yo te **di**?
R:   No. El **ratón** no es compatible con tu **teclado**.
V:   A mi no me gusta trabajar con el **ordenador** porque siempre se estropea cuando lo necesito.
R:   De todas formas, estoy contento porque **acabé** mi trabajo a tiempo y **después fui** a dar un paseo con Ana.
V:   ¿Dónde **fuisteis** a pasear?
R:   **Fuimos hasta** el centro de la ciudad. Caminamos **durante** una hora **hasta** que se **hizo** de noche. ¿Qué **hiciste** tú ayer?
V:   Yo ayer **fui** de excursión con Laura. **Fuimos** en auto desde aquí **hasta** la montaña y **después** comimos en un restaurante muy bonito.
R:   ¿Conocías esa ruta?
V:   Sí. **Estuve** allí hace muchos años. La semana pasada **leí** un artículo sobre ella y **quise** volver allí.
R:   ¿**Hicisteis** fotos?
V:   Sí, **hicimos** muchas fotos. Te las enseñaré algún día.

SpanishEasyAndFun.com

Plaza de San Francisco, centro histórico de Quito, Ecuador.

*Verónica sees Ricardo a little tired and asks him if everything is alright.*

Verónica: Ricardo, you look tired. Are you okay?

Ricardo: Yes, I am fine, thank you. Very tired, but fine.

V:   Why are you tired? What did you do yesterday?

R:   Yesterday I got up early and spent the whole day working at the computer.

V:   What happened?

R:   Last week the keyboard broke and I had to take it to be repaired. I just got it back yesterday and I had to get all my work done in one day.

V:   And the keyboard I gave you, didn't it work?

R:   No. It is not compatible with my mouse.

V:   I don't like working on the computer. It always breaks down when I need it.

R:   Anyway, I'm happy because I finished my work on time and after that I took a walk with Ana.

V:   Where did you take a walk?

R:   We went downtown. We walked for an hour until it got dark. What did you do yesterday?

V:   I went on a hike with Laura. We drove my car from here to the mountain and then we had lunch at a very nice restaurant.

R:   Have you been that way before?

V:   Yes. I went there many years ago. Last week I read an article about it and I wanted to go back to that place.

R:   Did you take some pictures?

V:   Yes, we took a lot of pictures. I'll show you some day.

# Hablemos español

**"Desde", "hasta" and "durante"**

We know that "**desde**" *(from)* and "**hasta**" *[(up) to]* can be prepositions of place:

| | | |
|---|---|---|
| **Desde** aquí no te puedo ver. | > | *I can't see you from here.* |
| Caminé **hasta** la estación. | > | *I walked up to the station.* |

But now we will study them as prepositions of time and conjunctions.

● **"Desde"** *(from, since)*:

| | | |
|---|---|---|
| Nosotros trabajamos **desde** las 9 de la mañana. | > | *We work from 9:00 a.m.* |
| Ese puente está ahí **desde** 1900. | > | *That bridge has been there since 1900.* |

● But it is also a conjunction that is followed by "**que + a sentence**".

| | | |
|---|---|---|
| Tengo pesadillas **desde que** (yo) vi esa película. | > | *I've had nightmares since I watched that film.* |

● **"Hasta"** *(until, to)*

| | | |
|---|---|---|
| Estuve en el hospital **hasta** las 3. | > | *I was in the hospital until 3:00.* |
| Ellos trabajaron desde enero **hasta** julio. | > | *They were working from January to July.* |

● It also functions as a conjuction, followed by "**que + a sentence**".

| | | |
|---|---|---|
| Él lo estudió **hasta que** (él) lo aprendió. | > | *He studied it until he learned it.* |

● **"Durante"** *(during, for)*

● It can precede a determinant and a noun that indicates an activity *(during)*.

| | | |
|---|---|---|
| No lo escuché **durante** la conferencia. | > | *I didn't listen to him during the conference.* |

● Or it can go before a period of time *(for)*.

| | | |
|---|---|---|
| Habló **durante** dos horas. | > | *He was speaking for two hours.* |

## b   Adverbs of time: "antes", "después" / "más tarde" / "luego"

| | | | |
|---|---|---|---|
| **después*** | *afterwards, after that* | **luego*** | *then* |
| **antes** | *before* | **más tarde*** | *later* |

⚙ These expressions have the same meaning, so they are interchangeable.

| | | |
|---|---|---|
| **Antes** estuve navegando por intenet. | > | *Before I was surfing the internet.* |
| ¿Vas **luego** al cine? | > | *Are you going to the movies later?* |
| ¿Viste a mi prima **antes**? | > | *Did you see my cousin before?* |

| | | |
|---|---|---|
| Me levanté temprano, **después** fui a trabajar y **más tarde** llamé a Juan. | > | *I got up early, after that I went to work and later I called Juan.* |

These adverbs stand alone although "antes" and "después" can also precede a noun or an infinitive, but, in these cases, we need the preposition "de" in between.

**antes de**   *before*
**después de**   *after*

$$\left.\begin{array}{l}\textbf{antes de}\\\textbf{después de}\end{array}\right\} \quad + \quad \left\{\begin{array}{l}\text{determinant + \underline{noun}}\\\underline{\text{infinitive}}\end{array}\right.$$

| | |
|---|---|
| Quiero estudiar un poco **antes de** <u>la clase</u>. > | *I want to study a little before the class.* |
| Nos fuimos a casa **después de** <u>la reunión</u>. > | *We went home after the meeting.* |

| | | |
|---|---|---|
| Yo tenía un perro **antes de** <u>comprar</u> este gato. | > | *I had a dog before buying this cat.* |
| **Después de** <u>ver</u> la televisión se acostó. | > | *After watching television he went to bed.* |

## c   Vocabulario: La computadora/el ordenador (The computer)

| | |
|---|---|
| **portátil**: *laptop computer* | **pantalla**: *screen* |
| **monitor**: *monitor* | **teclado**: *keyboard* |
| **ratón**: *mouse* | **alfombrilla del ratón**: *mousepad* |
| **memoria**: *memory* | **internet**: *the Internet* |
| **virus**: *virus* | **impresora**: *printer* |
| **escáner**: *scanner* | **altavoces**: *speakers* |
| **correo electrónico**: *email* | **contraseña**: *password* |
| **nombre de usuario**: *user name* | **navegar por internet**: *to surf the internet* |

# Gramática fácil

## a  The preterite of irregular verbs

- In the preterite there are some verbs that change the vowel in the stem ("e" for "i" or "o" for "u") for the third person singular (él, ella) and plural (ellos, ellas).

  Ex: **pedir** *[to ask (for), to order]*, **dormir** *(to sleep)*.

  |  | **PEDIR** | **DORMIR** |
  |---|---|---|
  | yo | pedí | dormí |
  | tú | pediste | dormiste |
  | usted-él-ella | pidió | durmió |
  | | | |
  | nosotros/as | pedimos | dormimos |
  | vosotros/as | pedisteis | dormisteis |
  | ustedes-ellos/as | pidieron | durmieron |

  El niño **durmió** tranquilamente.  >  *The boy slept quietly.*

  This pattern is also followed by the verbs: **preferir** *(to prefer)*, **mentir** *(to lie)*, **sentir[se]** *(to feel)*, **repetir** *(to repeat)*, **seguir** *(to follow)* or **morir** *(to die)*.

- Verbs ending in "**-car**", "**-gar**" and "**-zar**" require a spelling change in the "yo" form.

  Ex: **buscar** *(to look for)*, **pagar** *(to pay)*, **empezar** *(to start)*.

  |  | **BUSCAR** | **PAGAR** | **EMPEZAR** |
  |---|---|---|---|
  | yo | bus**qu**é | pa**gu**é | empe**c**é |
  | tú | buscaste | pagaste | empezaste |

  **Busqué** esa computadora portátil.  >  *I looked for that laptop.*

- When there is an unstressed "i" between vowels, it changes into "y".

  Ex: **leer** *(to read)*

  | leer | | |
  |---|---|---|
  | yo | leí | |
  | tú | leíste | |
  | usted-él-ella | le**y**ó | |
  | | | |
  | nosotros/as | leímos | |
  | vosotros/a | leísteis | |
  | ustedes-ellos/as | le**y**eron | |

  Other verbs following this pattern are: **tocar** *(to touch/play)*, **jugar** *(to play)* or **comenzar** *(to begin)*.

  Other verbs that follow this pattern are: **oír** *(to hear)*, **construir** *(to build)* or **creer** *(to believe)*.

  ¿Qué libro **leyó** Francisco?  >  *What book did Francisco read?*

SpanishEasyAndFun.com

- Some common verbs are irregular in the preterite. In these cases, the stress is on the stem for the first and third persons in singular (yo, usted-él-ella).

Ex: **saber** *(to know)*, **poder** *(can)*, **decir** *(to say)*

|  | SABER | PODER | DECIR |
|---|---|---|---|
| yo | **su**pe | **pu**de | **di**je |
| tú | supiste | pudiste | dijiste |
| usted-él-ella | **su**po | **pu**do | **di**jo |
|  |  |  |  |
| nosotros/as | supimos | pudimos | dijimos |
| vosotros/as | supisteis | pudisteis | dijisteis |
| ustedes-ellos/as | supieron | pudieron | dijeron |

We can see that these verbs are highly irregular.

| No **supe** nada de él. | > | *I didn't hear anything about him.* |
|---|---|---|
| ¿Qué **pudo** hacer Pedro? | > | *What could Pedro do?* |
| Mi madre no **dijo** eso. | > | *My mother didn't say that.* |

- The verbs "**ser**" *(to be)* and "**ir**" *(to go)* have the same irregular form in the preterite.

|  | SER - IR |
|---|---|
| yo | **fui** |
| tú | **fuiste** |
| usted-él-ella | **fue** |
|  |  |
| nosotros/as | **fuimos** |
| vosotros/as | **fuisteis** |
| ustedes-ellos/as | **fueron** |

| Él **fue** piloto durante cinco años. | > | *He was a pilot for five years.* |
|---|---|---|
| Él **fue** al teatro anoche. | > | *He went to the theater last night.* |

- Other important verbs with several irregularities are "**estar**" *(to be)* and "**hacer**" *(to do/make).*

|  | ESTAR | HACER |
|---|---|---|
| yo | **estuve** | **hice** |
| tú | **estuviste** | **hiciste** |
| usted-él-ella | **estuvo** | **hizo** |
|  |  |  |
| nosotros/as | **estuvimos** | **hicimos** |
| vosotros/as | **estuvisteis** | **hicisteis** |
| ustedes-ellos/as | **estuvieron** | **hicieron** |

| La semana pasada **estuve** en Madrid. | > | *I was in Madrid last week.* |
|---|---|---|

¿**Hiciste** los deberes ayer?     >     *Did you do your homework ysterday?*

● The preterite of the impersonal form "**hay**" *(there is, there are)* is "**hubo**".

**Hubo** muchos accidentes de     >     *There were a lot of traffic accidents*
tráfico el año pasado.                      *last year.*

## b    The verb "dar" (to give)

This verb has a special feature: although it ends with "-ar", in the preterite it is conjugated like verbs ending with "-ir". It is equivalent to *"gave"* in English.

| | DAR |
|---|---|
| yo | d**i** |
| tú | d**iste** |
| usted-él-ella | d**io** |
| nosotros/as | d**imos** |
| vosotros/as | d**isteis** |
| ustedes-ellos/as | d**ieron** |

Ellos nos **dieron** este libro.     >     *They gave us this book.*
¿Qué te **dio** ella?             >     *What did she give you?*

## c    The verb "tener" (to have)

The verb "**tener**" is also very irregular in the preterite and is conjugated in a similar way to the verb "estar". This tense corresponds to *"had"* in English (but it is also equivalent to *"was"/"were"* in many cases).

| | TENER |
|---|---|
| yo | **tuve** |
| tú | **tuviste** |
| usted-él-ella | **tuvo** |
| nosotros/as | **tuvimos** |
| vosotros/as | **tuvisteis** |
| ustedes-ellos/as | **tuvieron** |

Él no **tuvo** tiempo libre.     >     *He didn't have any free time.*
Anoche **tuve** frío.          >     *I was cold last night.*
No **tuvimos** suerte y perdimos     >     *We weren't lucky and lost the match.*
el partido.

**a** Fill in the gaps with the correct form of the verbs in the preterite.

1. Yo (comenzar) _____ a estudiar el año pasado.
2. Ellos no (traer) _____ el helado.
3. Juan (leer) _____ el libro en dos días.
4. Mis abuelos (tener) _____ problemas económicos.
5. Les (dar) _____ tú mis libros a mis primos.
6. Yo (pagar) _____ el hotel con un cheque.
7. Ella no me (decir) _____ la verdad.
8. Él (traducir) _____ todo el texto.
9. El muchacho se (caer) _____ del árbol y está en el hospital.
10. El millonario (contribuir) _____ con un millón de dólares.

**b** Choose the correct answer:

Which of these words is a synonym of "**después**"?
1. antes
2. luego
3. cuando
4. hasta
5. durante

**c** Match the words with their meanings.

1. teclado
2. contraseña
3. pantalla
4. ratón
5. altavoz

a. speaker
b. screen
c. mouse
d. keyboard
e. password

**d** Complete the sentences with the suitable adverb: **hasta**, **desde** or **durante**.

1. La escuela está cerrada _____ julio _____ septiembre.
2. _____ el verano solo trabajo medio día.
3. No veo a Tomás _____ el lunes.

••••••••••••••••••••••••••••••••••••••••••••••••••••••••••••••••••••••••••••••••••••

**d:** 1.- desde, hasta; 2.- durante; 3.- desde.

**c:** 1.-d; 2.- e; 3.- b; 4.- c; 5.- a.

**b:** 2.

**a:** 1.- comencé; 2.- trajeron; 3.- leyó; 4.- tuvieron; 5.- diste; 6.- pagué; 7.- dijo; 8.- tradujo; 9.- cayó; 10.- contribuyó.

**Key**

# Unidad 21
## Extremadura

### En esta unidad estudiaremos:

- **Diálogo**
- **Hablemos español:**
  **a)** Making suggestions. **b)** Adverbs of manner. **c)** Adverbs ending in "-mente". **d)** Vocabulario: Tiendas y comercios (Shops and stores).
- **Gramática fácil:**
  **a)** The imperfect. **b)** Joining sentences: "mientras" and "cuando".
- **Ejercicios**

---

*Emilio habla con Pilar y le pregunta acerca de lo que hizo el domingo anterior.*

Emilio: El domingo pasado **quería** verte, pero no te encontré en casa. **¿Estabas** con tu familia?

Pilar: No. Salí por la mañana y no volví hasta la tarde.

E: ¿Qué hiciste todo el día?

P: Como **era** un buen día y **hacía** sol decidí ir al campo, pero allí **llovía**. Entonces volví a la ciudad y fui al Museo de Ciencias Naturales.

E: ¿Es un museo interesante?

P: Muy interesante. Allí **había** animales, plantas, minerales, fósiles... **Mientras veía** todo eso **me acordaba** de mi madre. A ella **le gustaba** mucho ese museo. **Pasaba** horas allí. **¿Quieres** que te lleve algún día**?**

E: Vale, seguro que me lo explicas todo **perfectamente**.

P: ¿Tú qué hiciste?

E: Yo hice unas compras: fui a la **panadería**, a la **pescadería** y después fui al centro a una **tienda de ropa** a la que siempre **iba** cuando yo **era** joven. **Mientras paseaba lentamente** hacia el centro me encontré con una vecina.

P: ¿Y qué te contó?

E: Me dijo que la **zapatería** de mi barrio había cerrado. Es una pena porque allí los zapatos **eran** baratos.

P: Sí, es verdad, yo siempre **compraba** los zapatos allí **cuando vivía** al lado de tu casa.

SpanishEasyAndFun.com

Plaza Mayor de Cáceres, Extremadura, España.

*Emilio is talking to Pilar and asks her about what she did last Sunday.*

Emilio: Last Sunday I wanted to see you, but you weren't at home. Were you with your family?

Pilar: No. I went out in the morning and didn't come back until the afternoon.

E: What did you do all day long?

P: Since it was sunny and a nice day I decided to go to the country, but it was raining there. Then I came back to the city and went to the Museum of Natural Science.

E: Is it an interesting museum?

P: Very interesting. There were animals, plants, minerals, fossils... While I was seeing all that I remembered my mother. She liked that museum a lot. She spent hours there. Would you like to come with me some day?

E: Yes. I'm sure you will be able to explain everything to me.

P: What did you do?

E: I went shopping: I went to the bakery, to the fish market and then I went downtown to a clothing store I used to go to when I was young. As I slowly made my way downtown I met a neighbor.

P: What did she say?

E: She told me the shoe store next to my house closed. It's a pity because shoes were cheap there.

P: Yes. That's true. I used to buy shoes there when I lived next to you.

# Hablemos español

## a  Making suggestions

In order to make suggestions we can say:

- **¿Qué tal** (si + present)**?**

  | | | |
  |---|---|---|
  | **¿Qué tal** a las 5**?** | > | *How about at 5:00?* |
  | **¿Qué tal** <u>si</u> nos vemos a las 5**?** | > | *How about meeting at 5:00?* |

- **¿Quieres +** <u>infinitive</u>**?**

  | | | |
  |---|---|---|
  | **¿Quieres** <u>ir</u> al cine**?** | > | *Would you like to go to the movies?* |
  | **¿Quieres** <u>tomar</u> un café**?** | > | *Would you like to have a coffee?* |

- **¿Te apetece +** <u>infinitive / noun</u>**?**

  | | | |
  |---|---|---|
  | **¿Te apetece** <u>bailar</u>**?** | > | *Do you feel like dancing?* |
  | **¿Te apetece** <u>un trago</u>**?** | > | *Do you feel like a drink?* |

## b  Adverbs of manner

Adverbs of manner help us to understand *how* or *in what manner* the action is completed. These adverbs usually follow the verb they modify.

Some of these adverbs are:

| | |
|---|---|
| **bien** | *well* |
| **mal** | *badly, poorly* |
| **mejor** | *better* |
| **peor** | *worse* |
| **así** | *this way, like that* |
| **alto** (de intensidad) | *loudly* |
| **bajo** (de intensidad) | *softly* |
| **rápido, deprisa** | *quickly, fast* |
| **despacio, lento** | *slowly* |
| **duro, duramente** | *hard* |

| | | |
|---|---|---|
| Ella siempre habla **alto**. | > | *She always speaks loudly.* |
| ¿Puedes hablar más **despacio**, por favor? | > | *Can you speak more slowly, please?* |
| Canto **peor** que mi padre. | > | *I sing worse than my father.* |
| Él maneja **muy mal**. | > | *He drives very badly.* |

## c Adverbs ending in "-mente"

Most Spanish adverbs of manner are formed by adding "**-mente**" to the feminine singular form of the adjectives. This ending corresponds to "*-ly*" in English.

| lenta | ····➤ | lenta**mente** | *(slow* | ····➤ | *slowly)* |
| fácil | ····➤ | fácil**mente** | *(easy* | ····➤ | *easily)* |
| perfecta | ····➤ | perfecta**mente** | *(perfect* | ····➤ | *perfectly)* |

**solamente** = **solo** *(only)*
Be careful not to mistake **solo** *(only)* for **solo/a** *(alone).*
**Solo** tengo dos monedas.    *I only have two coins.*

—¿Vives con tus padres?                —*Do you live with your parents?*
—No, vivo **solo**.                            —*No, I live alone.*

Remember that when an adjective has a written accent, the adverb retains it.
rápida ····➤        rápidamente        *(quick* ····➤        *quickly)*

## d Vocabulario: Tiendas y comercios (Shops and stores)

**panadería**: *bakery*
**pescadería**: *fish market*
**verdulería**: *farmer's market*
**ferretería**: *hardware store*
**pastelería**: *pastry shop*
**librería**: *bookstore*
**tintorería**: *dry cleaner's*
**floristería**: *florist's*
**gasolinera**: *gas station*
**tienda de animales**: *pet shop*

**carnicería**: *butcher's*
**frutería**: *fruit shop*
**supermercado**: *supermarket*
**cafetería**: *coffee shop*
**farmacia**: *drugstore*
**tienda de ropa**: *clothing store*
**zapatería**: *shoe store*
**kiosko**: *kiosk*
**agencia de viajes**: *travel agency*
**agencia inmobiliaria**: *real estate agency*

# Gramática fácil

## a | The imperfect

With the preterite we can't express all the actions and events that took place in the past. There is another set of past tense forms, the imperfect, whose main function is to describe past actions or events.

To form the imperfect we have to add the following endings to the verb stems.
Ex: **hablar** *(to speak)*, **aprender** *(to learn)*, **escribir** *(to write)*.

|  | -AR **HABLAR** | -ER **APRENDER** | -IR **ESCRIBIR** |
|---|---|---|---|
| yo | habl**aba** | aprend**ía** | escrib**ía** |
| tú | habl**abas** | aprend**ías** | escrib**ías** |
| usted-él-ella | habl**aba** | aprend**ía** | escrib**ía** |
| | | | |
| nosotros/as | habl**ábamos** | aprend**íamos** | escrib**íamos** |
| vosotros/as | habl**ábais** | aprend**íais** | escrib**íais** |
| ustedes-ellos/as | habl**aban** | aprend**ían** | escrib**ían** |

Notice that the endings for "-er" and "-ir" verbs are exactly the same.

| —¿Qué **hacía** Guadalupe? | > | —¿What was Guadalupe doing? |
| —¿Ella **navegaba** por internet. | > | —She was surfing the internet. |

| —¿Dónde **estabas**? | > | —¿Where were you? |
| —¿**Estaba** en la cocina. | > | —¿I was in the kitchen. |

| —¿Con quién **hablaban** ustedes? | > | —¿Who were you talking to? |
| —¿**Hablábamos** con nuestra vecina. | > | —¿We were talking to our neighbor. |

Antes **escribíamos** cartas y ahora escribimos correos electrónicos.
*We wrote letters before and now we write emails.*

There are only three irregular verbs in the imperfect: "**ser**" *(to be)*, "**ver**" *(to see)* and "**ir**" *(to go)*:

|  | SER | VER | IR |
|---|---|---|---|
| yo | **era** | **veía** | **iba** |
| tú | **eras** | **veías** | **ibas** |
| usted-él-ella | **era** | **veía** | **iba** |
| | | | |
| nosotros/as | **éramos** | **veíamos** | **íbamos** |
| vosotros/as | **érais** | **veíais** | **íbais** |
| ustedes-ellos/as | **eran** | **veían** | **iban** |

SpanishEasyAndFun.com

| | | |
|---|---|---|
| Brenda **era** muy tímida. | > | *Brenda was very shy.* |
| ¿Dónde **ibas**? **Iba** a tu casa. | > | *Where were you going?* |
| | | *I was going to your house.* |
| Había niebla y no **veíamos** nada | > | *It was foggy and we couldn't see anything.* |

As we can see in the examples, the imperfect in Spanish is equivalent to some past tenses in English (depending on the context) and is frequently translated in ways other than the simple past in English.

💧 The impersonal form **"hay"** belongs to the verb **"haber"**, therefore its imperfect form is **"había"** *(there was/there were)*.

Hace veinte años no **había** tantos teléfonos móviles como hoy.
*Twenty years ago there weren't as many cell phones as today.*

💧 The imperfect is used:

  ◉ to describe a state or a situation in the past:

| | | |
|---|---|---|
| Susana **estaba** cansada cuando llegó a casa. | > | *Susana was tired when she got home.* |
| Aquí **había** un cuadro antes. | > | *There was a picture here before.* |

  ◉ to express habits or repeated actions or facts in the past:

| | | |
|---|---|---|
| A menudo **jugábamos** en la plaza. | > | *We often played in the square.* |
| Hace mucho tiempo me **gustaba** comer caramelos. | > | *I liked eating candy a long time ago.* |

  ◉ to refer to past actions or events that occurred over an unspecified time:

| | | |
|---|---|---|
| Los alumnos **salían** de la escuela. | > | *The students left the school.* |
| ¿Dónde **vivías**? **Vivía** en Londres. | > | *Where were you living? I was living in London.* |

  ◉ to indicate time or age in the past.

| | | |
|---|---|---|
| **Eran** las 6 de la tarde. | > | *It was 6:00 p.m.* |
| Ella **tenía** veinticinco años. | > | *She was twenty-five years old.* |

There are many words used to join sentences. They are called "linking words". In this unit we will work on two of these linking words: **mientras** *(while)* and **cuando** *(when)*.

● **"Mientras"** *(while)* can be defined as "during the time that". It means that the two actions joined in the same sentence by **"mientras"** are happening at the same time. "**Mientras**" is generally placed at the beginning of the sentence or in the middle (between the two clauses).

Yo leía **mientras** mi padre cocinaba.

*I was reading while my father was cooking.*

**Mientras** mi padre cocinaba, yo leía.

*While my father was cooking, I was reading.*

Sonó el teléfono **mientras** tú te duchabas.    **>**    *The phone rang while you were taking a shower.*

Voy al gimnasio **mientras** mis hijos están en la escuela.    **>**    *I go to the gym while my children are at school.*

**"Mientras"** or **"mientras tanto"**, as adverbs of time, are equivalent to *"meanwhile"*, or *"in the meantime"*.

Voy de compras. **Mientras (tanto)** tú puedes lavar el auto.    **>**    *I'm going shopping. Meanwhile you can wash the car.*

● **"Cuando"** *(when)* means "at the time that". It is also placed at the beginning or in the middle of a sentence.

**Cuando** los niños salieron de la escuela, sus padres los recogieron.    **>**    *When the children got out of school their parents picked them up.*

Me despierto **cuando** suena el despertador.    **>**    *I get up when the alarm clock rings.*

¿Qué haces **cuando** no puedes dormir?    **>**    *What do you do when you can't sleep?*

🖐 SpanishEasyAndFun.com

# Ejercicios de la **Unidad 21**

## a  Form adverbs by adding the ending "-mente"

**1** probable    _____
**2** frecuente    _____
**3** rápido    _____
**4** terrible    _____
**5** cierto    _____

## b  Fill in the gaps with the correct form of the imperfect.

**1** Nos vio cuando nosotros (ir) _____ al supermercado.
**2** ¿Con quién (hablar) _____ tú ?
**3** Por la mañana nosotros (tener) _____ frío.
**4** ¿Quién (ser) _____ ese hombre del traje azul?
**5** Ellos (abrir) _____ las ventanas porque (hacer) _____ calor.
**6** Cuando él (entrar) _____ en la habitación nunca (encender) _____. la luz.
**7** El niño no (jugar) _____ porque (tener) _____. sueño.
**8** Nosotros siempre (leer) _____ el periódico en la cafetería.
**9** Te vi mientras tú (caminar) _____. por el parque.
**10** ¿Vosotros (escribir) _____. artículos o novelas?

## c  Match the words with their meanings.

**1** carnicería            **a** drugstore
**2** verdulería            **b** greengrocer's
**3** farmacia            **c** bakery
**4** panadería            **d** pet shop
**5** tienda de animales    **e** butcher's

**Key**

**a:** 1.- probablemente; 2.- frecuentemente; 3.- rápidamente; 4.- terriblemente;
5.- ciertamente.
**b:** 1.- íbamos; 2.- hablabas; 3.- teníamos; 4.- era; 5.- abrían, hacía; 6.- entraba,
encendía;
7.- jugaba, tenía; 8.- leíamos; 9.- caminabas; 10.- escribíais.
**c:** 1.-e; 2.- b; 3.- a; 4.- c; 5.- d.

# Unidad 22
## Santo Domingo

### En esta unidad estudiaremos:

● **Diálogo**

● **Hablemos español:**
   **a)** The imperfect versus the preterite. **b)** Vocabulario: El cuerpo humano (The human body). **c)** The verb "doler". **d)** Giving advice.

● **Gramática fácil:**
   **a)** Relative pronouns. **b)** The relative pronoun "que". **c)** The relative pronoun "lo que". **d)** The relative pronoun "quien".

● **Ejercicios**

---

*Guillermo se encuentra a Rosalía y hablan sobre algunos problemas de salud.*

Guillermo: ¡Hola, Rosalía! ¿Cómo estás? Manuel me **dijo** que la semana pasada **estuviste** enferma, pero no recuerdo **lo que** te **pasaba**.

Rosalía: Estoy bien, gracias. Sí, la semana pasada **estuve** enferma. **Me dolían** la **espalda**, las **piernas** y los **brazos**. Creo **que tuve** gripe.

G: ¿**Viste** al médico?

R: No, no lo **hice**.

G: Y ahora, ¿**te duele** algo?

R: No, ya no **me duele** nada. Me siento muy bien.

G: De todas formas, **deberías** ver a un médico.

R: ¿Por qué?

G: Porque pareces cansada. No sé si aún tienes gripe.

R: Ya te he dicho que no **me duele** nada.

G: A mí **me duelen** las **rodillas**. Yo también **debería** ver a un médico. ¿Recuerdas el accidente **que tuve** el mes pasado? Las **rodillas me dolieron** en ese momento y ahora **me duelen** de nuevo.

R: Entonces tienes razón; creo **que deberías** ver a un médico. Él te dirá **lo que** te ocurre.

G: ¿Y qué es eso **que** tienes en la **mano**?

R: Son unos formularios **que** rellené sobre los días **que** no **fui** a trabajar la semana pasada. Ahora voy a la oficina y veré al gerente, **a quien** se los daré.

G: Muy bien. Yo voy a hacer algo de compra y vuelvo a mi casa. ¡Cuídate y hasta pronto!

R: ¡Hasta pronto, Guillermo!

SpanishEasyAndFun.com

Parque Colón, Ciudad Colonial de Santo Domingo, República Dominicana.

*Guillermo runs into Rosalía and they are talking about some health problems.*

Guillermo: Hello, Rosalía! How are you? Manuel told me you were sick last week
 but I don't remember what was wrong with you.
Rosalía: I'm fine, thank you. Yes, I was sick last week. My back, my legs and my
 arms ached. I think I had the flu.
G:   Did you see the doctor?
R:   No, I didn't.
G:   And now, do you have any aches and pains?
R:   No, now nothing hurts. I feel good.
G:   Anyway, you should see a doctor.
R:   Why?
G:   Because you look tired. I don't know if you still have the flu.
R:   I told you that nothing hurts now.
G:   My knees hurt. I should see a doctor too. Do you remember the accident I had
 last month? My knees hurt me then and they hurt now again.

R:   Then you're right; I think you should see a doctor. He will tell you what's
 wrong with you.
G:   And what's that you have in your hand?
R:   They're some forms I completed having to do with the days I didn't go to work
 last week. Now I'm going to the office and I'll see the manager and give him
 the forms.
G:   Okay. I'm going to do some shopping and then back home. Take care and see
 you soon!
R:   See you soon, Guillermo!

# Hablemos español

## a  The imperfect versus the preterite

So far we have studied two past tenses: the preterite and the imperfect. Let's look at the differences between them that will help us use these tenses properly.

- When we use the imperfect we are placed "within" a past fact, situation or event, and are describing something in process at that moment.

| | | |
|---|---|---|
| **Hacía** mucho frío. | > | *It was very cold.* |

But using the preterite we are placed "after" a past fact or event and mention a process already finished or completed.

| | | |
|---|---|---|
| **Hizo** mucho frío (ese día). | > | *It was very cold (that day).* |

- When using the imperfect we refer to a situation that has not been completed at a specific moment in the past. We are describing an ongoing situation at that time.

| | | |
|---|---|---|
| Ayer a las 8 yo **estaba** **visitando** a mi tía. | > | *Yesterday at 8:00 I was visiting my aunt.* |
| Cuando llegaste yo **estaba** **haciendo** un ejercicio. | > | *When you arrived I was doing an exercise.* |

The preterite shows an action that has already been completed at a specific moment in the past.

| | | |
|---|---|---|
| Ellos **trabajaron** hasta las 5. | > | *They were working until 5:00.* |
| **Hice** el ejercicio en dos minutos. | > | *I did the exercise in two minutes.* |

For this reason, when we talk about the "total duration" of an action we use the preterite, not the imperfect.

| | | |
|---|---|---|
| La semana pasada **trabajé** todos los días. | > | *Last week I worked everyday.* |
| **Estuvimos** en México <u>durante tres meses</u>. | > | *We were in Mexico for three months.* |
| Ellos **conversaron** <u>mucho tiempo</u>. | > | *They were talking for a long time.* |

- We use the imperfect to indicate features of objects or people:

| | | |
|---|---|---|
| Tu hermana **era** muy alta. | > | *Your sister was very tall.* |
| Los gatos **eran** negros. | > | *The cats were black.* |
| El vaso **estaba** lleno de agua. | > | *The glass was full of water.* |

SpanishEasyAndFun.com

● But the preterite is used when we refer to features of a process or an activity:

| | | |
|---|---|---|
| La reunión **estuvo/fue** interesante. | > | *The meeting was interesting.* |
| La fiesta **estuvo/fue** divertida. | > | *The party was fun.* |

Notice the difference between these two tenses:

| | | |
|---|---|---|
| **Yo conocía** a tu padre. | > | *I knew your father. (It was a past fact)* |
| **Yo conocí** a tu padre. | > | *I met your father. (We were introduced)* |
| | | |
| Ellos **traían** regalos. | > | *They used to bring presents.* |
| Ellos **trajeron** regalos. | > | *They brought presents (that time).* |

## b Vocabulario: El cuerpo humano (The human body)

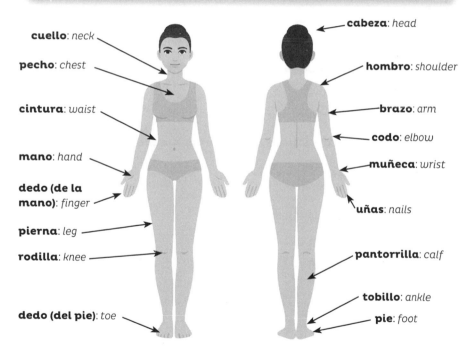

**cuello**: *neck*
**pecho**: *chest*
**cintura**: *waist*
**mano**: *hand*
**dedo (de la mano)**: *finger*
**pierna**: *leg*
**rodilla**: *knee*
**dedo (del pie)**: *toe*

**cabeza**: *head*
**hombro**: *shoulder*
**brazo**: *arm*
**codo**: *elbow*
**muñeca**: *wrist*
**uñas**: *nails*
**pantorrilla**: *calf*
**tobillo**: *ankle*
**pie**: *foot*

Remember that the parts of the body are preceded by articles in Spanish, and not by possessive adjectives:

| | | |
|---|---|---|
| Me duele **la** cabeza. | > | <u>My</u> head aches. |
| Él lleva un reloj en **la** muñeca derecha. | > | He is wearing a watch on <u>his</u> right wrist. |
| Ayer me dolían **los** pies. | > | <u>My</u> feet hurt yesterday. |

## c   The verb "doler"

When you don't feel well you can say:

**No me siento bien**
**No me encuentro bien** } *I don't fell well*

**Me siento mal**     *I feel bad.*
**Me siento fatal**   *I feel terrible.*

And when we want to state that a part of our body hurts, we can say:

|     |        | el  |                    |
| Me  | duele  | la  | + part of the body |
|     | duelen | los |                    |
|     |        | las |                    |

**(A mí) Me duele** la espalda.      >   *I have a backache.*
**(A mí) Me duelen** las rodillas.   >   *My knees hurt.*

If someone else has a specific pain:

**(A ti) Te** duele la cabeza.       >   *You have a headache.*
**(A ella) Le** duelen los brazos.   >   *Her arms hurt.*

Other ways to express pain are:

**Tengo (un) dolor en + el/la/los/las +  part of the body**

**Tengo un dolor en** el brazo.        >   *I have a pain in my arm.*
**Ellos tienen un dolor en** los pies. >   *Their feet hurt.*

or: **Tengo (un) dolor de + part of the body**

**Tengo dolor de** barriga.            >   *I have a stomachache.*
**Ella tiene un dolor de** cabeza terrible. >   *She has a terrible headache.*

## d   Giving advice

There are several ways that we can ask for and give advice, but the most common is to use the conditional form of the verb "**deber**" *(must, have to)*, that is, "**debería, deberías, etc.**" *(should).*
The form "**debería**" is followed by the pure infinitive form of the verb.

Ellos **deberían** venir con nosotros. >   *They should come with us.*
¿**Deberíamos** comprarnos ese auto?   >   *Should we buy that car?*
Ella no **debería** ir a esa reunión.  >   *She shouldn't go to that meeting.*

# Gramática fácil

## a Relative pronouns

Relative pronouns are those related to a noun that has just been stated.

Compré <u>un helado</u>.     >     *I bought an ice cream.*
<u>El helado</u> estaba delicioso.     >     *The ice cream was delicious.*

These two sentences can be joined by means of the relative pronoun "que", to avoid the repetition of the subject.

El helado **que** compré estaba delicioso. >     *The ice cream that I bought was delicious.*

## b The relative pronoun "que"

The most common relative pronoun is "**que**". It can be used to refer to both persons and things. "**Que**" is the Spanish equivalent of the English words: *who, whom, which,* and *that.*

Don't forget that the relative "**que**" has no graphic accent, not to be confused with the interrogative "**¿qué?**"

"**Que**" is usually followed by a verb, but it does not always function as the subject of that verb. In any case, it can <u>never</u> be omitted.

La película **que** (yo) vi fue interesante.   >   *The movie that I saw was interesting.*

Las naranjas **que** (nosotros) comemos   >   *The oranges that we eat are from*
son de California.                              *California.*

La novela **que** estoy leyendo es   >   *The novel (that) I am reading is very*
muy interesante.                           *interesting.*

El hombre **que** conocí es francés.   >   *The man who I met is French.*

Un carnicero es una persona **que**   >   *A butcher is a person who sells meat.*
vende carne.

## c    The relative pronoun "lo que"

To refer to "the thing that", we use "**lo que**" *(what):*

No entiendo **lo que** dices.              >    *I don't understand what you're saying.*
¿Quieres ver **lo que** compré?            >    *Do you want to see what I bought?*

## d    The relative pronoun "quien"

The relative pronoun "**quien**" and its plural form "**quienes**" are used when referring to people. They have no written accent mark, not to mistake them for "**¿quién?**"/ "**¿quiénes**"?

🔵 When the relative pronoun "que" refers to people and is not the subject of the verb that follows it, it can be replaced for **"a quien"**.

El hombre **que** (yo) conocí es francés.   =   El hombre **a quien** (yo) conocí es francés.
Silvia es la mujer **que** (tú) ayudaste.   =   Silvia es la mujer **a quien** (tú) ayudaste.

🔵 In this pair of sentences "que" and "a quien" are used indistinctly, but, <u>when the relative pronoun comes after a preposition, "que" is only used for things and "quien/ quienes" for people.</u>

Esa es la herramienta **con** <u>que</u> trabajo*.   >   *That is the tool I work with.*
Ella es la persona **en** <u>quien</u> estoy           >   *She is the person I am thinking about.*
pensando.
Estas son las personas **con** <u>quienes</u> vivo.   >   *These are the guys I am living with.*

🔵 Anyway, after any preposition, "quien" and "quienes" can be replaced for "**el/la/ los/las + que**".

Ella es la persona **en** <u>la que</u> estoy pensando.
Estas son las personas **con** <u>las que</u> vivo.

⭐ Although this sentence is correct, it is much more common to add the corresponding article just before "que".

Esa es la herramienta <u>con **la** que</u> trabajo.

🖐 SpanishEasyAndFun.com

**a** Fill in the gaps with the correct form of the preterite or the imperfect.

Cuando yo (**1** ser) _____ niño, (**2** tener) _____ que dormirme pronto porque me (**3** levantar) _____ temprano. Un día nos (**4** visitar) _____ mi tía Luisa y, mientras ella nos (**5** cuidar) _____, mis padres (**6** poder) _____ hacer otras cosas. Ella (**7** nacer) _____ en Argentina, pero sus padres (**8** ser) _____ españoles.

**b** Fill in the gaps with the suitable relative pronoun: **con la que, al que, a quien, lo que, en la que, que.**

**1** Aquel edificio _____. ven ustedes a la derecha es el ayuntamiento.
**2** La señora _____ Pedro está hablando es la directora.
**3** La casa _____ vivo tiene dos plantas.
**4** Aquel señor _____ María está saludando es nuestro profesor.
**5** El pueblo _____ vamos en verano está lejos.

**c** Choose the correct answer.

If you have a toothache, what should you do?
**1** Deberías beber agua fría.
**2** Deberías comer fruta.
**3** Deberías ir al dentista.

**d** Word search: find six parts of the human body.

| S | U | E | M | N | S | R |
|---|---|---|---|---|---|---|
| I | C | M | D | A | V | O |
| R | I | A | J | R | S | D |
| P | A | N | B | D | O | I |
| I | D | O | R | E | T | L |
| E | M | S | A | U | Z | L |
| A | O | L | Z | N | L | A |
| D | E | D | O | S | R | C |
| O | R | D | S | A | U | N |

# Unidad 23
## La Costa del Sol

### En esta unidad estudiaremos:

● **Diálogo**

● **Hablemos español:**
  **a)** Expressing possession. **b)** Possessive pronouns.
  **c)** Vocabulario: La escuela (The school).

● **Gramática fácil:**
  **a)** Durative actions in the past. **b)** The past participle.

● **Ejercicios**

---

*Guillermo ha vuelto de la escuela. Beatriz ve una mochila en casa.*

Beatriz: Guillermo, ¿**de quién es** esa **mochila**? Es parecida a **la de Luisa**, pero no es **la suya**.

Guillermo: Es **de Nacho**, uno de sus compañeros de clase. La trajo ella.

B: ¿Por qué se lleva cosas que no le pertenecen?

G: Ella sabe que no es **suya**, pero Nacho la olvidó en el **patio de la escuela**. Estaba **abierta** y los **cuadernos**, **lápices**, **gomas**, **reglas**, etc., estaban **tirados**. Luisa metió todo en la **mochila** y la trajo para devolverla mañana.

B: ¿Por qué no la guardaron allí?

G: No había nadie por allí. Los **profesores** y los **alumnos** ya se habían marchado. Además, **estaba lloviendo** y todo se **estaba mojando**.

B: Bueno, la pongo junto a **la suya**.

G: ¿Y ese bolso? ¿**De quién es**? ¿Es **tuyo**?

B: Em... Sí.

G: Pero **el tuyo** es negro ¿Es nuevo?

B: Sí. **El mío se estaba rompiendo** y me he comprado otro.

G: Pues hay más cosas que tenemos que cambiar, como el apartamento. **El nuestro** es pequeño para los niños. Me gusta **el de Miguel** y Lucía.

B: Sí, pero ellos pudieron comprarlo porque sus salarios son altos. **Los nuestros** no lo son.

G: Sí, tenemos que esperar un poco.

B: Además, su apartamento es más antiguo que **el nuestro**.

G: Tienes razón, **el nuestro** es más moderno y más bonito. Solo necesitamos una habitación más para los niños.

SpanishEasyAndFun.com

Costa del Sol, Málaga, España.

Guillermo has come back from school. Beatriz sees a backpack at home.

Beatriz: Guillermo, whose backpack is that? It looks like Luisa's but it's not hers.

Guillermo: It's Nacho's, one of her classmates. She brought it home.

B: Why does she take things that don't belong to her?

G: She knows it's not hers, but Nacho forgot it on the school playground. It was open and the notebooks, pencils, erasers, rulers, etc., were on the ground. Luisa put everything back in the backpack and brought it home to return it to him tomorrow.

B: Why didn't they keep it there?

G: There wasn't anyone there. The teachers and students had already left. It was raining and it was getting all wet.

B: Well, I'll put it next to hers.

G: And that purse? Whose is it? Is it yours?

B: Em... Yes.

G: But yours is black. Is it new?

B: Yes. Mine was breaking so I bought this one.

G: There are more things that we have to change too, like this apartment. Ours is small for the kids. I like Miguel and Lucía's.

B: Yes, but they could buy it because they have high salaries. Ours are not.

G: Yes, we'll have to wait a little.

B: Moreover, their apartment is older than ours.

G: You are right. Ours is more modern and beautiful. We only need one more room for the kids.

# Hablemos español

### a  Expressing possession

In order to ask who the owner of an object is we use **"¿De quién?"**.

| ¿De quién es esta mochila? | > | *Whose is this backpack?* |
| ¿De quién son esos lápices? | > | *Whose are those pencils?* |

Its plural form is **"¿de quiénes?"** if we ask about more than one owner:

| ¿De quiénes son estos cuadernos? | > | *Whose are these notebooks?* |

And to answer, we can use possessive pronouns or names (preceded by "de"):

| Esta mochila es **mía**. | > | *This backpack is mine.* |
| Esos lápices son **de Miguel**. | > | *These pencils are Miguel's.* |

### b  Possessive pronouns

Possessive pronouns express possession or relationship to something. They replace a possessive adjective and the noun of the object possessed:

| Ese es <u>mi celular</u>. | Ese es **mío**. | **Mío** | <u>mi celular</u>. |
| *That is my cell phone.* | *That one is mine.* | *Mine* | *my cell phone.* |

| **POSSESSIVE ADJECTIVES** | | **POSSESSIVE PRONOUNS** | |
|---|---|---|---|
| mi | *(my)* | (el) **mío** | *(mine)* |
| tu | *(your)* | (el) **tuyo** | *(yours)* |
| su, de usted | *(your)* | (el) **suyo** | *(yours)* |
| su*, de él | *(his)* | (el) **suyo*** | *(his)* |
| su*, de ella | *(her)* | (el) **suyo*** | *(hers)* |
| | | | |
| nuestro/a | *(our)* | (el) **nuestro** | *(ours)* |
| vuestro/a | *(your)* | (el) **vuestro** | *(yours)* |
| su, de ustedes | *(your)* | (el) **suyo** | *(yours)* |
| su, de ellos | *(their)* | (el) **suyo** | *(theirs)* |

⭐ "Su" is also used when we refer to animals or things as possessors (*its*).

Possessive pronouns have masculine, feminine, singular and plural forms, as they always agree in gender and number with the noun they replace. The article that

🖐 SpanishEasyAndFun.com

usually precedes a possessive pronoun also has to agree with it in gender and number.

| | | | |
|---|---|---|---|
| mi auto | ·····➤ el **mío** | tus libros | ·····➤ los **tuyos** |
| su hermana | ·····➤ la **suya** | nuestras camisas | ·····➤ las **nuestras** |

But there may, or may not, be an article after the verb "ser":

Ese pasaporte <u>es</u> (el) **mío**.      >      *That passport is mine.*

Aquellos diccionarios <u>son</u> **nuestros**.      >      *Those dictionaries are ours.*

🌑 The pronouns "**suyo, suya, suyos, suyas**" may refer to several persons. In order to avoid ambiguity, it is possible to use the following structure:

**de** + **subject pronoun** (él / ella / usted / ellos / ellas / ustedes)

El auto rojo es **de ella**.      >      *The red car is hers.*

Aquellos documentos son **de ellos**.      >      *Those documents are theirs.*

| | | |
|---|---|---|
| —Estoy pintando la suya (su casa). | > | —*I am painting theirs (their house).* |
| —¿La **de él**? | > | —*His?* |
| —No, la **de ellos**. | > | —*No, theirs.* |

Or we can use names instead of subject pronouns:

El auto rojo es **de María**.      >      *The red car is María's.*

Aquellos documentos son **de Luis y Jorge**.      >      *Those documents are Luis and Jorge's.*

---

## C  Vocabulario: La escuela (The school)

| | |
|---|---|
| **profesor, maestro**: *teacher* | **estudiante**: *student* |
| **alumno**: *student/pupil* | **pizarra**: *chalkboard* |
| **cuaderno**: *notebook* | **carpeta**: *folder* |
| **escritorio, pupitre**: *desk* | **mochila**: *backpack* |
| **portafolios**: *book bag* | **lápiz, lapicero**: *pencil* |
| **bolígrafo, pluma**: *pen* | **sacapuntas**: *pencil sharpener* |
| **goma de borrar**: *eraser* | **tinta**: *ink* |
| **lápices de colores**: *crayons* | **hoja de papel**: *sheet of paper* |
| **rotulador**: *marker* | **regla**: *ruler* |
| **tijeras**: *scissors* | **pegamento**: *glue* |

¿De quién es este **sacapuntas**?      >      *Whose is this pencil sharpener?*

Esa **mochila** es mía. La tuya es aquella.  >   *That backpack is mine. Yours is that one.*

# Gramática fácil

## a   Durative actions in the past

To express a durative action in the past we can use two tenses: the preterite and the imperfect, but in a continuous or progressive manner. In this case, both tenses are equivalent to the past continuous in English *(was/were + present participle)*.

🔵 The preterite continuous

| | | |
|---|---|---|
| yo | **estuve** | |
| tú | **estuviste** | |
| usted-él-ella | **estuvo** | + present participle |
| nosotros/as | **estuvimos** | |
| vosotros/as | **estuvisteis** | |
| ustedes-ellos/as | **estuvieron** | |

When using this tense we mean that the action was durative but that it was completed in the past.

Nosotros **estuvimos jugando** al tenis ayer.     >     *We were playing tennis yesterday.*

Ellos **estuvieron trabajando** para esa empresa hace dos años.     >     *They were working for that firm two years ago.*

**Estuve cenando** en ese restaurante la semana pasada.     >     *I was having dinner in that restaurant last week.*

SpanishEasyAndFun.com

# The imperfect continuous

| | |
|---|---|
| yo | **estaba** |
| tú | **estabas** |
| usted-él-ella | **estaba** |
| | |
| nosotros/as | **estábamos** |
| vosotros/as | **estabais** |
| ustedes-ellos/as | **estaban** |

+ present participle

| | | |
|---|---|---|
| Él **estaba jugando** al tenis cuando se cayó. | > | He was playing tennis when he fell down. |
| ¿Qué **estaba haciendo** ella? Ella **estaba nadando**. | > | What was she doing? She was swimming. |
| Yo **estaba hablando** con ella cuando alguien la llamó por teléfono. | > | I was talking to her when somebody called her. |

■ When using this tense we are refering to a durative action in progress at a certain moment in the past that was not yet completed.
This "certain moment" in the past may not appear explicitly, but it is understood in context.

| | | |
|---|---|---|
| ¿Qué **estaba haciendo** ella (cuando la viste)? Ella **estaba nadando**. | > | What was she doing (when you saw her)? She was swimming. |

■ This tense is also used when we refer to two durative past actions happening simultaneously.

| | | |
|---|---|---|
| Yo **estaba leyendo** mientras ellos **estaban haciendo** sus deberes. | > | I was reading while they were doing their homework. |

■ And when a single action "interrupted" another one in progress. In this case, the action that "interrupted" is expressed in the preterite.

| | | |
|---|---|---|
| **Estábamos viendo** la televisión cuando alguien **llamó** a la puerta. | > | We were watching television when somebody knocked at the door. |

## b  The past participle

Past participles are words that share some characteristics of verbs and adjectives. As verbs they are used when making the perfect tenses (see unit 24).

Past participles are formed by dropping the infinitive ending (-ar, -er, -ir) and adding "**-ado**" to the infinitive stem of "**-ar**" verbs and "**-ido**" to the stems of "**-er**" and "**-ir**" verbs.

| -AR VERBS | -ER VERBS | -IR VERBS |
|---|---|---|
| hablar – habl**ado** | correr – corr**ido** | vivir – viv**ido** |
| *to speak – spoken* | *to run – run* | *to live – lived* |

Some common verbs have irregular past participles:

| | | | | | |
|---|---|---|---|---|---|
| abrir | ····▶ | **abierto** | *(to open* | ····▶ | *opened)* |
| decir | ····▶ | **dicho** | *(to say* | ····▶ | *said)* |
| escribir | ····▶ | **escrito** | *(to write* | ····▶ | *written)* |
| hacer | ····▶ | **hecho** | *(to do/make* | ····▶ | *done/made)* |
| morir | ····▶ | **muerto** | *(to die* | ····▶ | *died)* |
| poner | ····▶ | **puesto** | *(to put* | ····▶ | *put)* |
| romper | ····▶ | **roto** | *(to break* | ····▶ | *broken)* |
| ver | ····▶ | **visto** | *(to see* | ····▶ | *seen)* |
| volver | ····▶ | **vuelto** | *(to come back* | ····▶ | *come back)* |

Many **past participles can be used as adjectives**; therefore, they have to agree in gender and number with the nouns they modify.

| | | |
|---|---|---|
| Yo estoy **cansado** y ellos están **aburridos**. | > | *I am tired and they are bored.* |
| La puerta estaba **cerrada** pero las ventanas estaban **abiertas**. | > | *The door was closed but the windows were open.* |

Remember that for "-er" and "-ir" verbs, if the stem ends in a vowel, an accent mark will be required, except for those verbs ending in "-uir" (construir, seguir, etc.).

| | | | | | |
|---|---|---|---|---|---|
| creer | ····▶ | cre**í**do | *(to believe* | ····▶ | *believed)* |
| construir | ····▶ | construido | *(to build* | ····▶ | *built)* |

# Ejercicios de la **Unidad 23**

## a
Use the suitable possessive pronoun.

1. ¿Es aquel vuestro coche? Sí, es el _____.
2. ¿Es esta su maleta, Sr. Pérez? Sí, es la _____.
3. ¿Son de ustedes estos sombreros? Sí, son los _____.
4. ¿Es esta la habitación de Luis? Sí, es la _____.
5. ¿Es de María este bolso? Sí, es el _____.

## b
Find the odd-one-out:

1. tinta – lápiz – árbol
2. goma – cuaderno – teléfono
3. botella – libro – pizarra
4. bolígrafo – mochila – planta
5. alumno – fuente – carpeta

## c
Choose the suitable participle (adjective) to complete the following sentences:
**hecho/a/os/as, resuelto/a/os/as, abierto/a/os/as, muerto/a, roto/a/os/as.**

1. ¿Has visto ese gato? Creo que está _____.
2. Esos problemas ya están _____.
3. Hace frío porque las ventanas están _____.
4. Ten cuidado. Esa silla está _____.
5. Este ejercicio ya está _____.

## d
Fill in the gaps with the verb in the past progressive: estuvieron almorzando, estaba bebiendo, estuvimos durmiendo, estuve cantando, estaban escuchando.

1. Yo _____ todo el día.
2. Él _____ cuando yo llegué.
3. Nosotros _____ durante toda la película.
4. Mis padres _____ el discurso del presidente.
5. Samuel y Linda _____ en casa el sábado pasado.

### Key

**a:** 1.- nuestro; 2.- mía; 3.- nuestros; 4.- suya; 5.- suyo.
**b:** 1.- árbol; 2.- teléfono; 3.- botella; 4.- planta; 5.- fuente.
**c:** 1.- muerto; 2.- resueltos; 3 – abiertas; 4 – rota; 5.- hecho.
**d:** 1.- estuve cantando; 2.- estaba bebiendo; 3.- estuvimos durmiendo; 4.- estaban escuchando; 5.- estuvieron almorzando.

Spanish: Easy and Fun

# Unidad 24
## Tikal

### En esta unidad estudiaremos:

⦿ **Diálogo**

⦿ **Hablemos español:**
a) Verbs followed by prepositions. b) Vocabulario: Actividades de ocio (Leisure activities).

⦿ **Gramática fácil:**
a) The present perfect. b) Uses of the present perfect. c) The adverbs "ya", "todavía" and "aún" + the present perfect.

⦿ **Ejercicios**

*Gustavo y Cristina hablan sobre distintos países.*

Cristina: Gustavo, ¿qué países **sueñas con** visitar?
Gustavo: No sé, ¿**has estado** alguna vez en China?
C: No, **aún** no **he estado** en China, pero es un país que quiero visitar. Estoy muy interesada en la cultura china.
G: Bueno, hay otros lugares que también son interesantes. Yo quiero volver a la República Dominicana.
C: ¿**Ya has estado** allí?
G: Sí, estuve allí hace tres años. Me encantó. Los dominicanos son muy alegres y las **playas** son maravillosas. También me gustan sus **fiestas**. El 27 de febrero es el **Día de la Independencia** y hay **música** por todas partes. A ellos les gusta mucho **bailar**. También hay **fuegos artificiales** por la noche. ¿**Has bailado** merengue alguna vez?
C: ¡Claro que sí! ¿Y tú? ¿**Has aprendido ya**?
G: Em..., bueno, no, **no he aprendido todavía**, pero yo no dejo de moverme cuando suena la **música**.
C: Bueno, eso es importante. A mí también me gustan esas **fiestas**. Por cierto, el próximo viernes voy a una **fiesta de los 15 años**.
G: ¡**Nunca he asistido** a ninguna! ¿Puedo ir contigo?
C: ¡Claro que sí! La chica que cumple los 15 es mi prima Ana, tú la conoces. **Se va a casar con** su novio Agustín dentro de 2 años.
G: Sí, aunque hace por lo menos 3 años que no nos vemos, nunca **me olvido de** ella.

SpanishEasyAndFun.com

Parque Nacional Tikal, departamento de Petén, Guatemala.

Gustavo and Cristina are talking about different countries.

Cristina: Gustavo, which countries do you dream of visiting?
Gustavo: I don't know, have you ever been to China?
C: No, I haven't been to China yet, but it is a country I want to visit. I am very interested in the Chinese culture.
G: Well, there are also other places which are interesting. I want to go back to the Dominican Republic.
C: Have you already been there?
G: Yes, I was there three years ago. I loved it. The Dominicans are very cheerful and the beaches are wonderful. I also like their celebrations. On February 27th it is Independence Day and there is music everywhere. They like dancing a lot. There are also fireworks at night. Have you ever danced merengue?

C: Yes, of course! And you? Have you already learned?
G: Err..., well, no, I haven't learned yet, but I don't stop moving when the music plays.
C: Well, that's important. I also like those celebrations. By the way, next Friday I'm going to a girl's 15th birthday party.
G: I've never been to one of those parties. Can I go with you?
C: Of course! You know the birthday girl. It's my cousin Ana. She is going to marry her boyfriend Agustín in two years.
G: Yes, although it's been at least 3 years since we've seen each other, but I never forgot her.

# Hablemos español

## a Verbs followed by prepositions

In Spanish there are many verbs followed by a preposition. After the preposition we usually find an infinitive, a pronoun, or a noun. The most common prepositions after verbs are **a**, **con**, **de**, **en**, **por** and **para**.

| | |
|---|---|
| aprender **a** | *to learn to* |
| ayudar **a** | *to help* |
| comenzar **a** | *to start to* |
| enseñar **a** | *to teach to* |
| soñar **con** | *to dream of/about* |
| casarse **con** | *to marry* |
| acordarse **de** | *to remember* |
| olvidarse **de** | *to forget* |
| salir **de** | *to leave (a place)* |
| entrar **en** | *to enter* |
| pensar **en** | *to think of/about* |
| ser **para** | *to be for* |
| servir **para** | *to be used for* |
| preocuparse **por** | *to worry about* |

| | | |
|---|---|---|
| Ellos <u>se olvidaron</u> **de** mí. | > | *They forgot me.* |
| ¿Quieres <u>casarte</u> **con**migo? | > | *Do you want to marry me?* |
| <u>Estoy pensando</u> **en** mi padre. | > | *I'm thinking about my father.* |

In Spanish, when there are two verbs together separated by a preposition, the first one is conjugated and the second one is always an infinitive.

| | | |
|---|---|---|
| Él <u>se acordó</u> **de** <u>comprar</u> pan. | > | *He remembered to buy some bread.* |
| <u>Estamos aprendiendo</u> **a** <u>esquiar</u>. | > | *We are learning to ski.* |
| Roberto <u>comenzó</u> **a** <u>andar</u> cuando tenía dos años. | > | *Roberto started to walk when he was two years old.* |

## b Vocabulario: Actividades de ocio (Leisure activities)

**ir de compras**: *to go shopping*
**ir a tomar un trago**: *to go for a drink*
**ir a nadar**: *to go swimming*
**jugar a las cartas**: *to play cards*
**practicar, hacer deporte**: *to do sports*
**ir al cine/teatro**: *to go to the movies/theater*
**reunirse con los amigos**: *to meet one's friends*

**ir al gimnasio**: *to go to the gym*
**ir a bailar**: *to go dancing*
**pintar**: *to paint*
**escuchar música**: *to listen to music*
**jardinería**: *gardening*
**pescar**: *to fish*
**cocinar**: *to cook*

SpanishEasyAndFun.com

# Gramática fácil

## a   The present perfect

The present perfect is formed by combining the present simple of the verb "haber" *(to have)* and the past participle of the main verb.

Subject + **present of "haber"** + **past participle**

| | | |
|---|---|---|
| yo | **he** | |
| tú | **has** | |
| usted-él-ella | **ha** | |
| nosotros/as | **hemos** | + **past participle** |
| vosotros/as | **habéis** | |
| ustedes-ellos/as | **han** | |

| | | |
|---|---|---|
| **He comido** paella. | > | *I have eaten paella.* |
| Tú **has traído** ese paquete. | > | *You have brought this package.* |
| Ellos **han estudiado** francés. | > | *They have studied French.* |
| Mi abuela **ha venido** desde Europa. | > | *My grandmother has come from Europe.* |
| Usted **ha bebido** mucho. | > | *You have drunk a lot.* |
| **Hemos hecho** nuestros deberes. | > | *We have done our homework.* |

● In order to structure negative sentences, "**no**" is placed before the verb "haber":

| | | |
|---|---|---|
| **No** he comprado el periódico. | > | *I haven't bought the newspaper.* |
| Ella **no** ha abierto la puerta. | > | *She hasn't opened the door.* |

● Direct or indirect object pronouns must also be placed just before the verb "haber":

| | | |
|---|---|---|
| Ellos **lo** han hecho. | > | *They have done it.* |
| Tú **me** has dado esa botella. | > | *You have given me that bottle.* |

● But if we find any of these pronouns and the negative "no" in a sentence, we have to place the "no" before the pronoun:

| | | |
|---|---|---|
| Ellos **no** lo han hecho. | > | *They haven't done it.* |
| Tú **no** me has dado esa botella. | > | *You haven't given me that bottle.* |

● When asking questions do not forget that the verb "haber" and the past participle always go together:

| | | |
|---|---|---|
| ¿**Han pintado** ellos la habitación? | > | *Have they painted the room?* |
| ¿No **ha llegado** ella? | > | *Hasn't she arrived?* |
| ¿Qué **has hecho**? | > | *What have you done?* |

With reflexive verbs, the pronouns always precede the verb "haber":

**Me** he lavado la cara.                            > *I have washed my face.*
¿Qué **te** has comprado?                          > *What have you bought for you?*

## b    Uses of the present perfect

The present perfect tense is used to express:

Unfinished actions, that is, actions that started in the past and still continue into the present.

**Hemos vivido** en Miami los últimos    >    *We have lived in Miami for the last two*
dos años.                                                    *years.*

**He tenido** este trabajo desde enero.  >    *I have had this job since January.*

Ella **ha sido** mi novia desde            >    *She has been my girlfriend since she*
que me conoció.                                          *met me.*

Ustedes **han navegado** por              >    *You have been surfing the Internet for*
internet durante dos horas.                        *two hours.*

Past actions or experiences, not stating when they occurred.

**He leído** "Guerra y Paz".                   >    *I have read "War and Peace".*
Él **ha trabajado** como pintor.           >    *He has worked as a painter.*
**Hemos limpiado** la casa.                  >    *We have cleaned the house.*
Ellos **han estado** en Europa.            >    *They have been to Europe.*

If we state when these actions took place, we use the preterite instead of the present perfect:

**Leí** "Guerra y Paz" hace muchos años.   >    *I read "War and Peace" many years ago.*
Él **trabajó** como pintor cuando            >    *He worked as a painter when he was*
tenía 25 años.                                             *25 years old.*
**Limpiamos** la casa ayer.                    >    *We cleaned the house yesterday.*
Ellos **fueron** a Europa en 2003.          >    *They went to Europe in 2003.*
tenía 25 años.

How often a past experience has occurred.

In this case we use "alguna vez" *(ever)* in the question and an adverb of frequency in the answer.

—¿Alguna vez **has llegado** tarde a una reunión? > —Have you ever been late for a meeting?

—No, nunca **he llegado** tarde a una reunión. > —No, I have never been late for a meeting.

—¿**Han perdido** ellos el tren alguna vez? > —Have they ever missed the train?

—Sí, ellos **han perdido** el tren muchas veces. > —Yes, they have missed the train many times.

—¿**Ha tenido** él pesadillas alguna vez? > —Has he ever had a nightmare?

—Sí, a veces **ha tenido** pesadillas. > —Yes, sometimes he has had nightmares.

Recent actions:

- When the period of time expressed is not over:

No **he leído** el periódico hoy. > I haven't read the newspaper today.

¿Qué **has hecho** esta semana? > What have you done this week?

Este año **he escrito** dos novelas. > This year I have written two novels.

- When we refer to actions that could have happened by the time they are described. In this case we almost always use the adverbs "ya" *(already, yet)*, "todavía" *(yet)* and "aún" *(yet)*.

● **"Ya"** *(already, yet)* means "by that moment" or "at an unspecified time before now". It is used in affirmative sentences and questions.

In affirmative sentences, "ya" can be placed before or after the verb or at the end of the sentence, although it is more common to find it before the verb.

| | | |
|---|---|---|
| **Ya** ha llegado la carta. | > | *The letter has already arrived.* |
| Hemos terminado **ya**. | > | *We have already finished.* |

In asking questions, "ya" may be placed in different positions: before or after the verb, or at the end of the sentence.

¿**Ya** ha llegado la carta?
¿Ha llegado **ya** la carta?
¿Ha llegado la carta **ya**?

● **"Todavía"** *(yet)* is used in negative sentences and may be placed in different positions: before the negative "no", after the verb, or at the end of the sentence.

**Todavía** no se han comido el bocadillo.
No se han comido **todavía** el bocadillo.   ▸ *They haven't eaten the sandwich yet.*
No se han comido el bocadillo **todavía**.

| | | |
|---|---|---|
| La carta no ha llegado **todavía**. | > | *The letter hasn't arrived yet.* |
| **Todavía** no hemos terminado. | > | *We haven't finished yet.* |

In this context, **"aún"** is a synonym of "**todavía**" and can be used in the same cases.

| | | |
|---|---|---|
| La carta no ha llegado **aún.** | > | *The letter hasn't arrived yet.* |
| **Aún** no hemos terminado. | > | *We haven't finished yet.* |

# Ejercicios de la **Unidad 24**

Fill in the gaps with the suitable preposition.

**1** Estamos aprendiendo _____ cocinar comida tailandesa. (a/en/de)
**2** Me olvidé _____ cerrar la puerta cuando salí. (en/de/por)
**3** Ellos están enseñándonos _____ nadar. (de/para/a)
**4** ¿Te acordaste _____ comprar pan? (por/en/de)
**5** Está comenzando _____ llover. Abre el paraguas. (a/para/de)
**6** Ella se casó _____ un alemán y se fue _____ vivir a Alemania (en/por/con)
(para/a/por)
**7** Richard vino _____ Francia para aprender español. (para/a/de)
**8** Las pastillas me ayudaron _____ dormir. (para/por/a)
**9** Las llaves sirven _____ abrir puertas. (para/de/a)
**10** Él se preocupa _____ hacer bien su trabajo. (a/en/por)

**b**  Complete the sentences with the following verbs in the present perfect:
**ha roto, has cocinado, han vuelto, he enviado, ha ido, han terminado, has apagado, hemos ido, ha hecho, hemos dormido.**

**1** Hoy _____ un día maravilloso.
**2** _____ muy mal esta noche.
**3** Ella _____ a la playa todos los días durante las vacaciones.
**4** _____ de Londres esta mañana.
**5** _____ a bailar dos veces este mes.
**6** ¿_____ alguna vez la pierna de cordero?
**7** ¿Ya _____ ustedes el ejercicio?
**8** ¿Quién _____ el despertador?
**9** No _____ todavía el correo electrónico al gerente.
**10** ¿_____ la luz?

# Unidad 25
## Segovia

**En esta unidad estudiaremos:**

◉ **Diálogo**

◉ **Hablemos español:**
   **a)** The imperative. **b)** Asking for and giving directions.

◉ **Gramática fácil:**
   **a)** The comparative of equality.

◉ **Ejercicios**

*Gloria es una señora mayor y pregunta por una dirección a Rafael, a quien se encuentra por la calle.*

Gloria: **¡Perdone!** ¡Buenos días!

Rafael: ¡Buenos días!

G:  Sé que hay una farmacia por aquí pero, ¿podría decirme dónde está? Tengo miedo a perderme.

R:  **No tenga miedo**. La farmacia está cerca de aquí. **Mire: cruce esta calle**; **siga adelante, doble la primera calle a la derecha** y allí está. **No tiene pérdida**.

G:  Muchas gracias.

R:  ¿Le puedo ayudar en algo más?

G:  Sí, por favor, **acompáñeme**.

R:  Parece asustada. ¿Se encuentra bien?

G:  Sí, estoy bien, pero yo vivo en un pueblo muy pequeño y en la ciudad me pierdo. Hay **tanta gente como** autos. Incluso tengo miedo de cruzar la calle.

R:  **No se preocupe**, señora. **No tema** nada. Yo le acompañaré.

G:  Muchas gracias, espero no causarle mucha molestia. Mi pueblo no es **tan grande como** esta ciudad, es muy tranquilo y no me gusta venir a la gran ciudad.

R:  La entiendo perfectamente. A mí también me gustan los pueblos tranquilos.

G:  ¿Cómo se llama usted?

R:  Rafael. **Mire**, ya hemos llegado. La farmacia está **justo aquí**.

G:  Encantada, Rafael. Muchas gracias. Es usted muy amable.

R:  De nada. ¡Buena suerte!

SpanishEasyAndFun.com

Acueducto de Segovia, España.

*Gloria is an elderly lady and is asking Rafael, whom she has met on the street, for directions.*

Gloria: Excuse me! Good morning!

Rafael: Good morning!

G: I know there is a drugstore around here but, could you tell me where it is? I'm afraid of getting lost.

R: Don't be afraid. The drugstore is near here. Look: cross this street, go straight ahead, turn at the first right and there it is. You can't miss it.

G: Thank you very much.

R: Is there anything else I can help you with?

G: Yes, please. Could you come with me?

R: You look frightened. Are you okay?

G: Yes, I'm fine, but I live in a very small town and I get lost in the city. There are so many people and cars. I am even afraid of crossing the street.

R: Don't worry, madam. Don't be afraid of anything. I'll go with you.

G: Thank you, I don't want to cause any inconvenience. My town is not as big as this city, it's very quiet and I don't like coming to the city.

R: I understand. I also like quiet towns.

G: What's your name?

R: Rafael. Look, we have arrived. The drugstore is right here.

G: Pleased to meet you, Rafael. Thank you very much. You are very kind.

R: You're welcome. Good luck!

# Hablemos español

## a The imperative

The imperative is a verb mood used to give a command, give instructions or make either affirmative or negative requests.

Imperatives are only addressed to the second person singular and plural (tú, usted, vosotros and ustedes). In addition, there is a way to imply both the and speaker and the listener (nosotros/as) in the same action. This is not a true imperative, but a way to express a suggestion. In English, its equivalent is *"let's + infinitive"*.

Imperatives are usually written between exclamation marks.

**Affirmative imperative:**

● **Tú**. Take the present tense and drop the final "s":

|  | PRESENT (INDICATIVE) | IMPERATIVE | |
|---|---|---|---|
| hablar | tú hablas | ¡Habla! | *Speak!* |
| comer | tú comes | ¡Come! | *Eat!* |
| abrir | tú abres | ¡Abre! | *Open!* |

| ¡**Mira** estas fotos! | > | *Look at these pictures!* |
|---|---|---|
| ¡Escucha esto**!** | > | *Listen to this!* |

● **Vosotros/as**. Take the infinitive and replace the final "r" with a "d":

|  | INFINITIVE | IMPERATIVE |
|---|---|---|
| hablar | ¡**Hablad!** | *Speak!* |
| comer | ¡**Comed!** | *Eat!* |
| abrir | ¡**Abrid!** | *Open!* |

| ¡Cerrad la puerta, por favor! | > | *Close the door, please!* |
|---|---|---|
| ¡Escribid un correo electrónico al gerente! | > | *Write an email to the manager!* |

SpanishEasyAndFun.com

## Affirmative and negative imperatives:

**Regular "-ar" verbs**: Take the present tense of the verb and change the "a" in the ending to "e".

|  | PRESENT TENSE | AFFIRMATIVE IMPERATIVE | NEGATIVE IMPERATIVE |
|---|---|---|---|
| tú | habl**a**s | (see above) | **no hables** |
| usted | habl**a** | **hable** | **no hable** |
| nosotros/as | habl**a**mos | **hablemos** | **no hablemos** |
| vosotros/as | habl**á**is | (see above) | **no habléis** |
| ustedes | habl**a**n | **hablen** | **no hablen** |

| ¡**Caminen** por ahí! | > | *Walk over there!* |
| ¡**Juguemos** al fútbol! | > | *Let's play soccer!* |
| ¡No **mires** estas fotos! | > | *Don't look at these pictures!* |
| ¡No **escuchéis** esto! | > | *Don't listen to this!* |
| ¡No **cierren** la puerta! | > | *Don't close the door!* |

**Regular "-er" verbs**: Take the present tense of the verb and change the "e" in the ending to "a".

|  | PRESENT TENSE | AFFIRMATIVE IMPERATIVE | NEGATIVE IMPERATIVE |
|---|---|---|---|
| tú | com**e**s | (see above) | **no comas** |
| usted | com**e** | **coma** | **no coma** |
| nosotros/as | com**e**mos | **comamos** | **no comamos** |
| vosotros/as | com**é**is | (see above) | **no comáis** |
| ustedes | com**e**n | **coman** | **no coman** |

| **Beba** un poco de leche. | > | *Drink a little milk.* |
| ¡**Lean** este artículo! | > | *Read this article!* |
| ¡No **enciendas** la luz! | > | *Don't turn on the light!* |
| ¡No **corran**! | > | *Don't run!* |

- **Regular "-ir" verbs**: Take the present tense of the verb and:

  - for "tú", "usted" and "ustedes", change the "e" in the ending to "a".
  - for "nosotros/as", change the "i" in the ending to "a".
  - for "vosotros/as", change the "í" in the ending to "ái"

|  | PRESENT TENSE | AFFIRMATIVE IMPERATIVE | NEGATIVE IMPERATIVE |
|---|---|---|---|
| tú | abres | (see above) | no abras |
| usted | abre | abra | no abra |
| nosotros/as | abrimos | abramos | no abramos |
| vosotros/as | abrís | (see above) | no abráis |
| ustedes | abren | abran | no abran |

| | | |
|---|---|---|
| ¡**Escriba** una carta al director! | > | Write a letter to the director! |
| ¡**Suban**! Estamos esperándolos. | > | Go upstairs! We are waiting for you. |
| ¡No **abras** las ventanas, por favor! | > | Don't open the windows, please! |

The imperative endings for "-er" and "-ir" verbs are identical when using regular verbs.

There are only eight irregular forms (here are the "tu" affirmative and negative forms):

| decir | ·····> | **di – no digas** | hacer | ·····> | **haz – no hagas** |
|---|---|---|---|---|---|
| ir | ·····> | **ve – no vayas** | poner | ·····> | **pon – no pongas** |
| salir | ·····> | **sal – no salgas** | ser | ·····> | **sé – no seas** |
| tener | ·····> | **ten – no tengas** | venir | ·····> | **ven – no vengas** |

| | | |
|---|---|---|
| ¡**Ven** aquí! | > | Come here! |
| **Pon** estas monedas en la mesa. | > | Put these coins on the table |
| ¡**Sal** de esta habitación! | > | Get out of this room! |
| **Ve** a la farmacia y **compra** jarabe para la tos. | > | Go to the drugstore and buy some cough syrup. |
| ¡No **vayas** a ese lugar! | > | Don't go to that place! |
| ¡No **vengas**! | > | Don't come! |
| ¡No **digas** nada! | > | Don't say anything! |

- **Reflexive or object pronouns are used with commands.**

  - When the command is affirmative, the pronouns are attached to the end of the verb.

| | | |
|---|---|---|
| ¡Leván**tate**! | > | Get up! |
| Di**me** lo que hiciste. | > | Tell me what you did. |

■ When the command is negative, the pronouns immediately precede the verb.

¡No **te** levantes!      >     *Don't get up!*

No **me** digas lo que hiciste.     >     *Don't tell me what you did.*

## b   Asking for and giving directions

Let's learn some verbs and expressions used when giving directions.

| | |
|---|---|
| **seguir la calle** | *go up the street* |
| **seguir recto** | *go straight ahead* |
| **cruzar la avenida** | *cross the avenue* |
| **caminar, ir hasta un lugar** | *walk /go up to a place* |
| **pasar por (delante de) un lugar** | *go past a place* |
| **doblar/girar a la izquierda** | *turn left* |
| **doblar/girar a la derecha** | *turn right* |
| **tomar la primera calle a la derecha** | *take the first right* |
| **tomar la segunda calle a la izquierda** | *take the second left* |
| **No tiene pérdida** | *You can't miss it* |

**Cruza** la calle.     >     *Go across the street.*

No **cruces** la calle.     >     *Don't go across the street.*

**Siga** recto hasta la esquina y **tome**   >     *Go straight to the corner and take the*
la primera calle a la izquierda.           *first street on the left.*

# Gramática fácil

## a   The comparative of equality

To say that two things share the same features we use the following structures:

■ With adjectives and adverbs:

| **tan + adjective/adverb + como** | *as + adjective/adverb + as* |
|---|---|

Ricardo es **tan** alto **como** Lucas.     >     *Ricardo is as tall as Lucas.*

Luis no toca el piano **tan** bien     >     *Luis doesn't play the piano as well as*
**como** Miguel.                   *Miguel.*

● With verbs:

To express the same quantity or the same thing(s):

| verb + lo mismo + (que) | verb + the same + (as) |
|---|---|

| Hoy hemos bebido **lo mismo** (que ayer). > | *Today we have drunk the same (as yesterday).* |
|---|---|
| Ella estudió **lo mismo que tú.** > | *She studied the same as you.* |

● With nouns:

◗ To express the same identity:

| **el mismo/los mismos + noun + (que)**<br>**la misma/las mismas** | *the same + noun + (as)* |
|---|---|

| Estoy leyendo **el mismo** <u>libro</u> **que** Marta. > | *I am reading the same book as Marta.* |
|---|---|
| Ella hace **las mismas** <u>cosas</u><br>**que** su novio. > | *She does the same things as her boyfriend.* |

And also:

| Marta y yo estamos leyendo **el**<br>**mismo** libro. > | *Marta and I are reading the same book.* |
|---|---|
| Ella y su novio hacen **las mismas** cosas. > | *She and her boyfriend do the same things.* |

◗ To express the same quantity:

| **tanto/ tanta + uncountable noun + como**<br>**tantos/tantas + countable noun + como** | *as much + uncountable noun + as*<br>*as many + countable noun + as* |
|---|---|

| No tengo **tanto** <u>dinero</u> **como tú.** > | *I don't have as much money as you.* |
|---|---|
| **Él bebe tanta** <u>leche</u> **como** su hijo. > | *He drinks as much milk as his son.* |
| Nosotros teníamos **tantos**<br><u>problemas</u> **como** ustedes. > | *We had as many problems as you.* |
| Ella comió **tantas** <u>manzanas</u> **como** yo. > | *She ate as many apples as I did.* |

SpanishEasyAndFun.com

# Ejercicios de la **Unidad 25**

### a
Match the sentences with their meanings.

**1** No conduzcas deprisa.
**2** Abre el armario.
**3** ¡Sal de aquí inmediatamente!
**4** No compres esos libros.
**5** Ve a casa de Pablo.

**a** Get out of here right now!
**b** Don't buy those books.
**c** Go to Pablo's house.
**d** Open the closet.
**e** Don't drive fast.

### b
Fill in the gaps with the correct verb form in the imperative.

**1** ¡_____ la puerta! (Cierras / No cierras / Cierra)
**2** _____ con atención. (Escuches / Escuchen / No escucha)
**3** _____ lo que le digo. (Haga / Haces / No haces)
**4** _____ el autobús 33. (No tomas / Tomas / Toma)
**5** _____ la luz. (Enciendes / No enciendan / No enciendes)

### c
Fill in the gaps with the following expressions:

**1** Vivo en la misma calle que ustedes.
**2** Luisa es tan simpática como su hermana.
**3** El algodón es tan blanco como la nieve.
**4** Tienen los mismos ojos que sus padres.
**5** Hay tantos niños como niñas en clase.
**6** Leonardo y yo hemos comido lo mismo.
**7** Los mejillones son tan caros como los calamares.
**8** En el parque hay tantas flores como en mi jardín.
**9** Hemos hecho los mismos ejercicios.
**10** Hablas español tan bien como los colombianos.

• • • • • • • • • • • • • • • • • • • • • • • • • • • • • • • • • • • • • • • • • • • • • • • • • •

# Unidad 26
## Isla de Pascua

### En esta unidad estudiaremos:

⦿ **Diálogo**

⦿ **Hablemos español:**
 **a)** Adjectives followed by prepositions. **b)** Uses of "algún", "ningún" and "cualquier". **c)** Vocabulario: Medios de transporte (Means of transport).

⦿ **Gramática fácil:**
 **a)** The comparative of superiority and inferiority.
 **b)** Irregular comparatives. **c)** The verbs "quedar" and "quedarse".

⦿ **Ejercicios**

---

*Luis e Isabel hablan sobre dos personas a las que conocen, pero a las que no ven mucho.*

Luis: Estoy **aburrido de** estudiar en casa. ¿Puedo ir contigo a la biblioteca **algún** día?

Isabel: ¡Claro! Ayer **me quedé** en la biblioteca hasta tarde y vi a Leo y a Javier.

L:  Yo los he visto muchas veces en **el autobús** y siempre los confundo. Son muy parecidos.

I:  Sí, son parecidos, pero Leo es **un poco más alto** que Javier.

L:  ¿Quién es **mayor**?

I:  Leo es **un poco mayor.** Los dos tienen los ojos marrones, pero Javier tiene los ojos **más grandes** y **más oscuros.**

L:  No estoy **segura de** cuál es el color de sus ojos, pero recuerdo que tienen el mismo peinado. Tienen el pelo largo.

I:  No. Ahora Leo tiene el cabello **mucho más corto** que Javier. Otra diferencia son las manos. Javier es pianista y sus **dedos** son **más largos y finos que** los de Leo, que es atleta. Pero **ninguno** tiene el pelo largo.

L:  Las **piernas** de los atletas son **más fuertes** que las **piernas** de los pianistas.

I:  Sí, **mucho más fuertes**. En general, todo el cuerpo.

L:  Bueno, los viste, pero ¿hablaste con ellos?

I:  Sí. Javier me dijo que está siempre viajando a todas partes desde que se compró su **auto** nuevo. Leo está muy **contento por** sus carreras. Ha participado en competiciones en muchos países y siempre viaja en **avión** con todo el equipo. Ahora están **más ocupados** y tienen **menos tiempo** para **quedar con** los amigos.

L:  Sí, la verdad es que hace mucho tiempo que no los veo.

I:  Me dijeron que van muchos días a la biblioteca para estudiar, todavía les **quedan algunas** asignaturas. Puede que **algún** día los veas tú también.

L:  ¡Espero no confundirlos la próxima vez!

SpanishEasyAndFun.com

Estatuas de Moáis en la Isla de Pascua, Chile.

Luis and Isabel are speaking about two people they know, but that they don't see very much.

Luis: I'm bored studying at home. Can I go to the library with you one day?

Isabel: Sure! Yesterday I was at the library until late and I saw Leo and Javier.

L: I have seen them several times on the bus and I always get them confused. They look so much alike.

I: Yes, they look alike but Leo is a bit taller than Javier.

L: Who is older?

I: Leo is a little older. They both have brown eyes, but Javier's eyes are bigger and darker.

L: I'm not sure what color eyes they have, but I remember that they have the same haircut. They both have long hair.

I: No. Leo's hair is much shorter than Javier's now. Another difference is their hands. Javier is a pianist and his fingers are longer and thinner than Teo's, who is an athlete. But neither of them have long hair.

L: An athlete's legs are stronger than a pianist's legs.

I: Yes, much stronger. In general the whole body is much stronger.

L: So you saw them, but did you talk to them?

I: Yes. Javier told me that he is always travelling everywhere since he bought his new car. Leo is very happy with his competitions. He has participated in competitions in many countries and he always travels by plane with his team. They said that they are busier now and that they have less time to spend with friends.

L: Yes, the truth is that I haven't seen them in a long time.

I: They told me they often go to the library to study because they still have some subjects left. So you may see them there some day.

L: I hope to not confuse them the next time!

# Hablemos español

## a Adjectives followed by prepositions

In Spanish we find many adjectives followed by prepositions. The most common prepositions found after adjectives are **"a"**, **"con"**, **"de"**, **"en"** and **"para"**.

Here is a list of some of these adjectives:

| | |
|---|---|
| (estar) **aburrido de** | *(to be) bored of* |
| (estar, ir) **acompañado de** | *(to be) accompanied by* |
| (ser) **adecuado para** | *(to be) suitable to/for* |
| (estar) **cansado de** | *(to be) tired of* |
| (estar) **contento con** | *(to be) happy with* |
| (estar) **contento por** | *(to be) happy for* |
| (estar) **contento de** | *(to be) happy about* |
| (ser) **difícil de** | *(to be) difficult to* |
| (estar) **dispuesto a** | *(to be) willing to* |
| (ser) **fácil de** | *(to be) easy to* |
| (estar) **harto de** | *(to be) fed up with* |
| (estar) **libre de** | *(to be) free of/from* |
| (ser) **el primero en** | *(to be) the first (one) to* |
| (ser) **responsable de** | *(to be) responsible for* |
| (estar) **seguro de** | *(to be) sure of* |
| (ser) **el último en** | *(to be) the last (one) to* |

When we use a verb after a preposition, it <u>must</u> be an infinitive.

| | | |
|---|---|---|
| Esto es **fácil de** comprender. | > | *This is easy to understand.* |
| Estoy **cansado de** estudiar. | > | *I am tired of studying.* |
| Mi madre estaba **harta de** cocinar. | > | *My mother was fed up with cooking.* |
| ¿Quién es **responsable de** eso? | > | *Who is responsible for that?* |

🖐 SpanishEasyAndFun.com

## b   Uses of "algún", "ningún" and "cualquier"

The indefinite adjectives "**algún**", "**ningún**" and "**cualquier**" always precede a noun with which they agree in gender and number. They refer to people or things, but not to a particular person or thing.

- "**Algún**" *(some, any)* is the shortened form of the pronoun "alguno" and is placed before a masculine singular noun. Its feminine and plural forms are: **alguna**, **algunos**, **algunas**.

| | | |
|---|---|---|
| ¿Tienes **algún** libro de historia? | > | *Do you have any history books?* |
| ¿Hay **alguna** luz encendida? | > | *Are there any lights on?* |
| He visto **algunos** perros en el parque. | > | *I have seen some dogs in the park.* |
| **Algunas** personas son inteligentes. | > | *Some people are intelligent.* |

- "**Ningún**" *(no, none)* is the shortened form of "ninguno" and goes before a masculine singular noun. Its feminine form is "**ninguna**" and it is not used with plural nouns. When "**ninguno/a**" precedes the verb, the sentence is affirmative. When they follow the verb, the sentence is negative.

| | | |
|---|---|---|
| **Ningún** alumno aprobó el examen. | > | *None of the students passed the exam* |
| **Ninguna** camisa está limpia. | > | *None of the shirts are clean.* |
| No oí **ningún** ruido. | > | *I didn't hear any noise.* |
| No tengo **ninguna** duda. | > | *I have no doubt.* |

- "**Cualquier**" *(any)* is the shortened form of "cualquiera" *(any at all)*. It is used before any noun in singular.

| | | |
|---|---|---|
| Visitaré a tu madre **cualquier** día. | > | *I will visit your mother on any day.* |
| **Cualquier** persona puede comprender esto. | > | *Any person can understand this.* |

## c   Vocabulario: Medios de transporte (Means of transport)

| | |
|---|---|
| **auto**: *car* | **taxi**: *taxi, cab* |
| **autobús**: *bus* | **furgoneta**: *van* |
| **camión**: *truck* | **camioneta**: *pickup truck* |
| **bicicleta**: *bicycle* | **motocicleta**: *motorcycle* |
| **tren**: *train* | **metro**: *subway* |
| **tranvía**: *streetcar, trolley* | **barco**: *ship, boat* |
| **crucero**: *cruise ship* | **plane**: *avión* |

| | | |
|---|---|---|
| ¿Usas **algún** **medio de transporte**? | > | *Do you use a means of transport?* |
| No he manejado nunca ningún **camión**. | > | *I have never driven a truck.* |

# Gramática fácil

## a  The comparative of superiority and inferiority

To compare two things and say that one of them is "superior" or "inferior" to the other, we use the following structures:

| **verb + más + que** | verb + more + than |
|---|---|
| **menos** | less |

Ella <u>estudia</u> **más que** su hermana.  ➤  *She studies more than her sister.*
Ahora Rosario <u>trabaja</u> **menos que** antes. ➤  *Now Rosario works less than before.*

|  |  | **adjective** |  |  |
|---|---|---|---|---|
| **más/menos** | + | **adverb** | + | **que** |
|  |  | **noun** |  |  |

more/less/fewer + adjective / adverb / noun + than

Ricardo es **más** <u>alto</u> **que** Francisco.  ➤  *Ricardo is taller than Francisco.*
Hoy me he levantado **más** <u>tarde</u> **que** ayer.  ➤  *Today I got up later than yesterday.*
Ellos tienen **menos** <u>hijos</u> **que** nosotros. ➤  *They have fewer children than us.*
Necesitamos **menos** <u>dinero</u> **que** ustedes.  ➤  *We need less money than you.*

## b  Irregular comparatives

The adjectives "**bueno**" *(good)*, "**malo**" *(bad)*, "**grande**" *(big)* and "**pequeño**" *(menor)* and the adverbs "**bien**" *(well)* and "**mal**" *(badly)* can have irregular forms to express the comparative of superiority.

🔹 "Bueno", "malo", "grande" and "pequeño" can be used as follows:

|  |  | **bueno** |  |  |
|---|---|---|---|---|
| **más** | + | **malo** | + | **que** |
|  |  | **grande** |  |  |
|  |  | **pequeño** |  |  |

🖐 SpanishEasyAndFun.com

But they can also have an irregular comparative:

más bueno / más bien = **mejor**   (better)

| | | |
|---|---|---|
| Esta tortilla está **mejor** que la otra. | > | This omelette is better than the other. |
| Hoy me siento **mejor** que ayer. | > | Today I feel better than yesterday. |

más malo / más mal = **peor**   (worse)

| | | |
|---|---|---|
| Mi resultado fue **peor** que el tuyo. | > | My result was worse than yours. |
| **Él baila peor** que ella. | > | He dances worse than her. |

más grande = **mayor***   más pequeño = **menor***

⚙ Both "mayor" and "menor" may refer to size or age, so their equivalents in English are:

"**mayor**" ⟶   "bigger" or "older"
"**menor**" ⟶   "smaller" or "younger"

| | | |
|---|---|---|
| Ella es **mayor** que yo. | > | She is older than me. |
| Su abuela es **menor** que su abuelo. | > | His grandmother is younger than his grandfather. |

🔘 "Mejor", "peor", "mayor" and "menor" do not have feminine forms, but they have plural forms: **mejores, peores, mayores** and **menores**, respectively.

| | | |
|---|---|---|
| Estas manzanas son **peores** que aquellas. | > | These apples are worse than those ones. |
| Ellos son un poco **mayores** que mis padres. | > | They are a little older than my parents. |

---

## C   The verbs "quedar" and "quedarse"

The verb "**quedar**" and the reflexive "**quedarse**" have different meanings in different contexts.

🔘 "**Quedar**":

▪ It can be a synonym of "to be" when we refer to the location of a place.

| | | |
|---|---|---|
| La estación **queda** lejos de aquí. | > | The station is far from here. |
| ¿Dónde **queda** el ayuntamiento? | > | Where is the town hall? |

It also means *"to be left"* or *"to have left"* to express how much of something is remaining. When you mean "to have left", you need an indirect object.

**Quedan** dos niños en la clase.  >  *There are two children left in the classroom.*

**Queda** poco café en la taza.  >  *There is little coffee left in the cup.*

Me **queda** algo de dinero.  >  *I have some money left.*

A Ricardo no le **queda** nada.  >  *Ricardo has nothing left.*

**"Quedarse":**

It is the equivalent of the verb *"to stay"*.

Ellos **se quedaron** en la cafetería mientras yo hacía la compra en supermercado.  >  *They stayed at the coffee shop while I was doing the shopping in the el supermarket.*

**"Quedarse"** may also imply a change of state. In this case it is equivalent to *"to become + adjective"*, *"to go + adjective"*, *"to get + adjective"*.

Él **se quedó** ciego cuando tenía cinco años.  >  *He went blind when he was five years old.*

Mi hermana **se quedó** embarazada hace dos meses.  >  *My sister got pregnant two months ago.*

It may also mean *"to go well with"*, *"to suit"*.

Ese vestido no **te queda** bien.  >  *That dress doesn't suit you.*

The expression **"quedarse con"** is used to indicate that something has been kept or retained.

Me quedé <u>con</u> sus libros.  >  *I kept his books.*

The expression **"quedarse sin"** means *"to run out of"*.

**Nos hemos quedado** <u>sin</u> azúcar otra vez.  >  *We have run out of sugar again.*

# Ejercicios de la **Unidad 26**

**a** Fill in the gaps with **más que, menos que or más... que, menos... que.**

**1** Hoy vivimos _____ antes.

**2** Nosotros ganamos _____ dinero _____ nuestros abuelos, pero ellos también gastaban _____ nosotros.

**3** Ayer llegué _____ tarde _____ anteayer porque perdí el autobús.

**4** Tengo _____ suerte _____ tú. No soy tan afortunado.

**b** Complete the sentences with the correct form of the verbs "**quedar**" or "**quedarse**" in the present indicative.

**1** ¿Dónde _____ la oficina de correos?

**2** ¿Dónde _____ ustedes cuando vienen a la ciudad?

**3** ¿Dónde _____ ustedes cuando vienen a la ciudad?

**4** A menudo nosotros _____ sin dinero.

**c** Fill in the gaps with the suitable indefinite adjective: **algún, ningún, ninguna** or **cualquier**.

**1** No he hecho _____ ejercicio todavía.

**2** Puedo comer _____ cosa. No te preocupes.

**3** ¿Hay _____ policía aquí?

**4** No tengo _____ duda sobre el tema.

**d** Word search: find the five means of transport.

| A | B | M | H | D | S | O | T |
|---|---|---|---|---|---|---|---|
| R | A | U | T | O | B | U | S |
| U | R | V | M | I | E | T | L |
| S | C | T | I | C | K | O | J |
| C | O | S | A | O | I | M | R |
| M | E | T | R | O | N | S | T |
| R | L | E | T | R | E | N | V |

**Key**

**a:** 1.– más que; 2.– más... que; 3.– más... que; 4.– menos... que; **b:** 1.– queda; 2.– se queda; 3.– se quedan; 4.– nos quedamos; **c:** 1.– ningún; 2.– cualquier; 3.– algún; 4.– ninguna. **d:** autobús, avión, barco, metro, tren.

# Unidad 27
## Toledo

### En esta unidad estudiaremos:

⦿ **Diálogo**

⦿ **Hablemos español:**
   **a)** Exclamaciones con "¡qué!". **b)** Expressing obligation and prohibition.
   **c)** Vocabulario: En el restaurante (At the restaurant).

   ⦿ **Gramática fácil:**
   **a)** Pronouns preceded by prepositions. **b)** The relative superlative.

⦿ **Ejercicios**

---

*Lidia Sánchez va a cenar a un restaurante. El camarero se encuentra en la entrada.*

Lidia: ¡Buenas noches!
Camarero: ¡Buenas noches, señora!
L:   **He reservado una mesa** para una persona a las nueve. Esta noche mi marido no viene **conmigo**. Soy Lidia Sánchez.
C:   Muy bien, señora Sánchez. Por aquí, por favor. Pero tendrá que apagar su cigarrillo. **Está prohibido** fumar en este lugar. ¿Prefiere esta mesa o aquella?
L:   Prefiero aquella. Me hace ilusión estar junto a la ventana y ver la ciudad desde allí. [Se sienta a la mesa] **¡Qué vistas tan bonitas!**
C:   ¿Qué desea beber?
L:   Una copa de vino tinto, por favor.
C:   Tenemos buenos vinos tintos. ¿Quiere uno español, uno chileno o uno francés?
L:   ¿Cuál recomienda?
C:   El español es una buena opción.
L:   Pues tomaré ese. ¿Me puede dar el **menú**, por favor?
C:   Aquí tiene. [Tras unos minutos, Lidia sabe qué pedir]
L:   Quisiera una crema de espárragos y un filete de solomillo **poco hecho**.
C:   Muy bien. ¿Desea algo más?
L:   No, nada más, de momento.
C:   [Le sirve el primer plato] Aquí tiene la crema de espárragos. **¡Buen provecho!**
L:   Muchas gracias.
C:   [Le retira el último plato] ¿Desea algo de **postre**?
L:   No gracias, la carne estaba exquisita. De hecho es **el solomillo más delicioso** que he comido en mi vida. Ahora **debo** irme. **Tengo que** hacer muchas cosas todavía. ¿Puede traerme la **cuenta**, por favor?

C:   ¡Por supuesto!

 SpanishEasyAndFun.com

Puerta de Alfonso VI, Toledo, España.

*Lidia Sánchez has gone to a restaurant for dinner. The waiter is at the entrance.*

Lidia: Good evening!

Waiter: Good evening, madam!

L:  I have reserved a table for one at nine. Tonight my husband is not coming with me. My name is Lidia Sánchez.

W:  Very good, Ms. Sánchez, this way please. But you will have to put out your cigarette. Smoking is forbidden here. Do you prefer this table or that one?

L:  I prefer that one. I like to be sitting by the window and see the city from there. [She sits at the table] What nice views!

W:  What would you like to drink?

L:  I'd like a glass of red wine, please.

W:  We have some good red wines. Would you like a Spanish one, a Chilean one or a French one?

L:  Which one do you recommend?

W:  The Spanish one is a good choice.

L:  I'll have that one, then. Could I have the menu, please?

W:  Here you are. [After a few minutes, Lidia knows what to order]

L:  I would like the cream of asparagus soup and a sirloin steak rare.

W:  Okay, would you like anything else?

L:  No, nothing else at the moment.

W:  [He is serving the first course] Here is your cream of asparagus soup. Enjoy your meal!

L:  Thank you very much.

W:  [He is taking away the last dish] Would you like any dessert?

L:  No, thank you. The meat was delicious. In fact, it's the most delicious sirloin steak I have ever eaten. Now I must go. I still have a lot to do. May I have the bill, please?

W:  Certainly!

# Hablemos español

## a Exclamaciones con "¡qué!"

In Spanish, many exclamations are formed with "**¡Qué!**".

"**¡Qué!**" functions as an intensifier of the adjective, adverb or noun that follows it. It is equivalent to *"What...!"*, *"What a...!"* or *"How...!"* in English.

● "**¡Qué!**" can be followed by:

● An adjective:

| | | |
|---|---|---|
| ¡**Qué** bonito! | > | *How nice!* |
| ¡**Qué** caro! | > | *How expensive!* |
| ¡**Qué** aburrida! | > | *How boring!* |
| ¡**Qué** interesante! | > | *How interesting!* |

● An adverb:

| | | |
|---|---|---|
| ¡**Qué** tarde! | > | *How late!* |
| ¡**Qué** lejos! | > | *How far away!* |

● A noun:

| | | |
|---|---|---|
| ¡**Qué** muchacha! | > | *What a girl!* |
| ¡**Qué** carácter! | > | *What a character!* |
| ¡**Qué** casa! | > | *What a house!* |
| ¡**Qué** tomates! | > | *What tomatoes!* |

● An adjective / adverb / noun + verb + (subject):

| | | |
|---|---|---|
| ¡**Qué** alta es (tu madre)! | > | *How tall your mother is!* |
| ¡**Qué** difícil es el ejercicio! | > | *How difficult the exercise is!* |
| ¡**Qué** tarde has llegado! | > | *How late you have arrived!* |
| ¡**Qué** bien vives! | > | *How well you live!* |
| ¡**Qué** nariz tiene Gregorio! | > | *What a nose Gregorio has!* |
| ¡**Qué** calor hace! | > | *How hot it is!* |

● When "**¡Qué!**" is followed by a noun there may be an adjective before the noun.

| | | |
|---|---|---|
| ¡**Qué** corbata! | > | *What a tie!* |
| ¡**Qué** buenas personas! | > | *What good people!* |

SpanishEasyAndFun.com

When an adjective follows the noun it has to be preceded by "<u>tan</u>" or "<u>más</u>".

| | | |
|---|---|---|
| ¡**Qué** corbata <u>tan</u> horrible! | > | *What a horrible tie!* |
| ¡**Qué** gente <u>más</u> ruidosa! | > | *What noisy people!* |
| ¡**Qué** música <u>más</u> maravillosa! | > | *What marvelous music!* |
| ¡**Qué** flores <u>tan</u> bonitas! | > | *What beautiful flowers!* |

## b   Expressing obligation and prohibition

In Spanish there are several ways to express **obligation**. Here are a few examples:

- "**deber +** <u>infinitive</u>" *(must + infinitive)*

| | | |
|---|---|---|
| **Debes** <u>estudiar</u> más. | > | *You must study harder.* |
| Usted **debe** <u>dejar</u> de fumar. | > | *You must stop smoking.* |

- "**tener + que +** <u>infinitive</u>" *(have to + infinitive)*

| | | |
|---|---|---|
| **Tenemos que** <u>levantarnos</u> temprano. | > | *We have to get up early* |
| **Ella tiene que** <u>alimentar</u> a sus hijos. | > | *She has to feed her children.* |

- "**hay que +** <u>infinitive</u>" *("it is necessary to + infinitive")*

This is an impersonal form (it has no subject), although we "understand" that the subject is "we" or "everybody".

| | | |
|---|---|---|
| ¡Fuego! ¡**Hay que** <u>salir</u> de aquí! | > | *Fire! We have to get out of here!* |
| **Hay que** <u>comer</u> muchos vegetales. | > | *We have to eat a lot of vegetables.* |

And now let's study some ways to express **prohibition**:

- "**Estar prohibido +** <u>infinitive</u>" *(to be forbidden/prohibited)*

| | | |
|---|---|---|
| **Está prohibido** fumar en este lugar. | > | *Smoking is forbidden in this place.* |

- "**No se puede +** <u>infinitive</u>" *(can't + infinitive)*

| | | |
|---|---|---|
| **No se puede** nadar en ese lago. | > | *You can't swim in that lake.* |

- "**No está permitido +** <u>infinitive</u>" *(not to be allowed to + infinitive)*

| | | |
|---|---|---|
| **No está permitido** poner la música alta. | > | *Playing loud music is not allowed.* |

**chef**: *chef*
**camarero/a**: *waiter/waitress*
**comida**: *meal, food*
**menú**: *menu*
**entrante**: *starter*
**plato principal**: *main course*
**menú de tres platos**: *three-course meal*
**libro de reclamaciones**: *complaint book*
**cuenta, factura**: *check*
**reservar una mesa**: *to book a table*
**tener una reserva**: *to have a reservation*
**recomendar**: *to recommend*
**pedir**: *to order*

**cocinero**: *cook*
**servir**: *to serve*
**bebida**: *drink*
**entremeses**: *hors d'oeuvres*
**primer plato**: *first course*
**postres**: *desserts*
**especialidad**: *specialty*
**carta de vinos**: *wine list*
**propina**: *tip*
**una mesa para dos**: *a table for two*
**comida para llevar**: *takeout, takeaway*

**restaurante de comida rápida**: *fast food restaurant*
**restaurante de autoservicio**: *self-service restaurant*
**Buen provecho!**: *Enjoy your meal!*

When ordering meat, the waiter will probably ask you if you want it:

**poco hecha /cruda**: *rare*
**hecha / a punto**: *medium*
**muy hecha / bien hecha**: *well done*

SpanishEasyAndFun.com

# Gramática fácil

## a Pronouns preceded by prepositions

When personal pronouns are preceded by a preposition, we have to use subject pronouns, except for "yo" and "tú" *. These two pronouns change for "mí" and "ti", respectively.

| PREPOSITIONS | | PRONOUNS | |
|---|---|---|---|
| **a** | (to) | **mí** | (me) |
| **con** | (with) | **ti** | (you) |
| **contra** | (against) | **usted** | (you) |
| **de** | (of, from) | **él** | (him) |
| **en** | (in, on) | **ella** | (her) |
| **hacia** | (towards) | **nosotros/as** | (us) |
| **para** | (for) | **vosotros/as** | (you) |
| **por** | (for, by) | **ustedes** | (you) |
| **sin** | (without) | **ellos/as** | (them) |

| | | |
|---|---|---|
| Ese regalo es **para ti**. | > | That gift is for you. |
| El perro corría **hacia ella**. | > | The dog was running towards her. |
| Ellos comenzaron la reunión **sin nosotros**. | > | They started the meeting without us. |
| Ella está luchando **contra mí**. | > | She is fighting against me. |
| Le di el libro **a ellos**. | > | I gave them the book. |
| ¿Te acuerdas **de mí**? | > | Do you remember me? |

An exception to this rule is the preposition "**entre**" (between, among).

| | | |
|---|---|---|
| No hay secretos **entre** tú y yo. | > | There are no secrets between you and me. |

When the preposition "**con**" (with) is followed by the pronouns "mí" or "ti", it becomes **"conmigo"** and **"contigo"**.

| | | |
|---|---|---|
| Ella fue al cine **conmigo**. | > | She went to the movies with me. |
| ¡Siempre estás hablando! No puedo estudiar **contigo**. | > | You are always talking! I can't study with you. |

## b The relative superlative

The relative superlative is used when we want to highlight an element or a quality over the rest. It is formed as follows:

**el/la/los/las** + noun + **más /menos** + adjective

> **de** + a group
>
> **que** + sentence

the + adjective + "-est" + noun
the + most + adjective + noun

> in (of) + a group
>
> that + sentence

Berta es **la** muchacha **más** alta **de** su clase. | > | *Berta is the tallest girl in her class.*
Estos son **los** trenes **más** rápidos **que** he visto. | > | *These are the fastest trains (that) I have seen.*

When the context makes clear the group of reference, we don't have to mention it:

Conozco a esas personas pero no sé quién es **la más inteligente**. (de ellas)
*I know those people but I don't know who is the most intelligent (of them).*

As with comparatives, there are some adjectives and adverbs whose superlative form is irregular:

| | | | |
|---|---|---|---|
| bueno / bien | ·······➤ | **el / la mejor, los / las mejores** | *the best* |
| malo / mal | ·······➤ | **el / la peor, los / las peores** | *the worst* |
| grande | ·······➤ | **el / la mayor, los / las mayores** | *the biggest/the oldest* |
| pequeño | ·······➤ | **el / la menor, los / las menores** | *the smallest/the youngest* |

Ha sido **la mejor** obra de teatro que he visto. | > | *It has been the best play I've ever seen.*

Fue **el peor** partido que jugamos. | > | *It was the worst game (that) we played.*

Enrique y Carlos son **los** hermanos **mayores**. | > | *Enrique and Carlos are the older brothers.*

**Las menores** de la clase son Rita y Lourdes. | > | *The youngest (students) in the class are Rita and Lourdes.*

SpanishEasyAndFun.com

**a** Match the expressions with their meanings.

1. ¡Qué muchacho tan listo!
2. ¡Qué suerte tenemos!
3. ¡Qué feliz soy!
4. ¡Qué ojos más bonitos!
5. ¡Qué sillón más cómodo!

a. What a comfortable armchair!
b. How happy I am!
c. What beautiful eyes!
d. What a clever boy!
e. How lucky we are!

**b** Complete the sentences with the suitable preposition: **a, con, contra, de, en, entre, hacia, para, por, sin.**

1. Esos caramelos son _____ ti.
2. ¿_____ ustedes les gusta el fútbol?
3. Ellos jugaron _____ nosotros.
4. Delante _____ mí hay una señorita.
5. Te amo. No puedo vivir _____ ti.
6. Lo recogeré e iré _____ él al cine.
7. El camión se dirige _____ ti.
8. Hay una mesa _____ tú y yo.
9. Yo no tenía tiempo y ella hizo el ejercicio _____ mí.
10. Pedro está muy interesado _____ ella.

**c** Fill in the gaps with the suitable expression: **el mejor, la mejor, el peor, la peor, la mayor.**

1. Este es _____ salmón que he comido. Está delicioso.
2. Ella es _____ estudiante de la clase. No aprueba ninguna asignatura.
3. Adela es _____ de las hermanas. Ya tiene 87 años.
4. Es _____ película que he visto este año. Los actores son muy buenos.
5. Ese es _____ auto que he tenido. Siempre está averiado.

• • • • • • • • • • • • • • • • • • • • • • • • • • • • • • • • • • • • • • • • • •

# Unidad 28
## Chichén Itzá

### En esta unidad estudiaremos:

◉ **Diálogo**

◉ **Hablemos español:**
  **a)** Expressing certainty and probability. **b)** Expressing future plans and intentions. **c)** "Ir a + infinitive». **d)** "Querer + infinitive".
  **e)** Vocabulario: El medio ambiente (The environment).

◉ **Gramática fácil:**
  **a)** The future tense. **b)** The future tense: time markers.
  **c)** Combining pronouns.

◉ **Ejercicios**

---

*Lucía ve a Mauricio distribuyendo la basura en distintos recipientes.*

Lucía: Veo que estás seleccionando la basura.

Mauricio: Sí. En un cubo pongo los **residuos orgánicos**, en otro pongo los **residuos plásticos** y en otro, el papel. Así **se podrán reciclar**.

L: Sí. Tenemos que ser más **ecológicos**.

M: **La semana que viene iré** a una conferencia sobre el **medio ambiente** y el **cambio climático**. **Vendrá** un experto a explicar la situación actual. **Probablemente será** un científico importante. ¿**Quieres venir** conmigo?

L: **Seguro que** es interesante. Sí, **iré** también a esa conferencia. **Quiero estar** informada de cosas que **van a** afectarnos directamente.

M: Este experto **hablará** de la **deforestación**, el uso de la **energía solar** y la capa de ozono. Si no cambiamos nuestra forma de vida, dentro de cien años no **habrá** bosques, muchas especies animales **desaparecerán** y los **residuos tóxicos serán** un gran problema.

L: Sí, la situación **será** terrible.

M: Entonces, ¿me **acompañarás**?

L: Sí. ¿Cuándo es?

M: **El próximo miércoles por la tarde**, a las siete. Es en el auditorio.

L: Bien. Como no tengo auto, **vendré** aquí y nos vamos juntos. ¿De acuerdo? Pero antes **voy a** llamar a mi madre para decirle que mi hijo **se quedará** con ella mientras estoy en la conferencia. **Se lo diré** mañana.

El Castillo, Chichén Itzá, México.

*Lucía sees Mauricio sorting the trash into different bins.*

*Lucía: I can see you are sorting the trash.*
*Mauricio: Yes, I put the biodegradable trash in one bin, the plastic trash in another and the paper in another one. Then they can be recycled.*
*L: Yes. Yes. We have to be more ecological.*
*M: Next week I am attending a conference about the environment and climate change. An expert is coming to explain the current situation. He will probably be an important scientist. Would you like to come with me?*

*L: It could be interesting. Yes, I'll go to that conference. I want to be informed about things that are going to affect us directly.*
*M: This expert will speak about deforestation, the use of solar energy and the ozone layer. If we don't change our way of life, in a hundred years there will be no forests, many animal species will disappear and toxic waste will become a big problem.*
*L: Yes, the situation will be terrible.*
*M: Then, will you come with me?*
*L: Yes. When is it?*
*M: Next Wednesday evening, at seven. It's in the auditorium.*
*L: Good, but since I don't have a car, I'll come here and we can go together. Is that okay? But before I will call my mother and tell her that my son will stay with her while I am at the conference. I'll tell her tomorrow.*

# Hablemos español

## a  Expressing certainty and probability

In order to express certainty about a future action or event we may use:

### Seguro que + present tense

| | |
|---|---|
| **Seguro que** mañana <u>hace</u> sol. | > | *It will be sunny tomorrow.* |
| **Seguro que** ella no me <u>llama</u>. | > | *I'm sure that she won't call me.* |
| **Seguro que** <u>almorzamos</u> habichuelas. | > | *I'm sure that we will have beans for lunch.* |

But if we are not sure that the action will happen we can say:

**probablemente + future tense**      if the action is probable to happen
**posiblemente + future tense**       if the action is possible to happen

Ella **probablemente** <u>ganará</u>
el premio. Es la gran favorita.

>  *She will probably win the prize. She is the big favorite.*

Él **posiblemente** <u>estudiará</u> en
la universidad.

>  *He may study at university.*

## b  Expressing future plans and intentions

We can express future plans and intentions in different ways:

🔹 With the present and future tenses:

El sábado **voy/iré** al cine.

>  *Next Saturday I am going to the movies.*

El año próximo **compraré** un
apartamento.

>  *Next year I'm going to buy an apartment.*

🔹 With the forms "**ir a + infinitive**" or "**querer + infinitive**".

## c  Ir a + infinitive

🔹 "**Ir a + infinitive**" *(be going to)* is used when making plans.
Although the action will take place in the future, "ir" is conjugated in the present.

**Voy a** <u>comprar</u> un televisor nuevo.    >    *I am going to buy a new television.*
Ellos no **van a** <u>cenar</u> en casa.    >    *They are not going to have dinner at home.*

¿**Vas a** <u>ir</u> al centro de la ciudad?    >    *Are you going downtown?*
Nosotros **vamos a** <u>hacer</u> negocios    >    *We are going to do business with a*
con una empresa mexicana.    *Mexican firm.*

🔹 "**Ir a + infinitive**" is also used to express a future prediction when there is some
evidence that the action will take place.

Está nublado. **Va a** <u>llover</u>.    >    *It is cloudy. It's going to rain.*

## d "Querer + infinitive"

"**Querer + infinitive**" *(want to + infinitive)* is used when expressing intentions.

**Quiero** <u>leer</u> ese libro.    >    *I want to read that book.*
¿**Quieres** <u>estudiar</u> japonés?    >    *Do you want to study Japanese?*
No **quiero** <u>hacer</u> nada.    >    *I don't want to do anything.*

## e Vocabulario: El medio ambiente (The environment)

**medio ambiente**: *environment*        **extinción**: *extinction*
**contaminar**: *to pollute*        **contaminación**: *pollution*
**residuos**: *waste*        **aguas residuales**: *sewage*
**ecológico**: *ecological*        **ecologista**: *ecologist*
**energía solar**: *solar energy*        **reciclar**: *to recycle*
**deforestación**: *deforestation*        **cambio climático**: *climate change*
**sustancias químicas**: *chemicals*        **calentamiento global**: *global warming*
**especies en peligro de extinción**: *endangered species*

Los ecologistas quieren conservar **especies en peligro de extinción**.
*Ecologists want to preserve endangered species.*

Esa empresa va a **reciclar** muchos **residuos**.
*That firm is going to recycle a lot of waste.*

# Gramática fácil

## a   The future tense

The future simple has the same endings for all verbs. These endings are:
Ex: **cantar** *(to sing)*.

|  | ENDING | VERB FORM |  |
|---|---|---|---|
| yo | **–é** | cantar**é** | *I will sing* |
| tú | **–ás** | cantar**ás** | *you will sing* |
| usted | **–á** | cantar**á** | *you will sing (formal)* |
| él | **–á** | cantar**á** | *he will sing* |
| ella | **–á** | cantar**á** | *she will sing* |
| nosotros/as | **–emos** | cantar**emos** | *we will sing* |
| vosotros/as | **– éis** | cantar**éis** | *you (all) will sing* |
| ustedes | **–án** | cantar**án** | *you (all) will sing* |
| ellos/as | **–án** | cantar**án** | *they will sing* |

| Miguel **hablará** en la reunión. | > | *Miguel will speak at the meeting.* |
|---|---|---|
| Mañana no **me levantaré** temprano. | > | *I won't get up early tomorrow.* |
| No **compraremos** ese auto. | > | *We won't buy that car.* |
| ¿Qué **estudiarán** ellos? | > | *What will they study?* |

But there are some verbs that have a change in the stem. Since the endings remain the same as for all the other verbs, we show only the "yo" form.

| | | |
|---|---|---|
| decir: **diré** | caber: **cabré** | hacer: **haré** |
| haber: **habré** | poder: **podré** | poner: **pondré** |
| saber: **sabré** | querer: **querré** | salir: **saldré** |
| tener: **tendré** | valer: **valdré** | venir: **vendré** |

| ¿**Podrás** venir a la fiesta? | > | *Will you be able to come to the party?* |
|---|---|---|
| No sé lo que **haremos** todavía. | > | *I don't know what we will do yet.* |
| Con este abrigo **tendrás** frío. | > | *With this coat you will be cold.* |
| Ellos no **dirán** nada. | > | *They will not say anything.* |

The future tense in Spanish may also be equivalent to *"be going to + infinitive"* or the present continuous in English .

| ¿Qué **harás** esta tarde? | > | *What <u>are you going to</u> do this afternoon?* |
|---|---|---|
| Mañana **almorzaré** con José. | > | *Tomorrow <u>I am having</u> lunch with José.* |

SpanishEasyAndFun.com

- The future tense is used to say what "will" happen or to make a future prediction.

Ellos **vendrán** el próximo mes.  >  *They will come next month.*
**Compraré** vino para la comida.  >  *I will buy some wine for the meal.*
Mañana **lloverá**.  >  *It will rain tomorrow.*

- The future of the impersonal form "hay" is "**habrá**" *(there will be)*.

**Habrá** mucha gente en el estadio.  >  *There will be a lot of people at the stadium.*
¿Qué **habrá** en esa caja?  >  *What will there be in that box?*

## b  The future tense: time markers

Some of the time expressions that are found with the future tense are:

**después**: *later*
**mañana**: *tomorrow*
**en el futuro**: *in the future*
**la próxima semana**: *next week*
**el próximo año**: *next year*

**más tarde**: *later*
**la próxima vez**: *next time*
**dentro de dos años**: *in two years*
**el próximo mes**: *next month*

**el/la próximo/a** + period of time = **el/la** + period of time + **que viene**

**El año que viene** iré a Brasil.  >  *Next year I will go to Brazil.*
¿Vendrás **después**?  >  *Will you come later?*
**Mañana** arreglaré el auto.  >  *I will fix the car tomorrow.*
Nos reuniremos **la próxima semana**. >  *We will meet next week.*

## c  Combining pronouns

🔹 There are **verbs** that may be combined with both a **direct object** and an **indirect object**. When both objects are pronouns and occur in a sentence, the indirect object is always placed before the direct object and both precede the verb.

$$\textbf{I.O.} \quad + \quad \textbf{D.O.} \quad + \quad \textbf{VERB}$$

Ella <u>me</u> regaló un libro           She gave me a book

Ella <u>me</u> <u>lo</u> regaló           She gave it to me
     I.O.  D.O.

| | | |
|---|---|---|
| Te lo dije | > | ("I said _it_ to <u>you</u>") |
| Me la compró | > | ("He bought _it_ for <u>me</u>") |

Rosa escribió una carta. ¿**Te la** mandó? > Rosa wrote a letter. Did she send it to you?

Juan pintó unos cuadros pero no **me los** enseñó. > Juan painted some pictures but he didn't show them to me.

Ellas leen unas revistas. Luego **nos las** darán. > They are reading some magazines. They will give them to us later.

🔹 When the indirect object pronouns "le" or "les" combine with a direct object pronoun (lo, la, los, las), "le" and "les" change into "se":

| | | | | | |
|---|---|---|---|---|---|
| le + lo | = | **se lo** | les + lo | = | **se lo** |
| le + la | = | **se la** | les + la | = | **se la** |
| le + los | = | **se los** | les + los | = | **se los** |
| le + las | = | **se las** | les + las | = | **se las** |

Ella **se la** vendió (la casa, a él). > She sold it to him (the house, to him).

No **se los** compro (los libros, para ustedes). > I don't buy them for you (the books, for them).

Yo **se las** he enviado (las cartas, a ella). > I have sent them to her (the letters, to her).

SpanishEasyAndFun.com

**a** Fill in the gaps with the verb in the future tense.

1. El año que viene todo _____ diferente. (ser)
2. Ellos no _____ más alcohol. (beber)
3. Ustedes _____ mucho dinero en ropa. (gastar)
4. Nosotros _____ a hablar chino. (aprender)
5. Tú _____ con nosotros a la fiesta (venir).
6. ¿Dónde _____, María? (estar)
7. Mañana nosotros _____ para Madrid. (salir)
8. Yo (poner) _____ la mesa y luego nosotros _____ (comer)
9. ¿A qué hora _____ tú? (venir)
10. ¿Quién _____ el vino? (comprar)

**b** Match the sentences with their meanings.

1. Él va a comprar una computadora.
2. ¿Queréis venir a la fiesta?
3. No vamos a subir al tren.
4. Ellos quieren visitarnos en julio.
5. ¿Qué vas a hacer?

a. What are you going to do?
b. Do you want to come to the party?
c. No, no es un libro.
d. They want to visit us in July.
e. He is going to buy a computer.

**c** Complete the sentences with both direct and indirect object pronouns.
(Ex.: Ella le puso el abrigo al bebé. – Ella **se lo** puso.)

1. Enviamos las cartas a tus primos. ____ ____ enviamos.
2. Ella dará un regalo a sus padres. ____ ____ dará.
3. Escribí una nota para Inés. ____ ____ escribí.
4. Pedro llevó un libro a Roberto. ____ ____ llevó.
5. Yo traje una revista para ti. ____ ____ traje.

# Unidad 29
## Ibiza

**En esta unidad estudiaremos:**

⦿ **Diálogo**

⦿ **Hablemos español:**
    **a)** The prepositions "para" and "por". **b)** Uses of the preposition "para".
    **c)** Uses of the preposition "por". **d)** Vocabulario: En el hotel (At the hotel).

⦿ **Gramática fácil:**
    **a)** Infinitives used as nouns. **b)** Ordinal numbers.

⦿ **Ejercicios**

*Gerardo llega a un hotel y habla con la recepcionista.*

Recepcionista: Buenas tardes! ¡Bienvenido!
Gerardo: Gracias. ¡Buenas tardes! Querría una habitación **para** esta noche, **por favor**.
R: ¿La tiene reservada?
G: No, no hice ninguna **reserva**.
R: ¿Quiere una **habitación sencilla** o **doble**?
G: Bueno, en realidad somos tres personas.
R: No tenemos habitaciones **para** tres personas, pero pueden ocupar una **habitación sencilla** y una **doble**.
G: ¿Cuánto cuestan?
R: 2.500 pesos **por** noche la **habitación sencilla** y 3.000 pesos la **doble**.
G: **Por** mí, está bien. **Reservo** las dos. ¿Puedo pagar con tarjeta de crédito?
R: **¡Por supuesto!** Aceptamos Visa y American Express.
G: Una cosa más. Yo necesito silencio **para** dormir. **Descansar** bien es muy importante para mí.
R: No se preocupe. Las habitaciones están insonorizadas **para** no escuchar ningún ruido. ¿Las habitaciones son **para** una noche o **para** más noches?
G: Solo **para** esta noche. Hemos venido **a descansar** y mañana tenemos que continuar el viaje. Vamos **para** la costa.
R: Bien. Necesito su pasaporte. Se lo devolveré **por** la mañana.
G: Aquí tiene.
R: ¿Puede firmar aquí? [Gabriel firma] Muy bien. Son las habitaciones 302 y 308, en la **tercera planta**, la **primera** y **cuarta** habitación a la derecha. Estas son las **llaves**.
G: Gracias.

🖐 SpanishEasyAndFun.com

Playa Cala Escondida, Ibiza, España.

*Gerardo has arrived at a hotel and is speaking to the receptionist.*

Receptionist: Good afternoon! Welcome!
Gerardo: Thank you. Good afternoon! I'd like a room for tonight, please.

R: Do you have a reservation?
G: No, I didn't make a reservation.
R: Would you like a single or a double room?
G: Well, in fact we are three people.
R: We don't have rooms for three people, but you can book a single room and a double room.
G: How much are they?
R: The single room is 2,500 pesos and the double room is 3,000 pesos per night .
G: For me it's okay. Then I'll book both of them. Can I pay by credit card?
R: Of course! We take Visa and American Express.
G: One more thing. I need quiet to sleep. Having a good nights sleep is very important to me.
R: Don't worry. The rooms are soundproofed to not hear any outside noises. Are the rooms for one or more nights?
G: Only for tonight. We have come to rest and tomorrow we have to continue with our trip.We are going to the coast.
R: Okay, I need your passport. I'll give it back to you in the morning.
G: Here you are.
R: Can you sign here? [Gerardo signs] Alright. They are rooms 302 and 308, on the third floor, the first and fourth rooms on the right. These are the keys.

G: Thank you.

# Hablemos español

## a   The prepositions "para" and "por"

The prepositions **"para"** and **"por"** are sometimes confusing for students of Spanish. In a very general sense **"para"** implies "destination" and **"por"** implies "source".

## b   Uses of the preposition "para"

**"Para"** has the following basic meanings:

🔵 **Destination or goal.**

| | |
|---|---|
| Parto **para** Cancún mañana. | > *I am leaving for Cancun tomorrow.* |
| Vamos **para** la oficina. | > *We are going to the office.* |
| Este regalo es **para** Susana. | > *This gift is for Susana.* |

🔵 **Purpose ("para + infinitive").**

| | |
|---|---|
| Tienes que estudiar **para** aprender. | > *You have to study in order to learn.* |
| Necesito un cuchillo **para** cortar pan en rodajas. | > *I need a knife to cut the bread in el slices.* |
| Tenemos que trabajar **para** pagar las facturas. | > *We have to work in order to pay the bills.* |

🔹 When this infinitive is negated, "no" is added between "para" and the "infinitive"

| | |
|---|---|
| Me quité los zapatos **para** no hacer ruido. | > *I took off my shoes to not make any noise.* |

🔹 The expression **"a + infinitive"** can sometimes be similar to **"para + infinitive"** in order to express purpose.

| | |
|---|---|
| He venido **a** ayudarte = He venido **para** ayudarte. | > *I have come to help you.* |

🔹 When a noun is placed after **"para"** we indicate "use" or "suitability":

| | |
|---|---|
| Esos platos son **para** el postre. | > *Those plates are for the dessert.* |
| Es un programa **para** niños. | > *It's a program for children.* |

🖐 SpanishEasyAndFun.com

Notice the difference between:

| | | |
|---|---|---|
| Una taza **de** café. | > | A cup of coffee. |
| Una taza **para** café. | > | A coffee cup, a cup for coffee. |

### To give a personal opinion.

| | | |
|---|---|---|
| **Para** <u>Sara</u>, nosotros estamos equivocados. | > | For Sara, we are wrong. |

## C   Uses of the preposition "por"

"**Por**" is used:

### To express approximate location (place or time).

In these cases "por" may be equivalent to *"by", "along", "during", "in", "over"* or *"through"*.

| | | |
|---|---|---|
| La oficina de correos está **por** <u>aquí</u>. | > | The post office is over here. |
| Mandé la carta **por** <u>correo</u>. | > | I sent the letter by mail. |
| Nosotros paseamos **por** <u>la ciudad</u>. | > | We walk through the city. |
| Llegamos **por** <u>la mañana</u>. | > | We arrived in the morning. |

### To express cause or reason.

| | | |
|---|---|---|
| No fuimos a la playa **por** <u>la lluvia</u>. | > | We didn't go to the beach because of the rain. |
| ¿**Por** <u>qué</u> has comprado eso? | > | Why have you bought that? |
| La castigaron **por** <u>llegar tarde</u>. | > | She was punished for being late. |

### To express exchange or substitution *(in exchange for / in place of).*

| | | |
|---|---|---|
| Yo lo compré **por** <u>mucho dinero</u>. | > | I bought it for a lot of money. |
| Ella habló **por** <u>su marido</u>. | > | She spoke for her husband. |

### To express the agent of an action.

| | | |
|---|---|---|
| La película fue dirigida **por** <u>Almodóvar</u>. | > | The film was directed by Almodóvar. |
| Don Quijote fue escrito **por** <u>Cervantes</u>. | > | Don Quixote was written by Cervantes. |

- **After certain verbs of motion, it means "in search of".**

| | | |
|---|---|---|
| Ella fue (a) **por** leche. | > | She went for milk. |
| Vengo (a) **por** las sillas. | > | I have come for the chairs. |

- **In some idiomatic expressions:**

| | |
|---|---|
| **por favor** | please |
| **por fin** | at last |
| **por ahora** | for the time being |
| **por casualidad** | by chance |
| **por cierto** | by the way |
| **por lo menos** | at least |
| **por lo tanto / por eso** | therefore |
| **por ejemplo** | for example |
| **por escrito** | in writing |
| **por lo general** | in general |
| **por lo visto** | apparently |
| **por supuesto** | of course |
| **¡Por Dios!** | For God's sake! |

| | | |
|---|---|---|
| **Por ahora** no tengo tiempo para ir al gimnasio. | > | For the time being I have no time to go to the gym. |
| No estaba invitado a la fiesta. **Por eso** no fui. | > | I wasn't invited to the party. Therefore, I didn't go. |

## d  Vocabulario:  En el hotel (At the hotel)

**vestíbulo**: lobby
**botones**: bellboy
**ascensor**: elevator
**reservar**: to book, to make a reservation
**reserva(ción)**: booking, reservation
**piso, planta**: floor
**llave magnética**: key card
**servicio de habitaciones**: room service
**registrarse**: to check in
**molestar**: to disturb
**hotel de tres estrellas**: three-star hotel

**recepción**: front desk
**recepcionista**: receptionist
**habitación sencilla**: single room
**habitación doble**: double room
**habitación disponible**: vacancy
**cancelar**: to cancel
**servicio de lavandería**: laundry service
**caja de seguridad**: safe
**registrar la salida**: to check out
**quedarse, permanecer**: to stay

# Gramática fácil

## a Infinitives used as nouns

The infinitive is the verb form that Spanish uses as a noun. Therefore it can be the subject or object of another verb:

| | | |
|---|---|---|
| **Ver** <u>es</u> **creer.** | > | *Seeing is believing.* |
| **Fumar** <u>es</u> dañino. | > | *Smoking is harmful.* |
| **Dormir** bien <u>es</u> necesario. | > | *Sleeping well is necessary.* |
| Me <u>gusta</u> **cantar**. | > | *I like singing.* |

## b Ordinal numbers

Ordinal numbers tell us the order or position of objects or elements.

Esta es la **cuarta** vez que vengo (he venido). > *This is the fourth time I have come here.*

El martes es el **segundo** día laborable de la semana. > *Tuesday is the second workday of the week.*

In Spanish, ordinal numbers are used most commonly for the numbers 10 and under. For larger numbers it is common to use cardinal numbers, especially in conversation.

| | | | |
|---|---|---|---|
| 1º | **primero** | 6º | **sexto** |
| 2º | **segundo** | 7º | **séptimo** |
| 3º | **tercero** | 8º | **octavo** |
| 4º | **cuarto** | 9º | **noveno** |
| 5º | **quinto** | 10º | **décimo** |

El rey Enrique VIII (octavo) tuvo seis esposas. > *King Henry VIII had six wives.*

Ayer celebramos nuestro 45º (cuarenta y cinco) aniversario. > *Yesterday we celebrated our 45th anniversary.*

Ordinal numbers are adjectives that have to agree in gender and number with the noun they modify:

Este es el **primer** <u>cuadro</u> que pinté. > *This is the first picture that I painted.*

| | | |
|---|---|---|
| Ella estará de viaje (durante) la **primera** semana de abril. | > | She will be on a trip for the first week of April. |
| Ya están llegando los **primeros** niños a la escuela. | > | The first children are already arriving at the school. |
| Son las **primeras** cartas que he recibido. | > | They are the first letters that I have received. |

🔷 When **"primero"** and **"tercero"** are followed by a singular masculine noun, the final "-o" is dropped:

| | | |
|---|---|---|
| Miguel es el **primer** mexicano que conocí. | > | Miguel is the first Mexican that I met. |
| Este es el **tercer** reloj que he comprado este año. | > | This is the third watch that I have bought this year. |

🔷 Ordinal numbers are represented by the cardinal number and the letter "o" in masculine or "a" in feminine. These forms are equivalent to "st", "nd", "rd" or "th" in English.

| | | | | |
|---|---|---|---|---|
| **1º – 1ª** | 1st | | **3º – 3ª** | 3rd |
| **2º – 2ª** | 2nd | | **15º – 15ª** | 15th |

🔷 Ordinal numbers can also function as pronouns. In this case, the articles "el, la, los, las" are used before the ordinal number. In English you use the pronouns "one/ones":

| | | |
|---|---|---|
| Hay dos muchachos en una fila. El **primero** es alto pero el **segundo** es bajo. | > | There are two boys in a row. The first one is tall but the second one is short. |

🖐 SpanishEasyAndFun.com

**a** Complete the sentences with **"para"** or **"por"**.

**1** ¿Tenéis algún plan _____ hoy?
**2** Esta noticia la he oído _____ la radio.
**3** Hicimos un viaje _____ toda Europa.
**4** Él trabaja _____ una empresa japonesa.
**5** Nosotros no pudimos viajar _____ la niebla.
**6** El alcohol no es bueno _____ la salud.
**7** Mándame _____ fax tus datos personales.
**8** Estos zapatos son buenos _____ la lluvia.
**9** Necesito dinero _____ comprar ropa.
**10** Cambié la computadora antigua _____ una más moderna.

**b** Choose the right infinitive to fill in the gaps: **hablar, aprender, ganar, comer, pintar, buscar, beber, ir, jugar, ver, viajar.**

**1** _____ al fútbol es su gran pasión.
**2** No es bueno _____ mucho café.
**3** Estoy muy interesado en _____ por África.
**4** Él sueña con _____ la lotería.
**5** A nosotros nos gusta _____ al cine los fines de semana.
**6** _____ palabras en un diccionario es bueno para _____ un idioma.
**7** _____ fruta es una costumbre saludable.
**8** Su gran problema es _____ en público.
**9** Solo pienso en . _____ a mi novia.
**10** _____ es una actividad muy creativa.

**c** Fill in the gaps with ordinal numbers:

**1** Marzo es el _____ mes del año.
**2** Él ya estuvo casado una vez. Este es su _____ matrimonio.
**3** Amstrong, Collins y Aldrin fueron los _____ hombres en llegar a la luna.
**4** La introducción está en las _____ páginas de un libro.
**5** El lunes es el _____ día laborable de la semana.

• • • • • • • • • • • • • • • • • • • • • • • • • • • • • • • • • • • •

**Key**

**a:** 1.- para; 2.- por; 3.- por; 4.- para; 5.- por; 6.- para; 7.- por; 8.- para; 9.- para; 10.- por.

**b:** 1.- jugar; 2.- beber; 3.- viajar; 4.- ganar; 5.- ir; 6.- buscar; aprender 7.- comer; 8.- hablar; 9.- ver; 10.- pintar.

**c:** 1- tercer; 2- segundo; 3- primeros; 4 – primeras; 5.- primer.

# Unidad 30
## Lago Titicaca

**En esta unidad estudiaremos:**

◉ **Diálogo**

◉ **Hablemos español:**
   **a)** Expressions on the telephone. **b)** Vocabulario: La salud y las enfermedades (Health and illnesses).

◉ **Gramática fácil:**
   **a)** The conditional mood. **b)** The absolute superlative.

◉ **Ejercicios**

---

*Felicidad llama por teléfono a su esposo, el Dr. López. Su ayudante recibe la llamada.*

Ayudante: **¿Sí? ¿Aló?**
Felicidad: ¡Buenas tardes!
A:  ¡Buenas tardes!
F:  **¿Podría hablar con** el Dr. López, **por favor?**
A:  Lo siento, pero el Dr. López **no está aquí en este momento**.
F:  Bueno. **¿Podría** decirle que llame a su hermana cuando llegue? Es **importantísimo**.
A:  No se preocupe. Se lo diré en cuanto llegue. **¿Quiere dejar algún otro mensaje** para él**?**
F:  Sí, dígale que ha llamado su esposa para decirle que su cuñado Juan ha tenido un accidente.
A:  **Espere en línea, por favor**. El doctor está llegando en este momento. **Le paso con** él.
F:  ¿Fermín?
Dr.:  Sí, soy yo.
F:  Soy Felicidad. Llamo para decirte que Juan ha tenido un accidente y ahora **está mareado** y **tiene vómitos**. Además, es **alérgico** a algunos **medicamentos** y no saben cuál puede tolerar.
Dr.:  Pero ¿qué le ha pasado?
F:  No lo sé. Tu hermana llamó muy nerviosa y solo me dijo eso. Llámala. Eso la tranquilizaría.
Dr.:  De acuerdo. La llamaré enseguida. Luego te contaré.

SpanishEasyAndFun.com

Islas flotantes de los Uros, Lago Titicaca, Puno, Perú.

*Felicidad called her husband Dr. López. His assistant answered the telephone.*

Assisstant: Hello?
Felicidad: Good afternoon!
A:   Good afternoon!
F:   Could I speak to Dr. López, please?
A:   I'm afraid Dr. López is not in at the moment.
F:   Okay. Could you tell him to phone his sister when he arrives? It's very important.
A:   Don't worry! I'll tell him as soon as he arrives. Would you like to leave any other message for him?
F:   Yes, tell him that his wife called to tell him that his brother-in-law has had an accident.
A:   Hold the line, please. The doctor is arriving right now. I'll put you through to him.
F:   Fermín?
Dr.: Speaking.
F:   This is  Felicidad. I'm calling to tell you that Juan has had an accident. Now he is dizzy and vomiting. He is also allergic to certain medications and they don't know which ones he can tolerate.
Dr.: But,what happened to him?
F:   I don't know. Your sister called me very nervous and  just told me that. Call her. It will calm her down.
Dr.: Alright. I'll call her right now.  Later I will tell you what happened.

# Hablemos español

## a  Expressions on the telephone

In this unit we will review some expressions that we can use when we make or receive a telephone call.

When the phone is ringing and we pick up the receiver we can say:

**¿Hola?**
**¿Aló?**
**¿Sí?**          *Hello?*
**¿Dígame?**
**¿Buenas?**

As a response we may hear:

| | |
|---|---|
| **Soy**... | *This is...* |
| **¿Puedo hablar con**..., por favor? | *May I speak to..., please?* |
| **¿Se puede poner**...? | *May I speak to...?* |

And we can answer:

| | |
|---|---|
| **Soy yo.** | *(Your name) Speaking.* |
| **Un momento, por favor**. | *Hang on / hold on / wait a second.* |
| **No está** en este momento. | *He/She is not in at the moment.* |

SpanishEasyAndFun.com

Let's review some other scenarios, and learn some common expressions used when speaking on the phone:

| | |
|---|---|
| **¿Quién (le) llama?** | *Who's calling?* |
| **¿De parte de quién?** | *Who's calling?* |
| **¿Con quién desea hablar?** | *Who would you like to speak to?* |
| **Se cortó/cayó la llamada.** | *The call was cut off.* |
| **Le paso (con)...** | *I'll put you through (to)...* |
| **Le llamo más tarde.** | *I'll call back later.* |
| **Espere en línea, por favor.** | *Hold the line, please/ please hold.* |
| **No se oye nada.** | *The line is dead.* |

With regard to messages, we can say:

| | |
|---|---|
| **¿Quiere dejar algún mensaje?** | *Would you like to leave a message?* |
| **¿Puedo tomar un mensaje?** | *Can I take a message?* |
| **Quiero dejar(le) un mensaje.** | *I would like to leave (him, her) a message.* |

When we make a call and no-one answers we may hear:

**Este es un contestador automático. Por favor, deje su mensaje después de la señal.**
*This is an answering machine. Please, leave your message after the beep.*

## b   Vocabulario: La salud y las enfermedades (Health and illnesses)

**salud**: *health*
**estar enfermo**: *to be ill/sick*
**tener fiebre**: *to have a fever/temperature*
**tener escalofríos**: *to have the shivers*
**tener la gripe**: *to have the flu*
**tener un resfriado**: *to have a cold*
**jarabe**: *syrup, cough medicine*
**dolor**: *pain, ache*
**dolor de cabeza**: *headache*
**romperse la pierna**: *to break one's leg*
**escayola**: *plaster cast*
**enfermera**: *nurse*
**quedarse en cama**: *to stay in bed*
**venda**: *bandage*
**tirita, curita**: *band-aid*
**remedio**: *cure*
**herida**: *injury, wound*

**enfermedad**: *illness, disease*
**estar mareado**: *to be dizzy*
**tener vómitos**: *to vomit*
**tener tos**: *to have a cough*
**tener diarrea**: *to have diarrhea*
**estornudar**: *to sneeze*
**ser alérgico a**: *to be allergic to*
**doler**: *to be in pain, to hurt*
**dolor de garganta**: *sore throat*
**ambulancia**: *ambulance*
**doctor, médico**: *doctor*
**cirujano**: *surgeon*
**receta**: *prescription*
**calmante**: *pain killer*
**pill**: *píldora*
**tablet**: *pastilla*
**termómetro**: *thermometer*

# Gramática fácil

## a The conditional mood

The conditional is used when referring to what somebody could or would do. It helps you talk about what would happen under certain circumstances.

🔘 As in the future, all verbs have the same endings that are added directly to the infinitive. They are conjugated as follows.

Ex: **jugar** *(to play)*.

|  | **ENDING** | **VERB FORM** |  |
|---|---|---|---|
| yo | **–ía** | jugar**ía** | *I would play* |
| tú | **–ías** | jugar**ías** | *you would play* |
| usted | **–ía** | jugar**ía** | *you would play (formal)* |
| él | **–ía** | jugar**ía** | *he would play* |
| ella | **–ía** | jugar**ía** | *she would play* |
| nosotros/as | **–íamos** | jugar**íamos** | *we would play* |
| vosotros/as | **-íais** | jugar**íais** | *you would play* |
| ustedes | **–ían** | jugar**ían** | *you (all) would play* |
| ellos/as | **–ían** | jugar**ían** | *they would play* |

| ¿Qué **tendrías** que hacer? | > | *What would you have to do?* |
|---|---|---|
| ¿Dónde les **gustaría** ir a ustedes? | > | *Where would you like to go?* |
| En su casa él **cocinaría** para todos. | > | *In his house he would cook for everyone.* |

🔘 If the verb has an irregular stem in the future, the same irregularity will remain in the conditional.

| decir | **diría** | cabe: | **cabría** | hacer | **haría** | haber | **habría** |
|---|---|---|---|---|---|---|---|
| poder | **podría** | poner | **pondría** | saber | **sabría** | querer | **querría** |
| salir | **saldría** | tener | **tendría** | valer | **valdría** | venir | **vendría** |

| ¿Qué le **diría** usted al presidente? | > | *What would you tell the president?* |
|---|---|---|
| Yo no **podría** ser actor. | > | *I couldn't be an actor.* |
| ¿Qué **harías** para conseguir un trabajo? | > | *What would you do to get a job?* |

🔘 The conditional is used to express the idea that in the past somebody thought or said something that would happen in the future.

| Ellos dijeron que **vendrían** con nosotros, pero no lo hicieron. | > | *They said (that) they would come with us, but they didn't.* |
|---|---|---|
| Yo pensé que **comprarías** el otro diccionario. | > | *I thought( that) you would buy the other dictionary.* |

SpanishEasyAndFun.com

In polite requests we often use the conditional form of "poder":

¿**Podría** decirme la hora, por favor?   >   *Could you tell me the time, please?*
¿**Podría** ayudarme, por favor?   >   *Could you help me, please?*

## b   The absolute superlative

Spanish has a form of the superlative, known as "the absolute superlative", which indicates that a person or thing possesses a quality to an unusual or extraordinary degree.

It is formed as follows:

$$\text{adjective / adverb} + \text{-ísimo / -ísima / -ísimos / -ísimas}$$

In English, its equivalent construction is: "*very* or *extraordinarily + adjective / adverb*".

fácil   ·····>   **facilísimo**   *(extraordinarily easy)*

The ending "**-ísimo/a/os/as**" is added to the singular form of the adjectives and some adverbs but:

● When adjectives or adverbs end in a vowel, this vowel is dropped before adding "**-ísimo**":

caro   ·····>   **carísimo**            lenta   ·····>   **lentísima**
interesante   ·····>   **interesantísimo**      tarde   ·····>   **tardísimo**

Me compré unas botas **carísimas**.   >   *I bought a very expensive pair of boots.*

Me tengo que ir. Es **tardísimo**.   >   *I have to go. It's very late.*

● When adjectives or adverbs end in a consonant you simply add "**-ísimo**":

difícil   ·····>   **dificilísimo**            útil   ·····>   **utilísimo**

Ese ejercicio es **dificilísimo**.   >   *That exercise is extraordinarily difficult.*

● When adjectives end in "-ble", you replace this ending for "**-bilísimo**":

amable   ·····>   **amabilísimo/a**      agradable   ·····>   **agradabilísimo/a**

Roberto es un hombre **amabilísimo**.   >   *Roberto is a very kind man.*

When the adverb ends in "-mente", first we separate this ending, we add "**-ísima**" to the adjective and then we add "-mente".

rápidamente ·····> **rapidísimamente**    peligrosamente ·····> **peligrosísimamente**

There are a few adjectives and adverbs that undergo a minor change in the superlative absolute:

| | | | |
|---|---|---|---|
| rico | ri**qu**ísimo | fresco | fres**qu**ísimo |
| largo | lar**gu**ísimo | antiguo | anti**qu**ísimo |
| fuerte | fo**r**tísimo | nuevo | n**o**vísimo |
| joven | joven**c**ísimo | poco | po**qu**ísimo |
| cerca | cer**qu**ísima | lejos | le**j**ísimos |

| | | |
|---|---|---|
| Él es un hombre **riquísimo**. | > | *He is a very rich man.* |
| Su casa está **cerquísima**. | > | *His house is very near.* |
| Está oscuro y veo **poquísimo**. | > | *It's dark and I can see very little.* |
| Este edificio es **antiquísimo**. | > | *This building is extraordinarily old.* |

There are also some irregular superlative forms:

| | | | | |
|---|---|---|---|---|
| bueno | ·····> | **buenísimo** | or | **óptimo** |
| malo | ·····> | **malísimo** | or | **pésimo** |
| grande | ·····> | **grandísimo** | or | **máximo** |
| pequeño | ·····> | **pequeñísimo** | or | **mínimo** |

Fue un partido **pésimo** (or **malísimo**). > *It was a terrible game.*
Es un detalle **mínimo** (or **pequeñísimo**). > *It is an insignificant detail.*

Colloquially, you can also add the word "**súper**" before the adjective or adverb to express this type of superlative:

La casa es **grandísima** = La casa es **súper grande**.    *The house is very big.*
¡Es **tardísimo**! = ¡Es **súper tarde**!    *It's very late.*

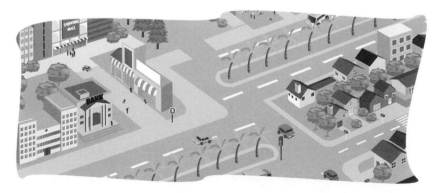

SpanishEasyAndFun.com

# Ejercicios de la **Unidad 30**

## a  Choose the correct answer:

Which expression do you use to ask "who's calling?" (on the telephone).

**1** ¿Con quién desea hablar?
**2** ¿De parte de quién?
**3** ¿Se puede poner?
**4** ¿Le llamo más tarde?
**5** ¿Con quién le paso?

## b  Match the expressions with their meanings.

**1** tener un resfriado
**2** tener gripe
**3** tener escalofríos
**4** tener fiebre
**5** tener tos

**a** to have a cough
**b** to have a flu
**c** to have a fever
**d** to have the shivers
**e** to have a cold

## b  Fill in the gaps with the correct form of the verbs, using the conditional mood.

**1** Ese cuadro (valer) _____ una fortuna.
**2** ¿Qué (hacer) _____ tú en mi lugar?
**3** Yo pensaba que ellos (tener) _____ más dinero.
**4** ¿Tú (bailar) _____ con él?
**5** ¿(poder) _____ usted decirme dónde está la ferretería?

## d  What is the absolute superlative form of the following adjectives or adverbs? (Ex: caro – **carísimo**)

**1** largo _____
**2** útil _____
**3** rico _____
**4** amable _____
**5** cerca _____

**Key**

**a:** 2.
**b:** 1.– e; 2.– b; 3.– d; 4.– c; 5.– a.
**c:** 1.– valdría; 2.– harías; 3.– tendrían; 4.– bailarías; 5.– Podría.
**d:** 1.– larguísimo; 2.– utilísimo; 3.– riquísimo; 4.– amabilísimo; 5.– cerquísima.

# Spanish Verbs

# HOW TO FORM THE PRESENT PARTICIPLE

## REGULAR VERBS

If the infinitive of the verb ends in -ar, the present participle is formed by replacing this ending by –ando.

Ex.: cantar – cant**ando**

In case the infinitive of the verb ends in -er or -ir, the present participle is formed by dropping these endings and replacing them by -iendo.

Ex.: hacer – hac**iendo**          escribir – escrib**iendo**

When necessary, to avoid the occurrence of three vowels together, the ending -iendo changes into -yendo.

Ex.: caer – ~~caiendo~~ – ca**yendo**          leer – ~~leiendo~~ – le**yendo**

oír – ~~oiendo~~ – o**yendo**          construir – ~~construiendo~~ - constru**yendo**

## IRREGULAR VERBS

Some verbs do not follow the rules quoted above and show other irregularities. Here are some of the most common ones:

conseguir – consiguiendo          corregir – corrigiendo
decir – diciendo          dormir – durmiendo
ir – yendo          morir – muriendo
pedir – pidiendo          poder – pudiendo
reír – riendo          repetir – repitiendo
seguir – siguiendo          sentir – sintiendo
servir – sirviendo          vestir – vistiendo

Among other functions, present participles are used to form continuous tenses:

No estás haciendo nada.          *You aren't doing anything.*
Silvia estaba sintiendo frío.          *Silvia was feeling cold.*

# HOW TO FORM THE PAST PARTICIPLE

## REGULAR VERBS

If the infinitive of the verb ends in -ar, the past participle is formed by replacing this ending by -ado.

Ex.: cantar – cant**ado**

In case the infinitive of the verb ends in -er or -ir, the past participle is formed by dropping these endings and replacing them by -ido.

Ex.: beber – beb**ido**        salir - sal**ido**

## IRREGULAR VERBS

Some verbs do not follow the rules quoted above and show other irregularities. Here are some of the most common ones:

| | |
|---|---|
| abrir – abierto | cubrir – cubierto |
| decir – dicho | descubrir – descubierto |
| devolver – devuelto | escribir – escrito |
| hacer – hecho | morir – muerto |
| poner – puesto | romper – roto |
| ver – visto | volver – vuelto |

Remember that, among other functions, past participles are used:
* To form compound tenses:
  Ellos han devuelto el dinero.        *They have given the money back.*

* To express the passive voice with the verb ser:
  Esos vehículos son fabricados        *Those vehicles are made*
  en Japón.        *in Japan.*

* To serve as adjectives, which must agree in gender and number with the noun they modify:
  Las puertas están abiertas.        *The doors are open.*
  El bebé está dormido.        *he baby is asleep.*

# AUXILIARY VERBS

**Auxiliary verbs** are very used in Spanish. There are four verbs that are considered auxiliary: haber, tener, estar and ser.

- **Haber** is used to form the compound tenses: pretérito perfecto de indicativo, pretérito pluscuamperfecto de indicativo, pretérito anterior, futuro perfecto, condicional compuesto, pretérito perfecto de subjuntivo and pretérito pluscuamperfecto de subjuntivo.

In all these tenses the verb **haber** is followed by a past participle.

The following tenses of **haber** are those used to form compound tenses:

## INDICATIVO

### PRESENTE

| | |
|---|---|
| (yo) | he |
| (tú) | has |
| (él/ella/usted) | ha |
| (nosotros) | hemos |
| (vosotros) | habéis |
| (ellos/ustedes) | han |

### PRETÉRITO IMPERFECTO

había
habías
había
habíamos
habíais
habían

### PRETÉRITO INDEFINIDO

| | |
|---|---|
| (yo) | hube |
| (tú) | hubiste |
| (él/ella/usted) | hubo |
| (nosotros) | hubimos |
| (vosotros) | hubisteis |
| (ellos/ustedes) | hubieron |

### FUTURO

habré
habrás
habrá
habremos
habréis
habrán

Example:

**He pintado** un cuadro hoy.
Cuando llegaste no **habíamos cenado** aún.

*I have painted a picture today.*
*When you arrived, we hadn't had dinner yet.*

SpanishEasyAndFun.com

# CONDICIONAL

## CONDICIONAL SIMPLE

| | |
|---|---|
| (yo) | habría |
| (tú) | habrías |
| (él/ella/usted) | habría |
| (nosotros) | habríamos |
| (vosotros) | habríais |
| (ellos/ustedes) | habrían |

# SUBJUNTIVO

## PRESENTE

| | |
|---|---|
| (yo) | haya |
| (tú) | hayas |
| (él/ella/usted) | haya |
| (nosotros) | hayamos |
| (vosotros) | hayáis |
| (ellos/ustedes) | hayan |

## PRETÉRITO IMPERFECTO (*)

hubiera / hubiese
hubieras / hubieses
hubiera / hubiese
hubiéramos / hubiésemos
hubierais / hubieseis
hubieran / hubiesen

(*) There are two forms, and both are correct.

- **Tener** is used as an auxiliary verb with the same meaning as **haber**, in certain contexts, when it forms the compound tenses. It is also followed by a past participle. Here are the simple tenses of the verb **tener** used to form compound tenses.

## INDICATIVO

### PRESENTE

| (yo) | tengo |
|---|---|
| (tú) | tienes |
| (él/ella/usted) | tiene |
| (nosotros) | tenemos |
| (vosotros) | tenéis |
| (ellos/ustedes) | tienen |

### PRETÉRITO IMPERFECTO

tenía
tenías
tenía
teníamos
teníais
tenían

### PRETÉRITO INDEFINIDO

| (yo) | tuve |
|---|---|
| (tú) | tuviste |
| (él/ella/usted) | tuvo |
| (nosotros) | tuvimos |
| (vosotros) | tuvisteis |
| (ellos/ustedes) | tuvieron |

### FUTURO

tendré
tendrás
tendrá
tendremos
tendréis
tendrán

Example:

**Tengo oído** que el director dimitirá.          *I have heard the director will resign.*

           SpanishEasyAndFun.com

# CONDICIONAL

## CONDICIONAL SIMPLE

| | |
|---|---|
| (yo) | tendría |
| (tú) | tendrías |
| (él/ella/usted) | tendría |
| (nosotros) | tendríamos |
| (vosotros) | tendríais |
| (ellos/ustedes) | tendrían |

# SUBJUNTIVO

## PRESENTE

| | | PRETÉRITO IMPERFECTO (*) |
|---|---|---|
| (yo) | tenga | tuviera / tuviese |
| (tú) | tengas | tuvieras / tuvieses |
| (él/ella/usted) | tenga | tuviera / tuviese |
| (nosotros) | tengamos | tuviéramos / tuviésemos |
| (vosotros) | tengáis | tuvierais / tuvieseis |
| (ellos/ustedes) | tengan | tuvieran / tuviesen |

(*) There are two forms, and both are correct.

Example:

Ojalá los estudiantes **tengan hechos** los deberes.

*I wish the students have done their homework.*

- **Estar** is used as an auxiliary verb when it is a part of continuous tenses. It is followed by a present participle.
  Here are the simple tenses of the verb **estar** used to form continuous tenses.

## INDICATIVO

**PRESENTE**

| | |
|---|---|
| (yo) | estoy |
| (tú) | estás |
| (él/ella/usted) | está |
| (nosotros) | estamos |
| (vosotros) | estáis |
| (ellos/ustedes) | están |

**PRETÉRITO IMPERFECTO**

estaba
estabas
estaba
estábamos
estabais
estaban

**PRETÉRITO INDEFINIDO**

| | |
|---|---|
| (yo) | estuve |
| (tú) | estuviste |
| (él/ella/usted) | estuvo |
| (nosotros) | estuvimos |
| (vosotros) | estuvisteis |
| (ellos/ustedes) | estuvieron |

**FUTURO**

estaré
estarás
estará
estaremos
estaréis
estarán

Example:

Supongo que **estarás viviendo** cómodamente.

*I suppose you are living comfortably.*

# CONDICIONAL

## CONDICIONAL SIMPLE

| | |
|---|---|
| (yo) | estaría |
| (tú) | estarías |
| (él/ella/usted) | estaría |
| (nosotros) | estaríamos |
| (vosotros) | estaríais |
| (ellos/ustedes) | estarían |

# SUBJUNTIVO

## PRESENTE

| | |
|---|---|
| (yo) | esté |
| (tú) | estés |
| (él/ella/usted) | esté |
| (nosotros) | estemos |
| (vosotros) | estéis |
| (ellos/ustedes) | estén |

## PRETÉRITO IMPERFECTO (*)

estuviera / estuviese
estuvieras / estuvieses
estuviera / estuviese
estuviéramos / estuviésemos
estuvierais / estuvieseis
estuvieran / estuviesen

(*) There are two forms, and both are correct.

Example:

No creemos que ellos **estén jugando** ahora.    *We don't think they are playing now.*

- **Ser** is used as an auxiliary verb to conjugate the passive voice of transitive verbs. It is followed by a past participle.

Here are the simple tenses of the verb **ser** used to form the passive voice.

## INDICATIVO

### PRESENTE

| (yo) | soy |
| (tú) | eres |
| (él/ella/usted) | es |
| (nosotros) | somos |
| (vosotros) | sois |
| (ellos/ustedes) | son |

### PRETÉRITO IMPERFECTO

| era |
| eras |
| era |
| éramos |
| erais |
| eran |

### PRETÉRITO INDEFINIDO

| (yo) | fui |
| (tú) | fuiste |
| (él/ella/usted) | fue |
| (nosotros) | fuimos |
| (vosotros) | fuisteis |
| (ellos/ustedes) | fueron |

### FUTURO

| seré |
| serás |
| será |
| seremos |
| seréis |
| serán |

Example:

Ese poema **fue escrito** por Neruda.     *That poem was written by Neruda.*
El desayuno **será servido** a las 2:00 p. m.     *Breakfast will be served at 2:00 p. m.*

SpanishEasyAndFun.com

# CONDICIONAL

## CONDICIONAL SIMPLE

| | |
|---|---|
| (yo) | sería |
| (tú) | serías |
| (él/ella/usted) | sería |
| (nosotros) | seríamos |
| (vosotros) | seríais |
| (ellos/ustedes) | serían |

# SUBJUNTIVO

## PRESENTE

| | |
|---|---|
| (yo) | sea |
| (tú) | seas |
| (él/ella/usted) | sea |
| (nosotros) | seamos |
| (vosotros) | seáis |
| (ellos/ustedes) | sean |

## PRETÉRITO IMPERFECTO (*)

fuera / fuese
fueras / fueses
fuera / fuese
fuéramos / fuésemos
fuerais / fueseis
fueran / fuesen

(*) There are two forms, and both are correct.

# REFLEXIVE VERBS

- Reflexive verbs are used to express actions that are performed on oneself. When conjugating reflexive verbs, reflexive pronouns (me, te, se, nos, os, se) must be placed just before the verbs and need to match with the corresponding subject pronoun.

  **Me lavo** todos los días.   *I wash myself every day.*

  Ella **se miraba** en el espejo.   *She looked at herself in the mirror.*

- In negative sentences, "no" must be used before the reflexive pronoun.

  **No te levantes** tarde.   *Don't get up late.*

  Mi abuelo **no se peina** porque es calvo.   *My grandfather doesn't comb himself because he is bald.*

- When we use reflexive verbs in the infinitive, reflexive pronouns must be attached to the end of the verb.

  Quiero **acostarme** temprano.   *I want to go to bed early.*

  Vamos a **sentirnos** felices en nuestra nueva casa.   *We are going to feel happy in our new house.*

  Ellos no desean **enojarse**.   *They don't want to get annoyed.*

Here are some of the most common reflexive verbs:

| | | | |
|---|---|---|---|
| aburrirse | *to get bored* | llamarse | *to be named* |
| acordarse | *to remember* | mirarse | *to look at oneself* |
| acostarse | *to go to bed / to lie down* | olvidarse | *to forget (about)* |
| afeitarse | *to shave oneself* | peinarse | *to comb oneself* |
| callarse | *to shut up* | ponerse | *to put on* |
| comprarse | *to buy (for oneself)* | presentarse | *to introduce oneself* |
| despedirse | *to say goodbye* | quitarse | *to take off* |
| despertarse | *to wake up* | sentirse | *to feel* |
| enojarse | *to get annoyed* | taparse | *to cover oneself up* |
| levantarse | *to get up* | volverse | *to become* |

# RECIPROCAL VERBS

- Reciprocal verbs are used to express actions performed and received by two or more people. When conjugating reciprocal verbs, we only use plural pronouns (nos, os, se). They need to match with the corresponding subject pronouns and are placed just before the verbs.

Mi hermano y mi cuñada **se aman**. *My brother and my sister-in-law love each other.*

**Nos hablamos** todos los días. *We talk to each other every day.*

Vosotros nunca **os peleáis**. *You never fight with each other.*

- In negative sentences, "no" must be used before the pronoun.

Están enfadados y **no se miran**. *They are angry and they don't look at each other.*

Estuvimos los dos en el concierto, pero **no nos vimos**. *We were both at the concert, but we didn't see each other.*

- When we use reciprocal verbs in the infinitive, the pronouns must be attached to the end of the verb.

Queremos **reunirnos** mañana temprano. *We want to meet early in the morning.*

Here are some of the most common reciprocal verbs:

| | | | |
|---|---|---|---|
| abrazarse | *to hug each other* | hablarse | *to talk to each other* |
| amarse | *to love each other* | llamarse | *to call each other* |
| ayudarse | *to help each other* | pelearse | *to fight to each other* |
| besarse | *to kiss each other* | reunirse | *to get together/to meet* |
| conocerse | *to get to know each other* | verse | *to see each other* |
| escribirse | *to write to each other* | | |

# ENDINGS OF SPANISH REGULAR VERBS

## INDICATIVO

### PRESENTE

|  | -AR | -ER | -IR |
|---|---|---|---|
| yo | -o | -o | -o |
| tú | -as | -es | -es |
| usted, él, ella | -a | -e | -e |
| nosotros/as | -amos | -emos | -imos |
| vosotros/as | -áis | -éis | -ís |
| ustedes, ellos, ellas | -an | -en | -en |

### PRESENTE CONTINUO

| yo | estoy | |
|---|---|---|
| tú | estás | |
| usted, él, ella | está | + gerund |
| nosotros/as | estamos | |
| vosotros/as | estáis | |
| ustedes, ellos, ellas | están | |

### PRETÉRITO INDEFINIDO

|  | -AR | -ER | -IR |
|---|---|---|---|
| yo | -é | -í | -í |
| tú | -aste | -iste | -iste |
| usted, él, ella | -ó | -ió | -ió |
| nosotros/as | -amos | -imos | -imos |
| vosotros/as | -asteis | -isteis | -isteis |
| ustedes, ellos, ellas | -aron | -ieron | -ieron |

### PRETÉRITO IMPERFECTO

|  | -AR | -ER | -IR |
|---|---|---|---|
| yo | -aba | -ía | -ía |
| tú | -abas | -ías | -ías |
| usted, él, ella | -aba | -ía | -ía |
| nosotros/as | -ábamos | -íamos | -íamos |
| vosotros/as | -abais | -íais | -íais |
| ustedes, ellos, ellas | -aban | -ían | -ían |

SpanishEasyAndFun.com

## PRETÉRITO PERFECTO

| | | |
|---|---|---|
| yo | he | |
| tú | has | |
| usted, él, ella | ha | |
| nosotros/as | hemos | + past participle |
| vosotros/as | habéis | |
| ustedes, ellos, ellas | han | |

## PRETÉRITO PLUSCUAMPERFECTO

| | | |
|---|---|---|
| yo | había | |
| tú | habías | |
| usted, él, ella | había | |
| nosotros/as | habíamos | + past participle |
| vosotros/as | habíais | |
| ustedes, ellos, ellas | habían | |

## FUTURO

| | | |
|---|---|---|
| yo | | −é |
| tú | | −ás |
| usted, él, ella | | −á |
| nosotros/as | infinitive + | −emos |
| vosotros/as | | −éis |
| ustedes, ellos, ellas | | −án |

## FUTURO PERFECTO

| | | |
|---|---|---|
| yo | habré | |
| tú | habrás | |
| usted, él, ella | habrá | |
| nosotros/as | habremos | + past participle |
| vosotros/as | habréis | |
| ustedes, ellos, ellas | habrán | |

# CONDICIONAL

## CONDICIONAL SIMPLE

| | | |
|---|---|---|
| yo | | −ía |
| tú | | −ías |
| usted, él, ella | infinitive + | −ía |
| nosotros/as | | −íamos |
| vosotros/as | | −íais |
| ustedes, ellos, ellas | | −ían |

## CONDICIONAL COMPUESTO

| | | |
|---|---|---|
| yo | habría | |
| tú | habrías | |
| usted, él, ella | habría | |
| nosotros/as | habríamos | + past participle |
| vosotros/as | habríais | |
| ustedes, ellos, ellas | habrían | |

# SUBJUNTIVO

## PRESENTE

| | −AR | −ER | −IR |
|---|---|---|---|
| yo | −e | −a | −a |
| tú | −es | −as | -as |
| usted, él, ella | −e | −a | −a |
| nosotros/as | −emos | −amos | −amos |
| vosotros/as | −éis | −áis | −áis |
| ustedes, ellos, ellas | −en | −an | −an |

## PRETÉRITO IMPERFECTO

| | −AR | −ER | −IR |
|---|---|---|---|
| yo | −ara/−ase | −iera/−iese | −iera/−iese |
| tú | −aras/−ases | −ieras/−ieses | −ieras/−ieses |
| usted, él, ella | −ara/−ase | −iera/−iese | −iera/−iese |
| nosotros/as | −áramos/−ásemos | −iéramos/−iésemos | −iéramos/−iésemos |
| vosotros/as | −arais/−aseis | −ierais/−ieseis | −ierais/−ieseis |
| ustedes, ellos, ellas | −aran/−asen | −ieran/−iesen | −ieran/−iesen |

SpanishEasyAndFun.com

## PRETÉRITO PERFECTO

| | | |
|---|---|---|
| yo | haya | |
| tú | hayas | |
| usted, él, ella | haya | |
| nosotros/as | hayamos | + past participle |
| vosotros/as | hayáis | |
| ustedes, ellos, ellas | hayan | |

## PRETÉRITO PLUSCUAMPERFECTO

| | | |
|---|---|---|
| yo | hubiera/hubiese | |
| tú | hubieras/hubieses | |
| usted, él, ella | hubiera/hubiese | |
| nosotros/as | hubiéramos/hubiésemos | + past participle |
| vosotros/as | hubierais/hubieseis | |
| ustedes, ellos, ellas | hubieran/hubiesen | |

# IMPERATIVO

## AFIRMATIVO

| | –AR | –ER | –IR |
|---|---|---|---|
| tú | –a | –e | –e |
| usted | –e | –a | –a |
| vosotros/as | –ad | –ed | –id |
| ustedes | –en | –an | –an |

## NEGATIVO

| | –AR | –ER | –IR |
|---|---|---|---|
| tú | –es | –as | –as |
| usted | –e | –a | –a |
| vosotros/as | –éis | –áis | –áis |
| ustedes | –en | –an | –an |

# "VOSOTROS" VERSUS "USTEDES" IN SPAIN'S SPANISH

We know that the second person plural in Spain's Spanish is different from that used in Latin America, which is the one that we have learned in this course.

The plural "you" is equivalent to "**vosotros, vosotras**" in Spain, when used informally, instead of "ustedes" (which is only used for formal treatment). The conjugation of the verbs for "ustedes" is the same as for "ellos, ellas", but it is different when we refer to "vosotros, vosotras". Here is a guide to show how to conjugate the different tenses for "**vosotros, vosotras**". The first person singular (yo) for each tense is also shown.

## INDICATIVO

### PRESENTE

#### VERBOS REGULARES

|            | *–ar (cantar)* | *–er (comer)* | *–ir (abrir)* |
|------------|----------------|---------------|---------------|
| yo         | canto          | como          | abro          |
| vosotros/as| **cantáis**    | **coméis**    | **abrís**     |

#### VERBOS IRREGULARES

|            | *ser*      | *estar*      |           |        |
|------------|------------|--------------|-----------|--------|
| yo         | soy        | estoy        |           |        |
| vosotros/as| **sois**   | **estáis**   |           |        |

|            | *pensar*   | *entender*   | *haber*   | *ir*   |
|------------|------------|--------------|-----------|--------|
| yo         | pienso     | entiendo     | he        | voy    |
| vosotros/as| **pensáis**| **entendéis**| **habéis**| **vais**|

### PRESENTE CONTINUO

|            | *hablar*             |
|------------|----------------------|
| yo         | estoy hablando       |
| vosotros/as| **estáis hablando**  |

## PRETÉRITO INDEFINIDO

### VERBOS REGULARES

| | *-ar (hablar)* | *–er (aprender)* | *–ir (escribir)* |
|---|---|---|---|
| yo | hablé | aprendí | escribí |
| vosotros/as | **hablasteis** | **aprendisteis** | **escribisteis** |

### VERBOS IRREGULARES

| | *pedir* | *ser* | *estar* | *hacer* |
|---|---|---|---|---|
| yo | pedi | fui | estuve | hice |
| vosotros/as | **pedisteis** | **fuisteis** | **estuvisteis** | **hicisteis** |

## PRETÉRITO IMPERFECTO

### VERBOS REGULARES

| | *hablar* | *aprender* | *escribir* |
|---|---|---|---|
| yo | hablaba | aprendía | escribía |
| vosotros/as | **hablabais** | **aprendíais** | **escribíais** |

### VERBOS IRREGULARES

| | *ser* | *ir* | *ver* |
|---|---|---|---|
| yo | era | iba | veía |
| vosotros/as | **erais** | **ibais** | **veíais** |

## PASADO CONTINUO

| | *hablar* |
|---|---|
| yo | estaba hablando |
| vosotros/as | **estabais hablando** |

## PRETÉRITO PERFECTO

| | *comprar* |
|---|---|
| yo | he comprado |
| vosotros/as | **habéis comprado** |

## PRETÉRITO PERFECTO CONTINUO

| | *comprar* |
|---|---|
| yo | he estado comprando |
| vosotros/as | **habéis estado comprando** |

| PRETÉRITO PLUSCUAMPERFECTO | | FUTURO | |
|---|---|---|---|
| | *comprar* | | *comprar* |
| yo | había comprado | yo | compraré |
| vosotros/as | **habíais comprado** | vosotros/as | **compraréis** |

## CONDICIONAL

| | SIMPLE | | COMPUESTO |
|---|---|---|---|
| | *comprar* | | *comprar* |
| yo | compraría | yo | habría comprado |
| vosotros/as | **compraríais** | vosotros/as | **habríais comprado** |

## SUBJUNTIVO

### PRESENTE

#### VERBOS REGULARES

| | *hablar* | *beber* | *vivir* |
|---|---|---|---|
| yo | hable | beba | viva |
| vosotros/as | **habléis** | **bebáis** | **viváis** |

#### VERBOS IRREGULARES

| | *volver* | *oír* | | | | |
|---|---|---|---|---|---|---|
| yo | vuelva | oiga | | | | |
| vosotros/as | **volváis** | **oigáis** | | | | |

| | *ser* | *ver* | *estar* | *saber* | *ir* | *haber* |
|---|---|---|---|---|---|---|
| yo | sea | vea | esté | sepa | vaya | haya |
| vosotros/as | **seáis** | **veáis** | **estéis** | **sepáis** | **vayáis** | **hayáis** |

#### PRETÉRITO IMPERFECTO

| | *hablar* | *beber* | *vivir* |
|---|---|---|---|
| yo | hablara or hablase | bebiera or bebiese | viviera or viviese |
| vosotros | **hablarais or hablaseis** | **bebierais or bebieseis** | **vivierais or vivieseis** |

SpanishEasyAndFun.com

## PRETÉRITO PERFECTO

| | *comprar* |
|---|---|
| yo | haya comprado |
| vosotros | **hayáis comprado** |

## PRETÉRITO PLUSCUAMPERFECTO

| | *comprar* |
|---|---|
| yo | hubiera comprado or hubiese comprado |
| vosotros | **hubierais comprado** or **hubieseis comprado** |

# IMPERATIVO

## VERBOS REGULARES

• AFFIRMATIVE SENTENCES:

| | *comer* | *escuchar* |
|---|---|---|
| vosotros | **comed** | **escuchad** |

• NEGATIVE SENTENCES:

| | *comer* | *escuchar* |
|---|---|---|
| vosotros | **no comáis** | **no escuchéis** |

## VERBOS IRREGULARES

• AFFIRMATIVE SENTENCES:

| | *hacer* | *tener* | *ir* | *venir* |
|---|---|---|---|---|
| vosotros | **haced** | **tened** | **id** | **venid** |

• NEGATIVE SENTENCES:

| | *hacer* | *tener* | *ir* | *venir* |
|---|---|---|---|---|
| vosotros | **no hagáis** | **no tengáis** | **no vayáis** | **no vengáis** |

The existence of this person (vosotros/as) in Spain's Spanish also implies:

**a)** Possessive adjectives and pronouns: **vuestro**, **vuestra**, **vuestros**, **vuestras** (*your*).

| | |
|---|---|
| Ese es vuestro amigo Andrés. | *That is your friend Andrés.* |
| Vuestras camisas están en el armario. | *Your shirts are in the wardrobe.* |

**b)** Reflexive pronoun: **os**

Vosotras os lavasteis el cabello con ese champú.  *You washed your hair with that shampoo.*

**c)** Indirect object pronoun: **os**

Os enseñaron la casa.  *You were shown the house.*

**d)** Direct object pronoun: **os**

Os vi en el parque.  *I saw you in the park.*

SpanishEasyAndFun.com

# USES OF THE DIFFERENT VERB TENSES IN SPANISH

## INDICATIVO (FORMAS SIMPLES)

### PRESENTE

This tense is used to talk about things that happen now, in the present. That is why we use this tense when we refer to facts, realities, current situations, etc.

Nosotros **trabajamos** como profesores.     *We work as teachers.*

### PRETÉRITO IMPERFECTO

This tense is used to talk about things that were habitual in the past, actions that were not completed, or characteristics and states that took place in the past.

Cuando **estaba** enamorado,     *When I was in love, I wrote love letters.*
**escribía** cartas de amor.

### PRETÉRITO INDEFINIDO

This tense is used to talk about past actions or states that have a clear ending point or when the action was completed.

Ayer **compré** un libro     *Yesterday I bought a very*
muy interesante.     *interesting book.*

### FUTURO

This tense is used to talk about actions that will take place in the future.

¿Qué **harás** mañana?     *What will you do tomorrow?*

# INDICATIVO (FORMAS COMPUESTAS)

## PRETÉRITO PERFECTO

This tense is used when we talk about actions that started and ended in the past, but very close to the moment we are talking about, as well as when we refer to past experiences, not saying when they took place.

Esta tarde **hemos visto** a Ricardo.

*We have seen Ricardo this afternoon.*

Nunca **he estado** en México.

*I have never been to Mexico.*

## PRETÉRITO PLUSCUAMPERFECTO

This tense is used to talk about an action that was completed before another action took place (or before a certain moment in the past), as well as to talk about actions that are implicit and happened in the past.

Fuimos al teatro porque ellos no **habían visto** esa obra.
*We went to the theater because they hadn't seen that play.*

## PRETÉRITO ANTERIOR

This tense is used to talk about an action that took place immediately before another one. This tense is not very common nowadays.

Cuando **hubimos terminado** nuestro trabajo, fuimos a dar un paseo.
*When we had finished our work, we went for a walk.*

## FUTURO PERFECTO

This tense is only used when we talk about future actions that will take place before another future action (or a certain moment in the future), as well as when we refer to actions that haven't happened yet, but we are very sure that they will happen.

**Habremos llegado** a Madrid antes del mediodía.
*We will have arrived in Madrid before noon.*

Estoy seguro de que mi hermana **habrá visitado** a mis primos.
*I am sure my sister will have visited my cousins.*

SpanishEasyAndFun.com

# CONDICIONAL

## CONDICIONAL SIMPLE

This tense is used to express desires, suggestions, advice, actions depending on a condition, hypothesis, or probabilities, among other situations.

Yo no lo **haría**. Es muy peligroso.
*I wouldn't do it. It's very dangerous.*

Si estuvieras en casa, me **ayudarías** a limpiarla.
*If you were at home, you would help me clean it.*

## CONDICIONAL COMPUESTO

This tense is used to talk about unreal past situations, that is, imaginary situations or desires that were never fulfilled. It is also used when you want to express that you would have done something in the past.

Si Juan hubiera estudiado más, **habría aprobado** el examen.
*If Juan had studied more, he would have passed the exam.*

Yo no **habría hecho** lo que hiciste tú.
*I wouldn't have done what you did.*

# SUBJUNTIVO

## PRESENTE

The present subjunctive is used in various ways; for example, it appears in all negative commands as well as all formal commands, and is used in dependent clauses to indicate doubt, among other functions.

Espero que ella **diga** la verdad.
*I hope she will tell the truth.*

No **abras** la ventana. Hace mucho frío.
*Don't open the window. It's very cold.*

## PRETÉRITO IMPERFECTO

This tense often refers to a previous experience, but can also refer to unlikely events or possibilities, doubts or wishes. It is also used in relative clauses with a non-existent, indefinite, or negated antecedent.

Quería que Carmen me **invitara** a su fiesta.
*I wanted Carmen to invite me to her party.*

Buscaba una casa que **tuviera** (o tuviese) un jardín.
*I was looking for house that had a garden.*

## PRETÉRITO PERFECTO

This tense is used to describe past actions that are connected to the present, as well as actions that will have happened by a certain moment in the future.

Es posible que ellos **hayan comprado** un vehículo nuevo.
*It's possible they have bought a new car.*

No creo que nos **hayamos visto** antes.
*I don't think we have seen each other before.*

## PRETÉRITO PLUSCUAMPERFECTO

This tense is used to talk about hypothetical situations in the past, past conditionals, and past actions that preceded other past actions.

Ojalá **hubieran (o hubiesen)** aprendido a nadar.
*I wish they had learned to swim.*

Si él **hubiera (o hubiese) tenido** mucho dinero, habría viajado por todo el mundo.
*If he had had a lot of money, he would have traveled around the world.*

# IMPERATIVO

This mood is used to give an order to someone, to suggest doing something, to provide recommendations, offer advice, prohibit actions or make a request.

**Olvida** lo que te dije.                    *Forget what I told you.*

**Juguemos** al tenis durante un rato.       *Let's play tennis for a while.*

No me **esperes**. Llegaré tarde.            *Don't wait for me. I'll arrive late.*

# REGULAR VERBS CONJUGATED IN ALL THE TENSES AND MOODS

| Infinitivo | Gerundio | Participio |
|---|---|---|
| hablar (-ar) | hablando | hablado |

## INDICATIVO

### PRESENTE

| (yo) | hablo |
|---|---|
| (tú) | hablas |
| (él/ella/usted) | habla |
| (nosotros) | hablamos |
| (vosotros) | habláis |
| (ellos/ustedes) | hablan |

### PRETÉRITO PERFECTO

he hablado
has hablado
ha hablado
hemos hablado
habéis hablado
han hablado

### PRETÉRITO IMPERFECTO

| (yo) | hablaba |
|---|---|
| (tú) | hablabas |
| (él/ella/usted) | hablaba |
| (nosotros) | hablábamos |
| (vosotros) | hablabais |
| (ellos/ustedes) | hablaban |

### PRETÉRITO PLUSCUAMPERFECTO

había hablado
habías hablado
había hablado
habíamos hablado
habíais hablado
habían hablado

### PRETÉRITO INDEFINIDO

| (yo) | hablé |
|---|---|
| (tú) | hablaste |
| (él/ella/usted) | habló |
| (nosotros) | hablamos |
| (vosotros) | hablasteis |
| (ellos/ustedes) | hablaron |

### PRETÉRITO ANTERIOR

hube hablado
hubiste hablado
hubo hablado
hubimos hablado
hubisteis hablado
hubieron hablado

### FUTURO

| (yo) | hablaré |
|---|---|
| (tú) | hablarás |
| (él/ella/usted) | hablará |
| (nosotros) | hablaremos |
| (vosotros) | hablaréis |
| (ellos/ustedes) | hablarán |

### FUTURO PERFECTO

habré hablado
habrás hablado
habrá hablado
habremos hablado
habréis hablado
habrán hablado

SpanishEasyAndFun.com

# CONDICIONAL

## CONDICIONAL SIMPLE

| | |
|---|---|
| (yo) | hablaría |
| (tú) | hablarías |
| (él/ella/usted) | hablaría |
| (nosotros) | hablaríamos |
| (vosotros) | hablaríais |
| (ellos/ustedes) | hablarían |

## CONDICIONAL COMPUESTO

| |
|---|
| habría hablado |
| habrías hablado |
| habría hablado |
| habríamos hablado |
| habríais hablado |
| habrían hablado |

# SUBJUNTIVO

## PRESENTE

| | |
|---|---|
| (yo) | hable |
| (tú) | hables |
| (él/ella/usted) | hable |
| (nosotros) | hablemos |
| (vosotros) | habléis |
| (ellos/ustedes) | hablen |

## PRETÉRITO PERFECTO

| |
|---|
| haya hablado |
| hayas hablado |
| haya hablado |
| hayamos hablado |
| hayáis hablado |
| hayan hablado |

## PRETÉRITO IMPERFECTO

| | |
|---|---|
| (yo) | hablara/hablase |
| (tú) | hablaras/hablases |
| (él/ella/usted) | hablara/hablase |
| (nosotros) | habláramos/hablásemos |
| (vosotros) | hablarais/hablaseis |
| (ellos/ustedes) | hablaran/hablasen |

## PRETÉRITO PLUSCUAMPERFECTO

| |
|---|
| hubiera/hubiese hablado |
| hubieras/hubieses hablado |
| hubiera/hubiese hablado |
| hubiéramos/hubiésemos hablado |
| hubierais/hubieseis hablado |
| hubieran/hubiesen hablado |

# IMPERATIVO

## AFIRMATIVO

| | |
|---|---|
| (tú) | habla |
| (él/ella/usted) | hable |
| (nosotros) | hablemos |
| (vosotros) | hablad |
| (ellos/ustedes) | hablen |

## NEGATIVO

| |
|---|
| no hables |
| no hable |
| no hablemos |
| no habléis |
| no hablen |

# REGULAR VERBS CONJUGATED IN ALL THE TENSES AND MOODS

| Infinitivo | Gerundio | Participio |
|---|---|---|
| temer (-er) | temiendo | temido |

## INDICATIVO

### PRESENTE

| | |
|---|---|
| (yo) | temo |
| (tú) | temes |
| (él/ella/usted) | teme |
| (nosotros) | tememos |
| (vosotros) | teméis |
| (ellos/ustedes) | temen |

### PRETÉRITO PERFECTO

he temido
has temido
ha temido
hemos temido
habéis temido
han temido

### PRETÉRITO IMPERFECTO

| | |
|---|---|
| (yo) | temía |
| (tú) | temías |
| (él/ella/usted) | temía |
| (nosotros) | temíamos |
| (vosotros) | temíais |
| (ellos/ustedes) | temían |

### PRETÉRITO PLUSCUAMPERFECTO

había temido
habías temido
había temido
habíamos temido
habíais temido
habían temido

### PRETÉRITO INDEFINIDO

| | |
|---|---|
| (yo) | temí |
| (tú) | temiste |
| (él/ella/usted) | temió |
| (nosotros) | temimos |
| (vosotros) | temisteis |
| (ellos/ustedes) | temieron |

### PRETÉRITO ANTERIOR

hube temido
hubiste temido
hubo temido
hubimos temido
hubisteis temido
hubieron temido

### FUTURO

| | |
|---|---|
| (yo) | temeré |
| (tú) | temerás |
| (él/ella/usted) | temerá |
| (nosotros) | temeremos |
| (vosotros) | temeréis |
| (ellos/ustedes) | temerán |

### FUTURO PERFECTO

habré temido
habrás temido
habrá temido
habremos temido
habréis temido
habrán temido

# CONDICIONAL

## CONDICIONAL SIMPLE

| | |
|---|---|
| (yo) | temería |
| (tú) | temerías |
| (él/ella/usted) | temería |
| (nosotros) | temeríamos |
| (vosotros) | temeríais |
| (ellos/ustedes) | temerían |

## CONDICIONAL COMPUESTO

habría temido
habrías temido
habría temido
habríamos temido
habríais temido
habrían temido

# SUBJUNTIVO

## PRESENTE

| | |
|---|---|
| (yo) | tema |
| (tú) | temas |
| (él/ella/usted) | tema |
| (nosotros) | temamos |
| (vosotros) | temáis |
| (ellos/ustedes) | teman |

## PRETÉRITO PERFECTO

haya temido
hayas temido
haya temido
hayamos temido
hayáis temido
hayan temido

## PRETÉRITO IMPERFECTO

| | |
|---|---|
| (yo) | temiera/temiese |
| (tú) | temieras/temieses |
| (él/ella/usted) | temiera/temiese |
| (nosotros) | temiéramos/temiésemos |
| (vosotros) | temierais/temieseis |
| (ellos/ustedes) | temieran/temiesen |

## PRETÉRITO PLUSCUAMPERFECTO

hubiera/hubiese temido
hubieras/hubieses temido
hubiera/hubiese temido
hubiéramos/hubiésemos temido
hubierais/hubieseis temido
hubieran/hubiesen temido

# IMPERATIVO

## AFIRMATIVO

| | |
|---|---|
| (tú) | teme |
| (él/ella/usted) | tema |
| (nosotros) | temamos |
| (vosotros) | temed |
| (ellos/ustedes) | teman |

## NEGATIVO

no temas
no tema
no temamos
no temáis
no teman

# REGULAR VERBS CONJUGATED IN ALL THE TENSES AND MOODS

| Infinitivo | Gerundio | Participio |
|------------|----------|------------|
| partir (-ir) | partiendo | partido |

## INDICATIVO

### PRESENTE

| | |
|---|---|
| (yo) | parto |
| (tú) | partes |
| (él/ella/usted) | parte |
| (nosotros) | partimos |
| (vosotros) | partís |
| (ellos/ustedes) | parten |

### PRETÉRITO PERFECTO

he partido
has partido
ha partido
hemos partido
habéis partido
han partido

### PRETÉRITO IMPERFECTO

| | |
|---|---|
| (yo) | partía |
| (tú) | partías |
| (él/ella/usted) | partía |
| (nosotros) | partíamos |
| (vosotros) | partíais |
| (ellos/ustedes) | partían |

### PRETÉRITO PLUSCUAMPERFECTO

había partido
habías partido
había partido
habíamos partido
habíais partido
habían partido

### PRETÉRITO INDEFINIDO

| | |
|---|---|
| (yo) | partí |
| (tú) | partiste |
| (él/ella/usted) | partió |
| (nosotros) | partimos |
| (vosotros) | partisteis |
| (ellos/ustedes) | partieron |

### PRETÉRITO ANTERIOR

hube partido
hubiste partido
hubo partido
hubimos partido
hubisteis partido
hubieron partido

### FUTURO

| | |
|---|---|
| (yo) | partiré |
| (tú) | partirás |
| (él/ella/usted) | partirá |
| (nosotros) | partiremos |
| (vosotros) | partiréis |
| (ellos/ustedes) | partirán |

### FUTURO PERFECTO

habré partido
habrás partido
habrá partido
habremos partido
habréis partido
habrán partido

SpanishEasyAndFun.com

# CONDICIONAL

## CONDICIONAL SIMPLE

| | |
|---|---|
| (yo) | partiría |
| (tú) | partirías |
| (él/ella/usted) | partiría |
| (nosotros) | partiríamos |
| (vosotros) | partiríais |
| (ellos/ustedes) | partirían |

## CONDICIONAL COMPUESTO

| |
|---|
| habría partido |
| habrías partido |
| habría partido |
| habríamos partido |
| habríais partido |
| habrían partido |

# SUBJUNTIVO

## PRESENTE

| | |
|---|---|
| (yo) | parta |
| (tú) | partas |
| (él/ella/usted) | parta |
| (nosotros) | partamos |
| (vosotros) | partáis |
| (ellos/ustedes) | partan |

## PRETÉRITO PERFECTO

| |
|---|
| haya partido |
| hayas partido |
| haya partido |
| hayamos partido |
| hayáis partido |
| hayan partido |

## PRETÉRITO IMPERFECTO

| | |
|---|---|
| (yo) | partiera/partiese |
| (tú) | partieras/partieses |
| (él/ella/usted) | partiera/partiese |
| (nosotros) | partiéramos/partiésemos |
| (vosotros) | partierais/partieseis |
| (ellos/ustedes) | partieran/partiesen |

## PRETÉRITO PLUSCUAMPERFECTO

| |
|---|
| hubiera/hubiese partido |
| hubieras/hubieses partido |
| hubiera/hubiese partido |
| hubiéramos/hubiésemos partido |
| hubierais/hubieseis partido |
| hubieran/hubiesen partido |

# IMPERATIVO

## AFIRMATIVO

| | |
|---|---|
| (tú) | parte |
| (él/ella/usted) | parta |
| (nosotros) | partamos |
| (vosotros) | partid |
| (ellos/ustedes) | partan |

## NEGATIVO

| |
|---|
| no partas |
| no parta |
| no partamos |
| no partáis |
| no partan |

# IRREGULAR VERBS CONJUGATED IN ALL THE TENSES AND MOODS

| Infinitivo | Gerundio | Participio |
|---|---|---|
| pensar | pensando | pensado |

## INDICATIVO

### PRESENTE

| | |
|---|---|
| (yo) | pienso |
| (tú) | piensas |
| (él/ella/usted) | piensa |
| (nosotros) | pensamos |
| (vosotros) | pensáis |
| (ellos/ustedes) | piensan |

### PRETÉRITO PERFECTO

he pensado
has pensado
ha pensado
hemos pensado
habéis pensado
han pensado

### PRETÉRITO IMPERFECTO

| | |
|---|---|
| (yo) | pensaba |
| (tú) | pensabas |
| (él/ella/usted) | pensaba |
| (nosotros) | pensábamos |
| (vosotros) | pensabais |
| (ellos/ustedes) | pensaban |

### PRETÉRITO PLUSCUAMPERFECTO

había pensado
habías pensado
había pensado
habíamos pensado
habíais pensado
habían pensado

### PRETÉRITO INDEFINIDO

| | |
|---|---|
| (yo) | pensé |
| (tú) | pensaste |
| (él/ella/usted) | pensó |
| (nosotros) | pensamos |
| (vosotros) | pensasteis |
| (ellos/ustedes) | pensaron |

### PRETÉRITO ANTERIOR

hube pensado
hubiste pensado
hubo pensado
hubimos pensado
hubisteis pensado
hubieron pensado

### FUTURO

| | |
|---|---|
| (yo) | pensaré |
| (tú) | pensarás |
| (él/ella/usted) | pensará |
| (nosotros) | pensaremos |
| (vosotros) | pensaréis |
| (ellos/ustedes) | pensarán |

### FUTURO PERFECTO

habré pensado
habrás pensado
habrá pensado
habremos pensado
habréis pensado
habrán pensado

SpanishEasyAndFun.com

## PRESENTE

| | |
|---|---|
| (yo) | piense |
| (tú) | pienses |
| (él/ella/usted) | piense |
| (nosotros) | pensemos |
| (vosotros) | penséis |
| (ellos/ustedes) | piensen |

## PRETÉRITO PERFECTO

haya pensado
hayas pensado
haya pensado
hayamos pensado
hayáis pensado
hayan pensado

# SUBJUNTIVO

## PRESENTE

| | |
|---|---|
| (yo) | piense |
| (tú) | pienses |
| (él/ella/usted) | piense |
| (nosotros) | pensemos |
| (vosotros) | penséis |
| (ellos/ustedes) | piensen |

## PRETÉRITO PERFECTO

haya pensado
hayas pensado
haya pensado
hayamos pensado
hayáis pensado
hayan pensado

## PRETÉRITO IMPERFECTO

| | |
|---|---|
| (yo) | pensara/pensase |
| (tú) | pensaras/pensases |
| (él/ella/usted) | pensara/pensase |
| (nosotros) | pensáramos/pensásemos |
| (vosotros) | pensarais/pensaseis |
| (ellos/ustedes) | pensaran/pensasen |

## PRETÉRITO PLUSCUAMPERFECTO

hubiera/hubiese pensado
hubieras/hubieses pensado
hubiera/hubiese pensado
hubiéramos/hubiésemos pensado
hubierais/hubieseis pensado
hubieran/hubiesen pensado

# IMPERATIVO

## AFIRMATIVO

| | |
|---|---|
| (tú) | piensa |
| (él/ella/usted) | piense |
| (nosotros) | pensemos |
| (vosotros) | pensad |
| (ellos/ustedes) | piensen |

## NEGATIVO

no pienses
no piense
no pensemos
no penséis
no piensen

| Infinitivo | Gerundio | Participio |
|---|---|---|
| hacer | haciendo | hecho |

## INDICATIVO

### PRESENTE

| (yo) | hago |
|---|---|
| (tú) | haces |
| (él/ella/usted) | hace |
| (nosotros) | hacemos |
| (vosotros) | hacéis |
| (ellos/ustedes) | hacen |

### PRETÉRITO PERFECTO

he hecho
has hecho
ha hecho
hemos hecho
habéis hecho
han hecho

### PRETÉRITO IMPERFECTO

| (yo) | hacía |
|---|---|
| (tú) | hacías |
| (él/ella/usted) | hacía |
| (nosotros) | hacíamos |
| (vosotros) | hacíais |
| (ellos/ustedes) | hacían |

### PRETÉRITO PLUSCUAMPERFECTO

había hecho
habías hecho
había hecho
habíamos hecho
habíais hecho
habían hecho

### PRETÉRITO INDEFINIDO

| (yo) | hice |
|---|---|
| (tú) | hiciste |
| (él/ella/usted) | hizo |
| (nosotros) | hicimos |
| (vosotros) | hicisteis |
| (ellos/ustedes) | hicieron |

### PRETÉRITO ANTERIOR

hube hecho
hubiste hecho
hubo hecho
hubimos hecho
hubisteis hecho
hubieron hecho

### FUTURO

| (yo) | haré |
|---|---|
| (tú) | harás |
| (él/ella/usted) | hará |
| (nosotros) | haremos |
| (vosotros) | haréis |
| (ellos/ustedes) | harán |

### FUTURO PERFECTO

habré hecho
habrás hecho
habrá hecho
habremos hecho
habréis hecho
habrán hecho

SpanishEasyAndFun.com

# CONDICIONAL

## CONDICIONAL SIMPLE

| | |
|---|---|
| (yo) | haría |
| (tú) | harías |
| (él/ella/usted) | haría |
| (nosotros) | haríamos |
| (vosotros) | haríais |
| (ellos/ustedes) | harían |

## CONDICIONAL COMPUESTO

habría hecho
habrías hecho
habría hecho
habríamos hecho
habríais hecho
habrían hecho

# SUBJUNTIVO

## PRESENTE

| | |
|---|---|
| (yo) | haga |
| (tú) | hagas |
| (él/ella/usted) | haga |
| (nosotros) | hagamos |
| (vosotros) | hagáis |
| (ellos/ustedes) | hagan |

## PRETÉRITO PERFECTO

haya hecho
hayas hecho (él/ella/usted)
haya hecho
hayamos hecho
hayáis hecho
hayan hecho

## PRETÉRITO IMPERFECTO

| | |
|---|---|
| (yo) | hiciera/hiciese |
| (tú) | hicieras/hicieses |
| (él/ella/usted) | hiciera/hiciese |
| (nosotros) | hiciéramos/hiciésemos |
| (vosotros) | hicierais/hicieseis |
| (ellos/ustedes) | hicieran/hiciesen |

## PRETÉRITO PLUSCUAMPERFECTO

hubiera/hubiese hecho
hubieras/hubieses hecho
hubiera/hubiese hecho
hubiéramos/hubiésemos hecho
hubierais/hubieseis hecho
hubieran/hubiesen hecho

# IMPERATIVO

## AFIRMATIVO

| | |
|---|---|
| (tú) | haz |
| (él/ella/usted) | haga |
| (nosotros) | hagamos |
| (vosotros) | haced |
| (ellos/ustedes) | hagan |

## NEGATIVO

no hagas
no haga
no hagamos
no hagáis
no hagan

# IRREGULAR VERBS CONJUGATED IN ALL THE TENSES AND MOODS

| Infinitivo | Gerundio | Participio |
|:---:|:---:|:---:|
| decir | diciendo | dicho |

## INDICATIVO

### PRESENTE

| (yo) | digo |
|---|---|
| (tú) | dices |
| (él/ella/usted) | dice |
| (nosotros) | decimos |
| (vosotros) | decís |
| (ellos/ustedes) | dicen |

### PRETÉRITO PERFECTO

he dicho
has dicho
ha dicho
hemos dicho
habéis dicho
han dicho

### PRETÉRITO IMPERFECTO

| (yo) | decía |
|---|---|
| (tú) | decías |
| (él/ella/usted) | decía |
| (nosotros) | decíamos |
| (vosotros) | decíais |
| (ellos/ustedes) | decían |

### PRETÉRITO PLUSCUAMPERFECTO

había dicho
habías dicho
había dicho
habíamos dicho
habíais dicho
habían dicho

### PRETÉRITO INDEFINIDO

| (yo) | dije |
|---|---|
| (tú) | dijiste |
| (él/ella/usted) | dijo |
| (nosotros) | dijimos |
| (vosotros) | dijisteis |
| (ellos/ustedes) | dijeron |

### PRETÉRITO ANTERIOR

hube dicho
hubiste dicho
hubo dicho
hubimos dicho
hubisteis dicho
hubieron dicho

### FUTURO

| (yo) | diré |
|---|---|
| (tú) | dirás |
| (él/ella/usted) | dirá |
| (nosotros) | diremos |
| (vosotros) | diréis |
| (ellos/ustedes) | dirán |

### FUTURO PERFECTO

habré dicho
habrás dicho
habrá dicho
habremos dicho
habréis dicho
habrán dicho

SpanishEasyAndFun.com

# CONDICIONAL

### CONDICIONAL SIMPLE

| | |
|---|---|
| (yo) | diría |
| (tú) | dirías |
| (él/ella/usted) | diría |
| (nosotros) | diríamos |
| (vosotros) | diríais |
| (ellos/ustedes) | dirían |

### CONDICIONAL COMPUESTO

habría dicho
habrías dicho
habría dicho
habríamos dicho
habríais dicho
habrían dicho

# SUBJUNTIVO

### PRESENTE

| | |
|---|---|
| (yo) | diga |
| (tú) | digas |
| (él/ella/usted) | diga |
| (nosotros) | digamos |
| (vosotros) | digáis |
| (ellos/ustedes) | digan |

### PRETÉRITO PERFECTO

haya dicho
hayas dicho
haya dicho
hayamos dicho
hayáis dicho
hayan dicho

### PRETÉRITO IMPERFECTO

| | |
|---|---|
| (yo) | dijera/dijese |
| (tú) | dijeras/dijeses |
| (él/ella/usted) | dijera/dijese |
| (nosotros) | dijéramos/dijésemos |
| (vosotros) | dijerais/dijeseis |
| (ellos/ustedes) | dijeran/dijeses |

### PRETÉRITO PLUSCUAMPERFECTO

hubiera/hubiese dicho
hubieras/hubieses dicho
hubiera/hubiese dicho
hubiéramos/hubiésemos dicho
hubierais/hubieseis dicho
hubieran/hubiesen dicho

# IMPERATIVO

### AFIRMATIVO

| | |
|---|---|
| (tú) | di |
| (él/ella/usted) | diga |
| (nosotros) | digamos |
| (vosotros) | decid |
| (ellos/ustedes) | digan |

### NEGATIVO

no digas
no diga
no digamos
no digáis
no digan

# Conversion Charts

# Length

SpanishEasyAndFun.com

## METRIC CONVERSIONS

| 1 centimeter | = | 10 millimeters | 1 cm | = | 10 mm |
|---|---|---|---|---|---|
| 1 meter | = | 100 centimeters | 1 m | = | 100 cm |
| 1 kilometer | = | 1000 meters | 1 km | = | 1000 m |

## US STANDARD CONVERSIONS

| 1 foot | = | 12 inches | 1 ft | = | 12 in |
|---|---|---|---|---|---|
| 1 yard | = | 3 feet | 1 yd | = | 3 ft |
| 1 yard | = | 36 inches | 1 yd | = | 36 in |
| 1 mile | = | 1760 yards | 1 mi | = | 1760 yd |

## METRIC->US STANDARD CONVERSIONS

| 1 millimeter | = | 0.03937 inches | 1 mm | = | 0.03937 in |
|---|---|---|---|---|---|
| 1 centimeter | = | 0.39370 inches | 1 cm | = | 0.39370 in |
| 1 meter | = | 39.37008 inches | 1 m | = | 39.37008 in |
| 1 meter | = | 3.28084 feet | 1 m | = | 3.28084 ft |
| 1 meter | = | 1.09361 yards | 1 m | = | 1.09361 yd |
| 1 kilometer | = | 1093.6133 yards | 1 km | = | 1093.6133 yd |
| 1 kilometer | = | 0.62137 miles | 1 km | = | 0.62137 mi |

## US STANDARD->METRIC CONVERSIONS

| 1 inch | = | 2.54 centimeters | 1 in | = | 2.54 cm |
|---|---|---|---|---|---|
| 1 foot | = | 30.48 centimeters | 1 ft | = | 30.48 cm |
| 1 yard | = | 91.44 centimeters | 1 yd | = | 91.44 cm |
| 1 yard | = | 0.9144 meters | 1 yd | = | 0.9144 m |
| 1 mile | = | 1609.344 meters | 1 mi | = | 1609.344 m |
| 1 mile | = | 1.609344 kilometers | 1 mi | = | 1.609344 km |

# Area

🖑SpanishEasyAndFun.com

## METRIC CONVERSIONS

| | | | | | |
|---|---|---|---|---|---|
| 1 sq centimeter | = | 100 sq millimeters | 1 sq cm | = | 100 sq mm |
| 1 sq meter | = | 10,000 sq centimeters | 1 sq m | = | 10,000 sq cm |
| 1 hectare | = | 10,000 sq meters | 1 ha | = | 10,000 sq m |
| 1 sq kilometer | = | 100 hectares | 1 sq km | = | 100 ha |
| 1 sq kilometer | = | 1 million sq meters | 1 sq km | = | 1,000,000 sq m |

## US STANDARD CONVERSIONS

| | | | | | |
|---|---|---|---|---|---|
| 1 sq foot | = | 144 sq inches | 1 sq ft | = | 144 sq in |
| 1 sq yard | = | 9 sq feet | 1 sq yd | = | 9 sq ft |
| 1 acre | = | 4840 sq yards | 1 acre | = | 4840 sq yd |
| 1 acre | = | 43,560 sq feet | 1 acre | = | 43,560 sq ft |
| 1 sq mile | = | 640 acres | 1 sq mi | = | 640 acres |

## METRIC->US STANDARD CONVERSIONS

| | | | | | |
|---|---|---|---|---|---|
| 1 sq centimeter | = | 0.15500 sq inches | 1 sq cm | = | 0.15500 sq in |
| 1 sq meter | = | 10.76391 sq feet | 1 sq m | = | 10.76391 sq ft |
| 1 sq meter | = | 1.19599 sq yards | 1 sq m | = | 1.19599 sq yd |
| 1 hectare | = | 2.47105 acres | 1 ha | = | 2.47105 acres |
| 1 sq kilometer | = | 0.386102 sq miles | 1 sq km | = | 0.386102 sq mi |

## US STANDARD->METRIC CONVERSIONS

| | | | | | |
|---|---|---|---|---|---|
| 1 sq inch | = | 6.4516 sq centimeters | 1 sq in | = | 6.4516 sq cm |
| 1 sq foot | = | 929.0304 sq centimeters | 1 sq ft | = | 929.0304 sq cm |
| 1 sq foot | = | 0.09290 sq meters | 1 sq ft | = | 0.09290 sq m |
| 1 sq yard | = | 0.83613 sq meters | 1 sq yd | = | 0.83613 sq m |
| 1 acre | = | 0.40469 hectares | 1 acre | = | 0.40469 ha |
| 1 sq mile | = | 258.99881 hectares | 1 sq mi | = | 258.99881 ha |
| 1 sq mile | = | 2.589988 sq kilometers | 1 sq mi | = | 2.589988 sq km |

# Volume

## METRIC CONVERSIONS

| | | | | | |
|---|---|---|---|---|---|
| 1 cubic centimeter | = | 1000 cubic millimeters | 1 cu cm | = | 1000 cu mm |
| 1 cubic meter | = | 1 million cubic centimeters | 1 cu m | = | 1,000,000 cu cm |

## US STANDARD CONVERSIONS

| | | | | | |
|---|---|---|---|---|---|
| 1 cubic foot | = | 1728 cubic inches | 1 cu ft | = | 1728 cu in |
| 1 cubic yard | = | 46,656 cubic inches | 1 cu yd | = | 46,656 cu in |
| 1 cubic yard | = | 27 cubic feet | 1 cu yd | = | 27 cu ft |

## METRIC->US STANDARD CONVERSIONS

| | | | | | |
|---|---|---|---|---|---|
| 1 cubic centimeter | = | 0.06102 cubic inches | 1 cuc m | = | 0.06102 cu in |
| 1 cubic meter | = | 35.31467 cubic feet | 1 cu m | = | 35.31467 cu ft |
| 1 cubic meter | = | 1.30795 cubic yards | 1 cu m | = | 1.30795 cu yd |

## US STANDARD->METRIC CONVERSIONS

| | | | | | |
|---|---|---|---|---|---|
| 1 cubic inch | = | 16.38706 cubic centimeters | 1 cu in | = | 16.38706 cu cm |
| 1 cubic foot | = | 0.02832 cubic meters | 1 cu ft | = | 0.02832 cu m |
| 1 cubic yard | = | 0.76455 cubic meters | 1 cu yd | = | 0.76455 cu m |

# Weight

## METRIC CONVERSIONS

| | | | | | |
|---|---|---|---|---|---|
| 1 gram | = | 1000 milligrams | 1 g | = | 1000 mg |
| 1 kilogram | = | 1000 grams | 1 kg | = | 1000 g |
| 1 tonne (1 megagram) | = | 1000 kilograms | 1 tonne (1 mg) | = | 1000 kg |

## US STANDARD CONVERSIONS

| | | | | | |
|---|---|---|---|---|---|
| 1 ounce | = | 16 drams | 1 oz | = | 16 dr |
| 1 pound | = | 16 ounces | 1 lb | = | 16 oz |
| 1 hundredweight | = | 100 pounds | 1 cwt | = | 100 lb |
| 1 ton (short) | = | 20 hundredweight | 1 ton | = | 20 cwt |
| 1 ton (short) | = | 2000 pounds | 1 ton | = | 2000 lb |

## METRIC->US STANDARD CONVERSIONS

| | | | | | |
|---|---|---|---|---|---|
| 1 gram | = | 0.035274 ounces | 1 g | = | 0.035274 oz |
| 1 kilogram | = | 2.20462 pounds | 1 kg | = | 2.20462 lb |
| 1 kilogram | = | 35.27396 ounces | 1 kg | = | 35.27396 oz |
| 1 tonne | = | 1.10231 ton (short) | 1 tonne | = | 1.10231 ton (short) |

## US STANDARD->METRIC CONVERSIONS

| | | | | | |
|---|---|---|---|---|---|
| 1 ounce | = | 28.34952 grams | 1 oz | = | 28.34952 g |
| 1 pound | = | 453.59237 grams | 1 lb | = | 453.59237 g |
| 1 pound | = | 0.45359 kilograms | 1 lb | = | 0.45359 kg |
| 1 hundredweight | = | 50.8023 kilograms | 1 cwt | = | 50.8023 kg |
| 1 ton (short) | = | 0.90718 tonnes | 1 ton (short) | = | 0.90718 tonnes |

# Liquid Volume

**Please note that these conversions work for US liquids only!**

## METRIC CONVERSIONS

| | | | | | |
|---|---|---|---|---|---|
| 1 centiliter | = | 10 milliliters | 1 cl | = | 10 ml |
| 1 liter | = | 1000 milliliters | 1 l | = | 1000 ml |

## US STANDARD CONVERSIONS

| | | | | | |
|---|---|---|---|---|---|
| 1 tablespoon | = | 3 teaspoons | 1 tbsp | = | 3 tsp |
| 1 fluid ounce | = | 2 tablespoons | 1 fl oz | = | 2 tbsp |
| 1 fluid ounce | = | 8 drams | 1 fl oz | = | 8 drams |
| 1 gill | = | 4 fluid ounces | 1 gi | = | 4 fl oz |
| 1 cup | = | 8 fluid ounces | 1 cup | = | 8 fl oz |
| 1 pint | = | 2 cups | 1 pt | = | 2 cups |
| 1 pint | = | 16 fluid ounces | 1 pt | = | 16 fl oz |
| 1 quart | = | 2 pints | 1 qt | = | 2 pt |
| 1 gallon | = | 4 quarts | 1 gal | = | 4 qt |
| 1 gallon | = | 128 fluid ounces | 1 gal | = | 128 fl oz |

1 gallon = 4 quarts = 8 pints = 16 cups = 128 fluid ounces

## METRIC->US STANDARD CONVERSIONS

| | | | | | |
|---|---|---|---|---|---|
| 1 milliliter | = | 0.033814 fluid ounces | 1 ml | = | 0.033814 fl oz |
| 1 liter | = | 33.814022 fluid ounces | 1 l | = | 33.814022 fl oz |
| 1 liter | = | 2.113376 pints | 1 l | = | 2.113376 pints |

## US STANDARD->METRIC CONVERSIONS

| | | | | | |
|---|---|---|---|---|---|
| 1 fluid ounce | = | 29.57353 milliliters | 1 fl oz | = | 29.57353 ml |
| 1 pint | = | 473.17648 milliliters | 1 pt | = | 473.17648 ml |
| 1 pint | = | 0.47318 liters | 1 pt | = | 0.47318 l |
| 1 gallon, liquid | = | 3.7854 liters | 1 gallon | = | 3.7854 l |

# Learn Spanish with the
# SPANISH IN 100 DAYS series!

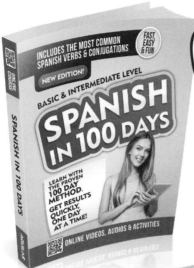

## SPANISH IN 100 DAYS
ISBN: 978-1-644737-66-8

Will teach you how to understand, speak, read and even write in **Spanish in only 100 days**!

## SPANISH EASY & FUN
ISBN: 978-1-644737-32-3

An immersive experience in the world of Spanish via language, culture, music, film, news, and community.

The best-selling **Spanish courses** in the United States!

## Photographs and illustrators:

### Cover and backcover
© Prostockstudio | Dreamstime.com
© Roman Samborskyi | Dreamstime.com
© Sanghyun Paek | Dreamstime.com
© Vladyslav Zakhareuych | Dreamstime.com
© wayhomestudio | Freepik.com

### Title page
© Tetiana Kozachok | Dreamstime.com

### Vignettes
© Agus Rusdiana | Dreamstime.com

### Spanish Units
© Abscent | Dreamstime.com (pág. 149)
© Aleutie | Dreamstime.com (pág. 205)
© Alexmillos | Dreamstime.com (pág. 63)
© Alhouik | Dreamstime.com (pág. 158)
© Andrés Cuenca | Dreamstime.com (pág. 79)
© Andrei Stancu | Dreamstime.com (pág. 217)
© Artisticco Llc | Dreamstime.com (pág. 147, 236, 262)
© Bogdan Lazar | Dreamstime.com (pág. 129)
© Burlesck | Dreamstime.com (pág. 100, 214)
© Ciro Zeno | Dreamstime.com (pág. 241)
© Diego Grandi | Dreamstime.com (pág. 31)
© Dimbar76 | Dreamstime.com (pág. 39)
© Ed Francissen | Dreamstime.com (pág. 71)
© Ekaterina Danilova | Dreamstime.com (pág. 141)
© Elenabsl | Dreamstime.com (pág. 25, 218)
© Ernest Akayeu | Dreamstime.com (pág. 26, 35, 36, 42, 50, 57, 66, 73, 82, 84, 92, 104, 109, 110, 115, 118, 124, 131, 171, 181, 213, 258)
© Francisco Crusat | Dreamstime.com (pág. 87)
© Galina Barskaya | Dreamstime.com (pág. 145)
© Golasza | Dreamstime.com (pág. 55)
© Irina Miroshnichenko | Dreamstime.com (pág. 195)
© Irina Siryanova | Dreamstime.com (pág. 28, 59, 67, 107, 108, 125, 134, 148, 190, 219)
© Irishka777 | Dreamstime.com (pág. 137)
© Javier Duran | Dreamstime.com (pág. 249)
© Jose Ramon Pizarro Garcia | Dreamstime.com (pág. 185)
© Jorisvo | Dreamstime.com (pág. 153)
© Kabasinki | Dreamstime.com (pág. 201)
© Kanokrat Tawokhat | Dreamstime.com (pág. 209)
© Kaye Oberstar | Dreamstime.com (pág. 193)
© LeOnid | Dreamstime.com (pág. 172)
© Lucas Viani | Dreamstime.com (pág. 169)
© Macrovector | Dreamstime.com (pág. 163, 222)
© Marketa Novakova | Dreamstime.com (pág. 47)
© Martin Schneiter | Dreamstime.com (pág. 257)
© Mast3r | Dreamstime.com (pág. 204)
© Microvone | Dreamstime.com (pág. 33, 81, 245)
© MrFly | Dreamstime.com (pág. 23)
© Olga Kurbatova | Dreamstime.com (pág. 52)
© Pavlo Syvak | Dreamstime.com (pág. 254)
© Phagenaars | Dreamstime.com (pág. 177)
© Plotnikov | Dreamstime.com (pág. 233)
© Norbert Buchholz | Dreamstime.com (pág. 68)
© Roberto Lusso | Dreamstime.com (pág. 113)
© Sergii Figurnyi | Dreamstime.com (pág. 103)
© Simone Matteo Giuseppe Manzoni | Dreamstime.com (pág. 161)
© Stefano Ember | Dreamstime.com (pág. 225)
© Tetiana Kozachok | Dreamstime.com (pág. 123, 226)
© Tifonimages | Dreamstime.com (pág. 95)
© Vera Zontova | Dreamstime.com (pág. 105)
© Vitalyedush | Dreamstime.com (pág. 121)

### Spanish Verbs
© Microvone | Dreamstime.com

### Conversion Chart
© Ernest Akayeu | Dreamstime.com

**Thank you for studying with us.**

For a full Spanish immersion, visit

SpanishEasyAndFun.com

to access online classes, videos,
activities, and interactive exercises.